MUDEATER

MUDEATER

AN AMERICAN BUFFALO HUNTER
AND THE SURRENDER OF LOUIS RIEL

JOHN D. PIHACH

University of Regina Press

Printed and bound in Canada at Marquis. The text of this book is printed on 100% post-consumer recycled paper with earth-friendly vegetable-based inks.

COVER AND TEXT DESIGN: Duncan Campbell, University of Regina Press
COPY EDITOR: Meaghan Craven
PROOFREADER: Kristine Douaud
INDEXER: Patricia Furdek
COVER ART: Robert Armstrong, circa 1925. Courtesy Glenbow Archives, NB-16-552.

Library and Archives Canada Cataloguing in Publication

Pihach, John D., author
    Mudeater : an American buffalo hunter and the surrender of Louis Riel / John D. Pihach.

Includes bibliographical references and index.
Issued in print and electronic formats.
ISBN 978-0-88977-458-2 (paperback).—ISBN 978-0-88977-462-9 (PDF).—ISBN 978-0-88977-463-6 (HTML)

1. Mudeater, Irvin, 1849-1940. 2. Wyandot Indians—Biography. 3. Riel Rebellion, 1885—Scouts and scouting. 4. Riel, Louis, 1844-1885. 5. Frontier and pioneer life—West (U.S.). 6. West (U.S.)—Biography. 7. Canada, Western—Biography. I. Title.

E99.H9M83 2017   970.004'97555   C2016-907119-7   C2016-907120-0

10   9   8   7   6   5   4   3   2   1

University of Regina Press, University of Regina
Regina, Saskatchewan, Canada, s4s 0A2
tel: (306) 585-4758 fax: (306) 585-4699
web: www.uofrpress.ca
email: uofrpress@uregina.ca

U OF R PRESS

We acknowledge the support of the Canada Council for the Arts for our publishing program. We acknowledge the financial support of the Government of Canada. / Nous reconnaissons l'appui financier du gouvernement du Canada. This publication was made possible through Creative Saskatchewan's Creative Industries Production Grant Program.

 Canada Council   Conseil des Arts
for the Arts   du Canada

 Canada

creative
SASKATCHEWAN

CONTENTS

PART TWO: ROBERT ARMSTRONG'S MEMOIR

ACKNOWLEDGEMENTS

I t is only by chance that Robert Armstrong came to my attention. During a conversation one day, my neighbour, Trevor Wheeler, informed me that his great-grandfather, Robert Armstrong, was the man who captured Louis Riel. Mr. Wheeler has my gratitude for sharing his knowledge of his ancestor with me and for informing me that Armstrong had written an account of his checkered life, that he had a copy of that memoir, and that a relative in the United States had the original manuscript. It is with the kind permission of Ella Melendrez, a resident of California and a granddaughter of Robert Armstrong, that the memoir is included in this book. Ella has been very co-operative and helpful, and I was touched when she travelled from California to visit me in Saskatchewan.

Armstrong's great-granddaughter, Eleanor Peppard, has my thanks, also, for supplying me with a photograph of Armstrong and some materials that were useful in my research. Thanks to another of Armstrong's great-granddaughters, Judy Lalonde, for answering some questions. My friend, Garry Radison, author of biographies of Wandering Spirit and Fine Day, read a draft of the manuscript and made valuable suggestions. My sister Maryellen Doucette saved me considerable time by typing Armstrong's handwritten manuscript. Thanks also to Elmer and Loretta McInnes, who took time off their work at the Kansas State Historical Society to look into matters related to this book. I am appreciative of the co-operative assistance provided by the staff at the Provincial Archives of Saskatchewan, Archives of Manitoba, Glenbow Archives, Special Collections at the University of Saskatchewan Library, and the Batoche Museum. Jamie Benson, at the Prince Albert Historical Society, has on several occasions been supportive and helpful. Barbara Becker, of the Miami (Oklahoma) Public Library, provided me with useful information, as did the late Louise Kiefer, the college historian at Baldwin-Wallace University. My thanks also to Robert Bluthardt, Russell Bohach, Golda Foster, Elizabeth Grindstaff, William B. Shillingberg, Bill Waiser, and others whom I contacted during my research.

Getting a book on the store shelves involves much more than submitting a manuscript to a publisher. My appreciation to the staff at the University of Regina Press who were engaged in the many stages of this process. In particular, I would like to acknowledge the work of David McLennan, editor, who guided the pre-publication stages of the book and fortified the manuscript with his insights; Donna Grant, managing editor; and Duncan Campbell, art director—congenial, talented professionals. I am also grateful to Meaghan Craven for her superb copy editing and comments.

INTRODUCTION

R obert Armstrong was born in Kansas in 1849. Before coming to Canada in 1882, he lived the life of a plainsman in the American West; he hunted buffalo for more than a decade, drove a stagecoach, and was caught up in skirmishes with the Indians of the Southwest. Soon after settling in Prince Albert, then part of the District of Saskatchewan, his life was interrupted by the 1885 conflict. Howard Angus Kennedy, a *Montreal Daily Witness* correspondent covering the North-West Resistance in 1885, met Robert Armstrong during that time and interviewed him again several decades later. In 1926 Kennedy wrote, "All over the Dominion, in fact from Halifax to Victoria, you will find veterans of 'the 85' with lively recollections of Bob as a scout and dispatch rider with General Middleton's command. Few, however, knew much more about him than the fact that he played the chief part in trailing and catching the fugitive Métis leader. . . . His famous deed of '85, big as it was in our national life, was only one of a hundred sensational incidents in his."[1] The "famous deed" that put Armstrong in the national spotlight was the apprehension of Louis Riel after the fall of Batoche.

This book tells the story of Robert Armstrong, examines his "famous deed," scrutinizes some of the "hundred sensational incidents" in his life, and, with the inclusion of his unpublished memoir, allows Armstrong to address us in his own voice.

In 1920 Robert Armstrong recited his life story to a family member. The handwritten manuscript, though preserved by his descendants, remained unpublished and forgotten until the publication of this book. However, Armstrong did show the memoir to several individuals who published brief summaries of it. Armstrong's personal account, to a large degree, is the testimony of someone who participated in the slaughter of the buffalo herds, their near extinction generating profound consequences for the Indigenous peoples of the Plains and for the social and political climate of the time. His revelations allow us a glimpse at the unrestrained era popularly known as the Old West or Wild West, where gritty individualism was a necessity and, in Armstrong's words, "law was but a myth or a story told but rarely enforced." Armstrong recalls his early years in his memoir, and his celebrated status in 1885 is recorded in brief in newspapers and books; nevertheless, there are at least four significant and sensational omissions in these accounts.

First, "Robert Armstrong" is an alias, a name he adopted after coming to Canada. Second, although the destruction of the buffalo herds ended his hunting career and may be part of the reason for his move to Canada in 1882, he actually came to Canada to escape justice in the United States. Third, in most accounts Armstrong is identified as an American, and in some documents his ethnic background is listed as Irish or English; in fact, he was the son of a Native American chief. Fourth, though Armstrong only makes scant reference to his family, his ancestry is unusual.

Armstrong's life in Canada was uneventful compared to his many adventures in the American West, yet it was in Canada that he emerged from the obscure life of a buffalo hunter and became a focus for the public eye. During the 1885 Resistance, three scouts—Robert Armstrong, Tom Hourie, and William Diehl—rode out together, located Riel, and brought him to General Middleton. Dissenting accounts by Armstrong and Hourie obscure what transpired when Riel encountered his captors. Both Armstrong and Hourie claim the principal role and credit the other scouts with minor, supporting contributions. Each alleges that Riel surrendered to and deferred to him, that Riel rode on the same horse with him, that Riel handed his pistol to him, and that he presented Riel to

Middleton. But Riel could have handed his note from Middleton offering safe passage to only one person, and he could only have handed one man his pistol. Finally, only one scout would have announced to Middleton that the man before him was Riel.

In his memoir, Armstrong addresses the issue, saying, "Certain other persons have at different times laid claim to Riels [sic] capture and right here I wish to say, that Louis Riel surrendered himself to me personally, and further, that he rode behind me on my horse for some few miles after which we walked the remainder of the distance to Gen. Middleton's camp at Guardepuis' [Gardepuis'] Crossing, and that upon arriving at said camp I personally delivered Riel a prisoner to General Middleton." In the same tone, Tom Hourie's father, Peter Hourie, relates that "no one but Tom could have done it. Armstrong and Deal [sic] were green horns at the trail. . . ." More than a century and a quarter after these events, Armstrong's and Hourie's conflicting claims, and the discrepancies appearing in later literature regarding this event, have not been resolved. Many historians do not assign a leading role to either of the two scouts, nor do they attempt to unknot the incompatible claims. Because Armstrong's place in Canadian history stems from his participation in Riel's apprehension, this book makes an effort to shed light on these unanswered questions and to reconstruct what may have happened on May 15, 1885.

Armstrong and Diehl both left personal accounts of Riel's capture, and accounts of Hourie's involvement in the event were written by Peter Hourie and other writers. Only those scouts and Riel knew what transpired, and all other credible reports have their source in what the scouts told reporters upon their arrival at Middleton's camp and what they may have said to other individuals present at the time or at a later date. Armstrong's version of events appears in contemporary newspaper columns, in later interviews, and in his memoir. Hourie's actions also were noted in newspapers and recorded by individuals who were acquainted with him, but the primary account of his activities and the source for later depictions of him as the principal participant is provided by his father, Peter. Diehl's description first appeared in telegram dispatches written by correspondents who were present when Diehl reported Riel's capture, in newspaper reports based on those telegrams, and then in an affidavit given by him years after Riel's capture.

As I began examining the story of Riel's capture, I also found myself scrutinizing other events Armstrong presents to the reader in his memoir. Armstrong's life story can be conveniently divided into the years before 1885, the year 1885, and the years after 1885. Chapter One, "Before Robert Armstrong," looks into Armstrong's roots—his Wyandot background, parents, and siblings. Chapter Two, "Youth to 1885," deals with his younger days, up to when he made Prince Albert home. His memoir, with the exception of the account of his participation in the 1885 Resistance, deals almost exclusively with his life on the American frontier, and, therefore, the second chapter of this book does not include many of the stories from the memoir. However, by referring to the small number of available documents and to the reports of those who witnessed several events that Armstrong recounts, it has been possible to broaden his narrative and, at the same time, evaluate some of the claims he makes in the memoir. Chapter Three, "1885," assesses his activities during that year of conflict but concentrates on the controversies related to apprehending Riel. In particular, attention is given to resolving the opposing views of Armstrong and Hourie and the question of who played the leading role. Armstrong was not involved in any newsmaking events after Riel's capture, and, in his memoir, he does not disclose much about what he did after 1885. Even so, it has been possible to gather details about his post-1885 years and thus complete the portrayal of his life story. Chapter Four, "1885 to 1940," introduces Armstrong's wife and children, looks at his return to and ten-year sojourn in Oklahoma, explores his retirement in Calgary, and concludes with his final days in California.

In Part Two, Robert Armstrong's Memoir—in suspension for a century—Armstrong speaks to us directly.[2] He was a consummate storyteller and so some of his claims relating to certain historical events appear unconvincing; all the same, his story vividly depicts the saga between the buffalo hunters and the Indians and is a reliable account of the savage nature of that series of encounters. Armstrong's language further illustrates and reminds us of the callous attitudes toward Indigenous peoples that prevailed in those days.

Appendices 1 and 2 are compilations of some of the multitude of accounts of Riel's apprehension by reporters, Middleton, later writers, the three scouts, and others. I point out the inconsistencies and errors in some of those reports, and the discrepancies found in the stories provided by the scouts.

A NOTE ON TERMINOLOGY

When referring to North American Indigenous peoples (excluding the Métis and Inuit), I have in a few instances made use of the term "First Nations" (commonly used in Canada), but terminology related to first peoples in the American and historical contexts proved problematic and awkward.

In the United States, Indigenous peoples have not adopted the term "First Nations," preferring instead to be called American Indians, Native Americans, or Indians, while some advocate First Americans. My impression, however, is that these relatively current terms are still evolving and not entirely satisfactory.

When I initially tried writing the terms "First Nations," "American Indians," or "Native Americans" into this story, a story set in a time long before these names were formulated, the result was sometimes jarring and incongruous—in fact, they became something like speed bumps in the narrative. When reading those terms, couched in the story, I felt their usage seemed forced and hence of dubious value.

To avoid this effect, and after hearing the opinions of a Cree Elder and other First Nations scholars, I decided to use the term "Indian" almost exclusively. Admittedly, though "Indian" has been (and still is) sometimes used in a demeaning way, and may have unfavourable connotations for some readers, I use the term in keeping with the English idiom of the era in which Armstrong lived and with no negative intentions.

MAPS

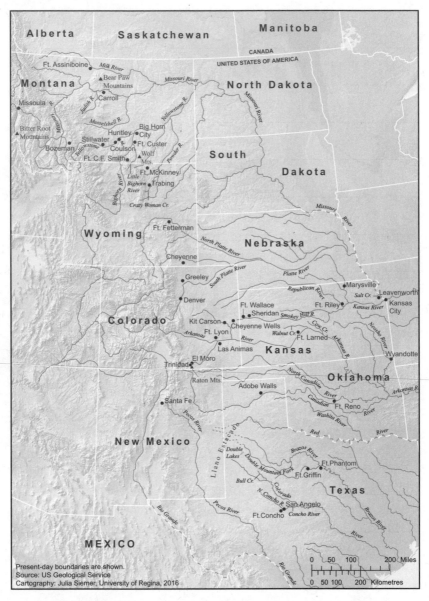

Present-day boundaries are shown.
Source: US Geological Service
Cartography: Julia Siemer, University of Regina, 2016

Map I. U.S. Plains, circa 1870s

Map 2. Southern and Central Saskatchewan and Alberta, circa 1880s

Part One

THE LIFE OF ROBERT ARMSTRONG

Chapter One

BEFORE ROBERT ARMSTRONG

IDENTITY

Robert Armstrong, prior to his name change, was Irvin Mudeater. This appears to be a fact known only to his family and some close acquaintances. Irvin was the son of Matthew Mudeater, a prominent member and chief of the Wyandots, and Nancy Pipe, a descendent of a Delaware chief. Armstrong does not reveal this in his memoir or elsewhere, but his son-in-law, to whom he dictated his memoir, does make an oblique reference to Armstrong's former surname when he says that Armstrong was known as "'Muddy' to the hunters and plainsmen of the great [American] South West."[1] Irvin Mudeater's motive for the name change was to shed a name associated with a crime he allegedly committed in the United States. His granddaughter, Ella Melendrez, writes, "I heard that Grandpa Armstrong changed his name when he went to Canada because of trouble with the law in the United States. He crossed the border to avoid capture."[2] Of course, he may have had additional personal reasons for the name change that now are impossible to determine.

He had relatives with the surname Armstrong (in his memoir he mentions a cousin called Si Armstrong), so it would be natural to assume that he chose the surname of a kinsman.[3] However, that is not the case. Melendrez recalls, "He did change his name in

Prince Albert to Armstrong. I'm not sure of the year but probably before he married Grandma. According to Mother, he took the name of Armstrong because he enjoyed being a scout for somebody by that name. I'm sure it was somebody he knew."[4] He used the Armstrong name for more than two decades in Canada, but when he moved back to the United States and resided there for ten years, he reverted to his former name, Mudeater.[5] Upon his return to Canada, he once again became Robert Armstrong.

Figuring out just how Armstrong self-identified involves turning to guesswork. He grew up Wyandot, albeit as an American citizen, in contrast with the majority of Native Americans at the time. Most of his adult life, however, was spent apart; he lived among white men and fully participated in their ways. His sense of being different from the Plains Indians of the Southwest is apparent when he refers to the Kiowa, Comanche, and other tribes as "savages" and "Redskins." In the 1901 Census of Canada, Armstrong presented himself as a white Presbyterian Englishman.[6] All the same, he must have felt some bond to his roots since, after returning to the United States in 1904, he specified in the 1910 U.S. Federal Census that he was Indian, even though some of his siblings declared that they were white.[7] For decades Armstrong was listed in the annual Wyandot census conducted by the Quapaw Agency, and later his children were registered as well.[8] When back in Canada, he claimed his racial or tribal origin was "Irish."[9] Shortly before his death, in the 1940 U.S. Federal Census, he repudiated his Indian roots and described himself as being white.[10] It is fair to conclude that Armstrong represented himself variously and according to the community in which he was living at the time.

WYANDOT HISTORY

The Wyandots (also, Wendats, Wyandotts, Wyandottes), a tribe connected to the Huron Confederacy, experienced many migrations during their history.[11] In the seventeenth century they were forced to move from their long-term home in Ontario to several locations in the upper Great Lakes region. In the early 1700s, they settled in the Detroit region, and by mid-century they started to migrate to the southern shore of Lake Erie (in the vicinity of Sandusky, Ohio). Beginning in the 1800s, the Wyandots were compelled to surrender much of their Ohio lands to accommodate encroaching white settlers. As the number of settlers in the area increased, the U.S. government proposed to resettle the Wyandots and other tribes to west of the Mississippi. A treaty was signed in 1842 whereby the Wyandots would be moved to the area of the state of Kansas. When some seven hundred tribal members arrived there in July 1843, they were not satisfied with the location proposed for them so they purchased land from the Delawares at the place where the Kansas and Missouri Rivers meet—in fact, where Kansas City, Kansas, is today. In the several months between their arrival and the time when they established their homes, many Wyandots died of illness and were buried on a hillside in what was later to be named the Huron Indian Cemetery, which now is usually referred to as the Wyandot National Burial Ground.[12] Years of negotiations passed before the Wyandots received the government's promised compensation for the loss of their properties in Ohio. Not every Wyandot was removed to Kansas, however, and small Wyandot communities continued to exist in Michigan and Canada.

In spite of floods, epidemics, and other problems experienced in the first few years at their new location, the Wyandots developed farms, some businesses, and a ferry across the Kansas (Kaw) River. Many Wyandots had been educated at a mission school in Ohio and a number of them had entered professions. Several of the leading members of the tribe had mixed white and Native ancestry, and some were white people who had been adopted by the tribe. The Wyandots, when still in Ohio, had taken on many of the practices of so-called "civilization" and occupied themselves in agriculture and commercial activities in Kansas. They subsequently negotiated a treaty with the federal government in 1855 whereby tribal members could become U.S. citizens. (This Wyandot society, when contrasted with the cultures of other Indians of the Southwest at the time, might explain Armstrong's feelings of being distinct from other Indian peoples and also his sense of belonging to the white cultural world.) The treaty required the dissolution of tribal government and dividing up the reserve land to make it available for individual ownership.

Soon after 1855, the Wyandots experienced their most difficult decade. Division of communal land into individual plots had fostered the incursion of white settlers who brought with them their various vices and hostile pro-slavery and anti-slavery factions. The Wyandot Christians, from their days in Ohio, belonged to the Methodist Episcopalian Church and were opposed to slavery. However, in Kansas, one of the church's ministers was from the South and his promotion of the opposite view divided the congregation with the result that two separate churches were built, both of which were subsequently burned by opposing groups in 1856, long before the start of the Civil War. The misery of the times prompted Chief Matthew Mudeater (Armstrong's father) to lead about two hundred Wyandots to Indian Territory in 1857, to a region now called Ottawa County, Oklahoma, where they settled on reserve land offered to them by the Senecas. This migration was carried out without the consent of the federal authorities, and it was not until 1867 that a reservation for the Wyandots in Oklahoma was formalized by treaty.

During the Civil War, the Wyandots who remained in Kansas and those in Indian Territory suffered tremendously and were made destitute. When the Confederate Army advanced on Indian Territory in 1862, the Wyandots fled back to Kansas. In 1865 a number of them began returning to their former places in Oklahoma. Factionalism originating in 1855 between those who favoured citizenship (the Citizen's Party headed by Matthew Mudeater) and those who opposed dissolving tribal status for citizenship (the Indian Party) led to internal dissention that lasted many decades.

After signing the 1867 treaty that provided for a Wyandot reservation in Indian Territory, many Wyandots still residing in Kansas decided to move to Oklahoma, where Indian tribal organization had now been re-established. Some of the Wyandots who had relinquished status in favour of citizenship requested to have their tribal status reinstated. Through adoptions and petitions, individual members of the Citizen Party were able to rejoin the tribe. In 1876 the Wyandotte Council chose Chief Mudeater and two other delegates to travel to Washington in order to secure funds owed to the Wyandots from prior treaties and obligations.

Just as the reservation in Kansas had been partitioned decades earlier, the reservation in Oklahoma was broken up. The Dawes Act of 1887 prescribed the partitioning of reserve land and for allotments to be given to individuals registered on the annual census rolls of the Wyandot Indians at the Quapaw Agency. Once the allotments were made, the Wyandotte Association, with Alfred Mudeater (Armstrong's brother) as vice-president, leased land from the allottees for a town site to be located in the area of a post office named Grand River. The town, named Wyandotte, was to become the cultural and administrative centre for the Wyandots of Oklahoma. Today there are four Wyandot Nations—the Wyandotte Nation of Oklahoma, the Wyandot Nation of Kansas, the Huron-Wendat of Wendake (Quebec), and the Wyandot Nation of Anderdon in Michigan.

ARMSTRONG'S ANCESTORS

Armstrong's ancestry is not typical. Notwithstanding his lineage from Wyandot and Delaware chiefs, two generations earlier, Armstrong actually did have a white paternal great-grandfather. His occasional reference to being English or Irish, therefore, has some justification, even though he would have had little experience of English culture as a child. His father, Matthew Mudeater, was the son of "Russia" Mudeater, who, in turn, was the son of a white man, who had been adopted as a boy by the Wyandots. Several versions of this story and of the origin of the name Mudeater are found in William Connelley's *Provisional Government of Nebraska Territory and the Journals of William Walker*:

> The name Mudeater is an honored one in the Wyandot Nation. There are different accounts of the manner in which it became fixed as a family name. Alfred J. Mudeater, Esq., [Armstrong's brother] of Wyandotte, Indian Territory, gave me substantially the following: A war party of Wyandots went up the Big Sandy River about the time of

the Revolutionary War, for the purpose, as he said, of falling upon the Cherokees, but much more probably for the purpose of raiding the settlements west of New River in Virginia, or along the Watauga in what is now East Tennessee. This party went down a valley after passing the head waters of the Big Sandy River. This valley was inhabited by white settlers who fled at the approach of the Indians, who passed on and went far beyond it. They were gone for about two weeks, when they returned up this same valley to again reach the waters of the Big Sandy, which they would descend on their way home. As they were marching up this little valley they saw a small boy run down to the creek some distance ahead of them and disappear in the bushes that fringed the stream. Some of the warriors hastened to the point where the boy was last seen but he was nowhere to be found. The other warriors of the party came up and a close and systematic search was instituted for the fugitive. One of them noticed that the creek had cut in under the roots of some trees, leaving a mass of roots and earth overhanging the water. He plunged into the stream and looked under this overhanging mass. He saw a boy's legs at the farthest corner of the cavity thus found, and, seizing him by the feet, drew him forth.

The child, for he was nothing more, being only about six or seven years old, was famished and emaciated. So extreme had been his sufferings from hunger that he had been eating the soapstone found along the bed of the creek. This soapstone and clay were smeared about his mouth and over his face. The Indians, with that aptness for which they are famous in the bestowal of names, called him Mud Eater, a name which he retained ever after. The warriors gave him food, and carried him with them to their town on the Sandusky. He said that his people had either abandoned him or forgotten him in their hasty flight from the Indians, and he had been left to starve, or to whatever fate might befall him. The Indians adopted him and he grew up among them and married a Wyandot woman.

The Hon. Frank H. Betton, of Wyandotte County, Kansas, who married Kim Susanah Mudeater, the sister of Alfred J. Mudeater, Esq. [also Armstrong's sister], who gave me the foregoing account, believes it possible that the name may have been bestowed from the habits of the turtle which burrows in the mud, and which might be said to be a mud eater. This is a plausible and tenable theory, and it is quite possible that it is correct, if the boy was adopted by the Big Turtle Clan, or the Mud Turtle Clan.

He related to me another tradition. A party of Wyandots went to visit another tribe, perhaps the Shawnees, or the Delawares. Arrived at the spring at which the village supply of water was obtained they beheld an emaciated white boy eating clay from its banks. He was a captive and had been adopted and had almost starved. The Wyandots from compassion bought him and adopted him into their tribe, and gave him the name of Mud Eater, from the circumstance which caused his purchase and adoption into the Wyandot Nation. The improbable part of this version of the matter lies in the assertion that he had been starved after adoption. This could not have been, unless the whole tribe was starving. It was contrary to all Indian customs to withhold food from anyone. While one had food all had it.[13]

According to Connelley, who was the author and editor of several books on the histories of Nebraska and Kansas, the adopted white boy called Mud Eater eventually married a Wyandot, and they had a son named "Russia" Mudeater. The personal name "Russia" seems improbable—more likely it is an adaptation or corruption of a Wyandot name that sounds similar.[14] "Russia" Mudeater married a daughter of Adam Brown, another white boy who had been adopted by the Wyandots and who later became their chief. One of their children was Matthew Mudeater, Armstrong's father. There is no further information about "Russia" Mudeater, but the death of his wife, Armstrong's grandmother, is noted in Provisional Governor of Nebraska Territory William Walker's diary entries for March 1848:

Tuesday, 28—Clear and frosty morning . . . To-day at 12 o'clock the widow Mudeater departed this life, a worthy and good woman gathered to her fathers.

Wednesday, 29—Clear and frosty morning. 4° below "freezing." Attended the funeral of the widow Mudeater.[15]

The widow Mudeater (1788–March 28, 1848) was buried in the Huron Cemetery in Kansas City.[16] Presumably, her husband, "Russia," had died earlier in Ohio. Robert Armstrong, thus, had white and Indigenous roots. The identity of the white boy adopted by the Wyandots will likely be forever a mystery.

MATTHEW MUDEATER, FATHER OF ROBERT ARMSTRONG

Matthew Mudeater, father of Robert Armstrong, was born on February 12, 1812.[17] His wife, Nancy Pipe (Armstrong's mother), was "a direct descendant of Hopocan, or Captain Pipe, Chief of the Wolf Clan, and afterwards Head Chief of all the Delawares, and who burned Colonel Crawford at the stake in what is now Crawford County, Ohio."[18] Matthew Mudeater, in one instance, stated that he and his wife were born in Canada; in another, Ohio.[19] In all likelihood, he was born in Canada, though Nancy may have been born in Ohio. An 1836 map of the Huron (Wyandot) Reserve shows Matthew Mudeater as the owner of some land in the southern tip of Ontario, just across the Detroit River from Michigan.[20] The couple had been educated at the Methodist Episcopal Church School in Upper Sandusky, Ohio, and both were described as being "exceedingly fair and handsome."[21] Three of their children—Silas, Susanah, and Dawson—were born in Ohio.[22]

In the summer of 1843, the Mudeaters were part of the Wyandot exodus from Ohio to Kansas. From that pivotal year onward, Matthew Mudeater was politically and socially active, engaging in diverse activities for the betterment of his community. As mentioned previously, soon after arriving at their destination, and not willing to settle far from established communities, the Wyandots purchased land from the Delawares. Mudeater's name appears as one of the signatories of that purchase agreement. In their new location, Matthew Mudeater "lived two miles west of the mouth of the Kansas River and had a fine orchard."[23]

Mudeater's ambition was noted by visitors to the area: "The Wyandot nation continued to improve their lands, so that they would be a credit to the most skillful of 'white agriculturists'. In fact, every missionary who came among them expressed his surprise at their skill in this direction. Matthew Mudeater, James Charloe and George I. Clark were especially distinguished for the energy manifested in making improvements, planting orchards, etc."[24] In March 1848, William Walker also remarked on Mudeater's proficiency as a farmer: "Thursday, 16 . . . Beautiful morning . . . Called upon the Grammar school. Went to M. Mudeater and engaged ten bushels of potatoes. Friday, 17 . . . Mr. Mudeater brought the potatoes I contracted for yesterday. Warm day, pleasant evening."[25] In the 1860 U.S. Federal Census, Matthew Mudeater valued his real estate at eight thousand dollars and his personal estate at one thousand dollars. In the same census, his daughter Susannah, age nineteen, who married Frank Betton in 1860, had real estate worth $1,200, more than that of her husband.

Matthew Mudeater was elected chief of the Wyandots for several terms. Between some terms he served as a council member, and his home was often used as a council meeting place. The *Kansas City Star* described the fire that "destroyed the home [Armstrong's childhood home] of the Chief of the Wyandotte Indians in the 'Forties and Fifties'" [1840s and 1850s], thus:

> The burning of the old Mudeater home west of Kansas City, Kas., early yesterday morning marked the passing of an interesting relic of border times. Many historic memories centered around the old log house. Not only was it the tribal palace of the Wyandotte Indians for many years, but it stood as a landmark ever since 1845. As the city grew each year the old log house became a stranger sight.
>
> The old Mudeater house, as it was known, was probably the oldest in the vicinity of Kansas City, Kas. Matthew

Mudeater was in 1845, at the time it was built, the head chief of the Wyandottes. Under the log roof the great council of the Wyandottes was held in 1855, at which it was decided to accept the offer of the United States government of land in the Indian Territory and under which the Wyandottes surrendered their tribal possessions in Wyandotte County. [This is incorrect—in 1855 the Wyandottes accepted United States citizenship while surrendering their tribal possessions in Wyandotte County] . . . and his home was a place where at parties and receptions the whites and the Indians met to pass away the winter evenings.[26]

In the early 1850s, Matthew Mudeater played a part in establishing the Territory of Kansas. As a member of a delegation, he travelled to Washington in 1855 to sign the treaty permitting the Wyandots to become U.S. citizens, which required the dissolution of their reservation and tribal status. After the signing, reserve land was partitioned and individual tribal members received allotments. Mudeater's property amounted to 360 acres.[27] Allotments were not made to those judged to be incompetent or to orphans, but provisions were made for those individuals by assigning guardians for them. Matthew Mudeater, a guardian for several individuals, received four thousand dollars to provide for his wards.[28] Years later, in 1871, a commission examined how some of these guardianship cases were handled. John Sarahass testified that Matthew Mudeater "was guardian for a great many persons, but does not remember what disposition was made of the funds in his hands; he thought him a liberal guardian, and that his settlements before the council were satisfactory; that at such settlements, to the best of his recollection, very little, if any, money was usually left in his hands."[29]

The dissolution of the reservation and subsequent white settlement created numerous problems, including theft of the Wyandots' animals and other property. In 1858 Matthew Mudeater and Silas Armstrong wrote to the acting commissioner of Indian Affairs that "There are at this time trespassers on the Wyandott lands and who are now occupying the same as they claim by virtue of 'Preemption

Law'. These settlers are destroying timber and otherwise interfering with the rights of the Wyandotts."[30]

As mentioned earlier, prior to the Civil War, fighting between pro-slavery and anti-slavery groups destroyed two churches as well as other properties. On July 1 and 4, 1859, Mudeater testified before Commissioner Kingman and requested financial compensation for the loss of the Wyandot churches:

> Matthew Mudeater, being duly sworn, says: That he is a Wyandott; lives about 2½ miles from the city of Wyandott; lived there at the time the two churches were burned in Wyandott; did not see the fire; and does not know who set them on fire, or why they were burned; both of the churches were burned. I have heard the testimony of the two preceding witnesses, and concur with them in their statements as to the buildings and the values given to them; I was acquainted with the buildings; have seen them often.[31]

The host of tribulations in the 1850s prompted Chief Mudeater, in 1857, to lead a group of about two hundred disheartened Wyandots out of Kansas Territory to Indian Territory in what is now the state of Oklahoma. At the same time, some individuals left Kansas for Ohio, Michigan, and Canada. Though he escorted the band of two hundred to Oklahoma, it appears that Mudeater did not move there at that time. His testimony in 1859 regarding the church fire and other records place him in Kansas after having led the group to Indian Territory. Further, the minutes of the National Council show him receiving fifty dollars for "Repairs to the National Grave Yard" in April 1859, when he was "appointed a committee of one to ascertain how many graves of deceased Chiefs could be found in Wyandott."[32] The 1865 Kansas State Census confirms that Mudeater was still a resident of Kansas at that time.

In 1865 (after the end of the Civil War), some of the Wyandots who had fled to Kansas during the war began returning to their homes in Oklahoma. The Mudeaters did move to Oklahoma later that year or soon after. The following years were marked by wrangling over whether or not those who gave up status to become citizens in 1855 should be allowed to live on the reservation in Indian Territory. Mudeater, a staunch proponent of adopting U.S. citizenship, must have been disappointed by the way things turned out. Difficulties with the white settlers and the impoverishment of the Wyandot community during the Civil War, however, led him to change his mind. In an 1867 Wyandotte tribal roll, Matthew Mudeater reports being destitute and wishing his name and those of his family members to be on the tribal roll.[33] His tribal status was reinstated on June 3, 1872.

In 1875 Matthew Mudeater, Nicholas Cotter, and John Sarahass journeyed to Washington DC, to settle unresolved matters relating to earlier agreements. At the same time, they posed for a photograph and were interviewed by John Wesley Powell, director of the Bureau of Ethnology at the Smithsonian Institute. In his report to the Smithsonian, Powell included a description of Wyandot traditions as they had been related to him in the interview.[34] Matthew Mudeater died on August 20, 1878. He was buried in Bland Cemetery alongside his wife, Nancy, who had died three years earlier.[35]

Robert Armstrong's father was a man of action—a successful entrepreneur who was also a dedicated public servant. Matthew Mudeater was a prominent Wyandot chief, and the tribal meetings held in his home must have been witnessed by the young Armstrong. He, like Moses leading the Israelites out of Egypt, led his distressed people out of Kansas to Indian Territory in Oklahoma. He was his people's representative and met with high officials in Washington.

It is astonishing that, in his memoir, Armstrong would not have a word to say about his father's noteworthy activities. But all Armstrong reveals about his father is that he took him buffalo hunting. Perhaps he found his father's other activities boring, and only the excitement of the hunt impressed him. His memoir is about his life, of course, and he may have felt that Matthew Mudeater's only relevant contribution to his story was his first experience on the buffalo range. Either that, or he may have had an ulterior motive. In his memoir, Armstrong avoids all mention of his Indian ancestry, and while in Canada he consistently portrayed himself as an American or of English or Irish descent. If he were to speak of his father's work, necessarily, he would have had to inform his readers of his original Indian identity, a disadvantageous fact in a society that idolized him for his role in arresting the Métis leader.

ARMSTRONG'S SIBLINGS

In his memoir, Armstrong hardly broaches the subject of his siblings. He speaks of attending school with an unnamed brother and makes a passing remark about his sister, Sue. During his first years away from home, Armstrong periodically visited his parents and siblings. However, after about the age of twenty-five, thirty years would pass before he saw any of them again. He recollects that after being away for such a protracted time, his family had assumed that he had been killed in some pistol fight years earlier. Though absent for three decades, Armstrong must have had infrequent contact with his family, or news about him had trickled down south because, while living in Saskatchewan, the names of his children began appearing in the annual Wyandot Census in Oklahoma.[36]

Robert Armstrong, the middle child in a family of nine, was born on January 21, 1849.[37] William Walker's journals provide the following information about Matthew and Nancy Mudeater's children: Silas, died in infancy; Susanah, born in Ohio, March 5, 1841; Thomas Dawson, born February 1843; Zelinda, 1845; Mary, 1847; Irvin [Robert Armstrong], 1849; Benjamin, 1851; Infant who died; Alfred J., 1855; Matthew, 1857; and Ida, 1859.[38] In most records Dawson replaces Thomas Dawson and, at least in one instance, Kim Susanah is substituted for Susanah (more frequently spelled Susannah).[39]

Ida, the youngest in the family, attended school in Wyandotte, Oklahoma, after the family had moved there from Kansas. She would have been about thirteen when the teacher at the school remarked, "We had in the school Ida Mudeater, Elizabeth Choplog, Margaret Splitlog, Susan Bearskin, Susan Swahas, and many other odd names. All the Indian children like to smoke, and when they went home they usually brought back a pipe and tobacco, which they hid near the mission, and then there was great glee among them. I had to be very watchful to keep them from this vice."[40] From July to September 1886, Ida worked as a laundress at the Cheyenne Boarding School, and from April to June 1887 as a domestic at the Arapaho Boarding School.[41]

Little is known about Matthew Jr. It is not clear whether he or his father is the one referred to in an essay titled "New Fruits in 1879," in which Matthew Mudeater is cited as the grower of a cultivated variety of peach called 'Wyandotte Chief'.[42]

Alfred Mudeater "was appointed in 1896 by James Walker, an Indian agent, to help plat the town of Wyandotte. He was a businessman owning a hay and feed store located at the end of North Main Street. Alfred served as mayor in 1901 and again several times later. He married Julia Robitaille, a postmistress. They owned and operated a grocery store and a hotel on the east corner of Main and Broadway."[43] In the acknowledgements in one of his books, William Connelley reports, "I wish to mention particularly the services and aid that Mr. Alfred Mudeater and his excellent wife gave to this work. In addition to the generous hospitality which I enjoyed in their home, Mr. Mudeater was always ready to take me to any part of the Wyandot Reserve that I desired to visit, or to send for and bring any Wyandot to his house that I desired to see and converse with."[44]

Alfred died on July 19, 1929. The announcement of his death in the *Miami* (OK) *Daily News-Record* (an Oklahoma paper) informs that:

Alfred Mudeater, 80-year-old Wyandotte Indian and virtually a life-time resident of Ottawa County, was found dead in his bed at his home in Wyandotte at 8 o'clock this morning. Mudeater had been in apparent good health, except for slight chills, of which he had been complaining for the last several days. . . . In addition to the store, which he owned at the time of his death and operated until about ten years ago, he conducted a hotel which became popular in this part of the state because of the home-cooked meals served there. Fellow-townsmen said that many times there would be people from a dozen nearby towns at the Sunday dinners.

Mudeater was known over the state by both the people of his own tribe and whites. Not typically Indian, he showed no backwardness about talking or acting, and was an ardent believer in the rights of self-expression. . . . Mudeater, it was reported had no relatives in the state. He had no children, but he has a brother [Armstrong] who is in Canada. His wife preceded him in death.[45]

Benjamin was the brother who, with Armstrong, went off to attend school for a brief time in Berea, Ohio. There was a school in Kansas City that the Mudeaters would have attended, but the trip to Ohio was for schooling beyond what was possible where they lived. When an Indian police service was established in Wyandotte, Benjamin served on it. The 1900 Census reports his occupation as farmer, but in 1910, under "occupation," simply "own income" was recorded.[46] Benjamin and his wife, Sydnie (also, Sidney), a white woman from Kentucky, had several children, among them Susan, Catherine, and Doane. The graves of three infants in Bland Cemetery almost certainly are those of Benjamin's children. Benjamin died sometime in late 1924 or early 1925. His widow and her two grown children, Catherine and Doane, moved to Phoenix, Arizona, in 1925; and later in that decade, the family moved to San Diego and to other places in California.[47]

Zelinda, because the name Mudeater appears on her headstone, most likely was not married. She is buried beside her parents in Bland Cemetery. The inscription reads: "Zelinda, Daughter of M. and N. Mudeater, died 11 May 1884, aged 39 years, 2 months, and 2 days."

Armstrong's sister, Mary, "was educated at a private school in Portsmouth, N.H. [New Hampshire], and on her return married Scott Armstrong, son of Silas Armstrong, formerly a chief of the Wyandottes."[48]

Dawson, in 1880, was living in his sister Susannah's household in Kansas. At the time he was thirty-seven years old, and according to the 1880 U.S. Federal Census of Kansas, considered himself white, and was an engineer at a mill.[49] (Susannah's husband Frank Betton was a mill owner in 1880.) He died in 1887 and was buried in Woodland Cemetery in Kansas City, the same cemetery where his sister Susannah would be interred.

Susannah, the only sibling Armstrong mentions by name, impressed her brother with her courage. She defied Civil War raiders trying to enter the family house: "With my boyish eyes I have seen these fellows raid our home while my sister Sue, whose fighting spirit was second to none, has stood in the doorway, defying the men to set foot inside. Even with a saber pointing at her breast she refused to give ground until dragged indoors by my mother to avoid possible bloodshed."

Susannah married Frank Betton, a man involved in several business ventures and who eventually became the labor statistics commissioner for the state of Kansas. In *History of the State of Kansas*, William Cutler writes that Frank H. Betton "was married in Wyandotte, March 8, 1860, to Susanna Mudeater, an accomplished and educated daughter of Matthew Mudeater, head chief of the Wyandotte nation."[50] Two years before his death in 1906, Mr. Betton described their wedding, which took place in the Matthew Mudeater home in Kansas: "I well remember the time, Mr. Betton said yesterday. Father Barnett, a Methodist missionary among the Indians, performed the ceremony. There was such a crowd inside the doors were blockaded and I had to crawl in through the window."[51]

Susannah's obituary in the *Kansas City* (MO) *Times* on August 23, 1912, contributes additional information:

> Mrs. Susannah Betton, a child of the Wyandotte tribe of Indians, died yesterday at her home on a farm near Pomeroy [now within the limits of Kansas City, Kansas] after residing sixty-nine years in Wyandotte County. She was a daughter of Matthew Mudeater, one of the first of the Indian tribe[s] from which Wyandotte County derived its name, to settle on the hills across the Kaw. Mrs. Betton was 2 years old when she was brought by her father to Wyandotte County from Upper Sandusky, O. [Ohio], where she was born March 5, 1841. Mrs. Betton was married to Frank H. Betton, an early white settler, March 8, 1860. Mr. Betton was state labor commissioner in Kansas

in 1885. Mrs. Betton is survived by six children. They are: Matthew T. Betton, Ernest L. Betton, Miss Cora Betton and Miss Florence Betton of the Kansas side, and Frank H. Betton and Mrs. Sue B. Campbell of this city. . . .[52]

Curiously, both Susannah and Armstrong chose to name their daughters Cora and Florence. But perhaps that is where the family resemblance begins and ends. Unlike his parents and siblings who remained in Kansas and Oklahoma and took up conventional occupations, Armstrong chose to live in reckless ways on the fringes of civilization.

Chapter Two

YOUTH TO 1885

BOYHOOD, WAGON TRAINS, AND SCHOOL

Robert Armstrong was born six years after his family had been removed from Ohio and resettled to where Kansas City, Kansas, is today. In those six years before his birth, his father prospered from the productive farm and orchard he had established. (Armstrong refers to his father's property as a "ranch.") It is not surprising that the earliest childhood memory Armstrong relates is accompanying his father on a buffalo hunt. Being only ten years old at the time, he was "almost scared stiff when we rode into the thick of a stampeding herd, Father shooting with all possible speed to down as many as he could before they got out of range." Armstrong, like most boys of that time, felt he had arrived at manhood at around fourteen or fifteen. Indeed, boys of that era participated in what would now be considered adult work. At age fourteen, Billy Dixon, of Adobe Walls fame, hired on as an oxen driver, and Mark Withers, a Texas cattle driver, reports being only thirteen when he made his first trip on the trail.[1] By the age of sixteen, Armstrong had endured the perils of the Civil War and twice accompanied wagon trains leaving Kansas for Colorado and Santa Fe.

Hard times befell the Mudeater family prior to and during the Civil War. The devastation, according to Armstrong, ensued not from armies battling on their property but from looting by both Union and Confederate soldiers and, above all, by two groups of marauders: the Quantrill Raiders and the Red Legs. These bands brought misfortune to most of the Wyandots. The Quantrill Raiders were associated with the Confederate Army while the criminal gangs disguised as the Red Legs supported the Union forces. When he was fifteen, Armstrong says he "enlisted in the . . . ." Unfortunately, this unfinished sentence continues on one of the two missing pages of his manuscript. Presumably he enlisted in one of several Kansas regiments in which Wyandots served. His name, however, is not on any of the regiment rolls, but that may be because, though he enlisted, he was not accepted. The 1865 Kansas State Census asks for the regiment and company of those who were in the military—the space for the answer is left blank for all the listed Mudeaters, including Irvin, making it unlikely that anyone in the family was formally in the army.

Howard Angus Kennedy, who interviewed Armstrong in 1926, provides a clue about what might be on that missing page: "In the civil war, the boy [Armstrong] squeezed into a Kansas regiment. He was soon squeezed out again, as not tall enough for Uncle Sam. But he was not too small to drive a six mule team for the army, and was doing that when a southern force swooped down and captured him."[2] The gap in the memoir makes it impossible to determine when and for how long his Civil War activities lasted. If, as Armstrong says, he enlisted at age fifteen then he would have done so sometime in 1864, in which case his involvement would have been brief.[3]

Armstrong's first experience with a wagon train nearly cost him his life. During the Civil War, part of the army on the frontier was withdrawn for duty in the East, emboldening the Indian raiders, who now felt free of retribution. In the summer of 1864, "drivers of freight wagons were afraid to cross the plains, and the Denver area began running short of food. Mail service to Santa Fe was stopped because of Kiowa strikes against stage stations and coaches."[4] In this troubled time, Armstrong hired on "with the Blanchard outfit." Andrew Blanchard, based in Leavenworth, Kansas, was the leader of a convoy consisting of fourteen wagons. His train joined with several others to form a caravan of ninety-five wagons and over one hundred armed men, which set off on the Santa Fe Trail. During the summer of 1864 and earlier, because freighting parties and other travellers were frequently attacked by the Kiowa, Comanche, and Cheyenne, only very large groups were permitted to travel beyond Fort Larned.[5]

Armstrong recollects that about a week of preparations preceded the caravan's departure and that drivers were hard to come by: "There were several other outfits preparing for the train which puts me in mind of one small outfit owned by an old man who was of a religious turn of mind. Drivers were scarce and one day, whilst his outfit was loading up, a certain man passed him heading for some other outfit. The old man called out to him, 'Hello there, can you drive bulls?' The man turned and replied, 'Yes, I can drive 'em to hell and back.' The old man returned, 'I'm not freighting there this year, you can go on.'"

In mid-August, the sizeable formation of oxen and mules towing wagons, bullwhackers goading them on, cattle herds, and armed men on horseback began the westward trek. On August 21, 1864, during a rest stop near the Arkansas River, the group was attacked by Cheyenne warriors at about one in the afternoon. While parts of Armstrong's account of this encounter are questionable, his description of his rather non-heroic part in the episode suggests that he was caught up in this raid. When Armstrong first spotted trouble, he and a companion were bathing in a river. In his dash back to camp, he lost his boots in the mud and, to save his life, had to run over prickly pear cacti. Meanwhile, Blanchard, unaware of the large war party, rode out after several warriors whom he had spotted near his herd. He was shot, lanced in the shoulder, and had an arrow shot through his back and through his stomach. According to Colonel Milton Moore, who was with the wagon train and whose account of the event is given in W. H. Ryus's book about the Santa Fe trail, the attackers drove off all Blanchard's stock except two oxen while the other trains were, for the most part, unaffected. (Armstrong, however, says only one blind mule was left.) After dark, Blanchard's night herdsman, using Blanchard's surviving horse, volunteered to take a message to Fort Larned.[6] According to Armstrong, that same night, "two men left camp with the blind mule to obtain assistance from Fort Leonard [Larned]." Colonel Moore says the messenger left on Blanchard's pony.[7] Though Blanchard lost his animals, the other groups would still have had many horses, so, even if the messenger did not leave on Blanchard's pony, it is hard to accept that he went off on a blind mule. On the other hand, Armstrong may have not meant his readers to take "blind mule" literally.

After the fight, several of Blanchard's men and Armstrong practised scalping on the dead bodies that were left behind: "As they left several dead near the corral we decided to try our hand at scalping, which, by the way, was considered quite legitimate in those days and thought nothing of anyway. I took my first scalp at the Big Bend of the Arkansas River."

Away from home for a long period for the first time, Armstrong was just a teenager when this calamity befell him. Did this first experience with an Indian raid and his brush with death have a formative effect? It would seem that, rather than feeling fear or revulsion, he reacted with excitement and anticipation of further adventure, for, after the incident, he did not choose the safety of settled communities but remained in the danger zone for more than a decade, living through similar experiences many times. It is doubtful, though, that he would have attempted scalping if the older men in his group did not engage in it, perhaps goading and teasing him to show his grit and do likewise. His trip with the Blanchard wagon train may have been a catalyst to his adopting the view that the Indians of the Southwest were alien and that he was a white frontiersman.

Early in 1865, Armstrong once again accompanied a freighting party that was transporting goods and escorting a herd of cattle from Fort Leavenworth to Denver, a trip lasting almost three months. The expedition was uneventful, and Armstrong chose to make a hurried trip home by stagecoach, which took only one week, while the returning wagon teams rambled along for nearly a month. Armstrong's hasty return may have been connected with his intention to attend school that fall. Also, Matthew Mudeater had purchased some land in Oklahoma in 1865. As noted previously, however, it is not clear just when the Mudeater family actually left their Kansas home.

Though he speaks of learning to ride, rope, and shoot at a very early age, Armstrong does not mention anything about his earliest schooling. (The first school house in the Wyandot community was built near his father's home.) After practising scalping and experiencing other frontier-life activities, it is unexpected to hear him say that he, his brother Benjamin, and some friends set off to attend school at Baldwin University in Berea, Ohio. The group enrolled in the Preparatory Department and the Commercial Department for the 1865–1866 school term. The Preparatory Department provided something similar to a high-school education and prepared students to handle college work.[8] Apparently, the lure of the West was stronger than the tedium of a classroom—the brothers returned home before completing their first year. Irvin went to see Principal John Wheeler, who gave him the money Irvin's father had provided for his boys' education. The money enabled the pair to return home "with the least trouble." It is tempting to believe that Armstrong's father had pressured the boys to enroll in the school program. His wish to have his children educated is evident by Mary's attendance at a private school in New Hampshire and Susannah being described as "an accomplished and educated daughter of Matthew Mudeater."[9] The decision to abandon further schooling profoundly altered the course of Armstrong's life (and no doubt disappointed his father). Instead of a career in business or in a profession, he chose an unpredictable course, one of dangerous adventure and excitement.

ADVENTURING IN THE SOUTHWEST

By 1868 Armstrong was hauling for construction crews working on the Union Pacific Railway (later the Kansas Pacific Railway), which was being built from Kansas City to Denver. Indian raids on the railway and the workmen were a frequent occurrence; consequently, in addition to employing an occasional armed escort, construction workers carried guns as well as shovels. In August 1868 the track reached the point where the makeshift town of Sheridan, Kansas, would sprout up when construction halted and did not resume until October 1869. About this time, Armstrong met and joined Buffalo Bill's crew. Buffalo Bill (William Cody) was scouting for the army, but in 1867 he obtained a leave in order to fulfill a contract to supply meat for the crews building the railroad. In his autobiography, Cody says he hunted buffalo for the railroad for twelve months. Other sources mention eighteen months and also that an eight-month contract lasted until May 1868.[10] Thus, for the first half of 1868, Armstrong and Cody were both in the same place and in the employ of the railroad.

Initially, Cody had a wagon with four mules, one driver, and two butchers. Cody would shoot the buffalo; the driver would manoeuvre the wagon alongside the dead animals, and after the butchers carved out the choice cuts and loaded them up, they would head for home, often fighting off Indian attacks. The crew had rehearsed for these attacks and would form a stockade with the wagon and the meat, which would be tossed to the ground to serve as a barricade. Cody reported that during his time with the railroad, "I had five men killed . . . three drivers and the others butchers."[11] Armstrong, who had "hired out to him with my team and wagon to haul his supplies," most likely had been hired to replace one of the three dead drivers.

When William Cody's contract was up, Armstrong had the opportunity to continue supplying meat for the railroad workers on his own. From that time until his buffalo-hunting days ended many years later, he would do the hunting while his hired men did the skinning and butchering. Armstrong describes Sheridan in the fall of 1868 as being a "lively place with its saloons, gambling halls, and dance halls running full blast; the town was full of hard men, many of whom died suddenly and in their boots, gun play being right frequent and deadly." His account is supported by others: "The town was host to every bad element on the Kansas plains including gamblers, horse thieves, buffalo hunters, murderers, and prostitutes. Often it was not an exaggeration to say that Sheridan had a 'dead man for breakfast every morning' . . . Indeed, throughout Sheridan's turbulent history [two years] more than thirty men died by hanging, and nearly 100 died either in Indian raids or in shootouts among themselves."[12] The short-lived town was named after General Sheridan who, after service in the Civil War, was appointed in 1867 to head the Department of the Missouri, an administrative area that included most of the western plains. As commander, Sheridan directed the many campaigns against the tribes of that region. When General Sheridan passed by the town of Sheridan, he reportedly said that "the conditions reminded him of the Battle of Shenandoah, due to the reckless use of weapons in the town."[13]

The many camps that dotted the buffalo ranges typically included a hunter, several skinners, and a driver with mules and a wagon. After the hunt, the carcasses were skinned and the hides stretched and pegged to the ground. When dried, they were stacked and eventually hauled to collection points or markets. The crew would have had tents, other makeshift shelters, or else slept on the ground, wrapped in robes, as Armstrong informs:

> I had a crew of six men in my camp who did most of the skinning and as it was necessary to kill from seventy to eighty or one hundred head per day to keep them going, I was kept pretty busy. My hunting outfit consisted of mules and wagons and riding horses or mules, food, and supplies for six or seven men sufficient to last us several weeks. We usually took along a keg of "fire water", often very poor dope too; but as everybody was strong and healthy through living outdoors and eating nothing but plain coarse food, the after effects of its use were seldom alarming. We mostly slept on the ground with robes for bed and cover so that we were warm and comfortable.

For the next four years after departing Sheridan (from late 1868 to the winter of 1873), Armstrong operated from a base near Fort Wallace, Kansas, occasionally travelling to Denver and places south. During those four years, for the most part, he continued with the slaughter of the buffalo, sometimes for its meat, but more often for the hides, which he sold in Fort Wallace. Also during this period, in a switch from hunting, he briefly scouted with Abner T. ("Sharp") Grover and escorted two separate "recreational hunter" groups from England and the East.

Fort Wallace was established in 1865 near the western end of Kansas. Like other forts, its purpose was to make safe the westward movement of white settlement. Soldiers escorted wagon trains, protected construction crews building the railway, pursued outlaws, and battled with the hostile tribes. George Armstrong Custer, commander of the U.S. 7th Cavalry Regiment, spent the spring and early summer of 1867 in the Fort Wallace area, campaigning against the Cheyenne and Sioux. Guiding him at this time was William Comstock, described by Custer as the best scout he had ever employed: ". . . our guide was a young white man known on the Plains as 'Will Comstock.' No Indian knew the country more thoroughly than did Comstock. He was perfectly familiar with every divide, water-course, and strip of timber for hundreds of miles in either direction. He knew the dress and peculiarities of every Indian tribe, and spoke the languages of many of them."[14] In January 1968, when Custer was no longer at Fort Wallace, Comstock shot a wood contractor who had cheated him and was brought before a judge who dismissed the case. However, Comstock did not return to scouting but retired to his ranch, and only after he was assured by General Sheridan that there would be no repercussions for the killing did he return to scouting.

Meanwhile, in the autumn of 1868, while Armstrong was still at Sheridan, a wagon train was attacked near Sheridan. Major Forsyth at Fort Wallace, who was directed to find the raiders, took with him Comstock and the scout Abner T. Grover. The two were sent to locate a Cheyenne chief, which they did, but, in circumstances that are still disputed, Comstock was killed. Grover, though wounded, made it back to Fort Wallace. Forsyth's expedition ended disastrously with his second-in-command, Lieutenant Beecher, being killed at what came to be called the Battle of Beecher Island. Though doubtful, some residents at Fort Wallace, including Armstrong, believed Comstock was shot by his companion, Grover.[15] Another rumour at the fort was that Comstock was part Indian, even though that claim also seems untrue.[16] (Armstrong thought he was part Cherokee.)

Grover replaced Comstock as chief guide at Fort Wallace. He was often called "Sharp" Grover or Abner "Sharp" Grover: hence

Armstrong's recollection that he scouted with Sharp, which could only have happened before February 1869, as Sharp was killed at that time. His was part of a series of unusual scout deaths at the fort, beginning with William Comstock.

Since Comstock was killed in August 1868 while Armstrong was still in Sheridan, Armstrong's version of events could only be what was the "talk of the town" when he got to Fort Wallace at the end of the year. The rumour that Sharp killed his fellow scout must have been convincing to Armstrong for he says, "Comstock, however, got his from a man named Sharp." In his memoir, Armstrong describes with considerable detail the deaths that occurred during his stay at Fort Wallace, specifically the murder of the wood contractor, White (actually Wyatt) by Comstock;[17] the killing of Sharp Grover by a man he calls Mooney (Moody in other sources);[18] and the subsequent slaying of Mooney by yet another scout, Langford, who in turn was lynched by a vigilante group.

Departing from his routine, in the summer of 1871, Armstrong served as a guide for two recreational excursions—a pastime popular among the well-to-do of the eastern United States and Europe who wanted to experience the exotic West. The most famous of these excursions was that of the Grand Duke Alexis of Russia, who was accompanied by General Sheridan, with Custer and Cody acting as guides. Armstrong, while on a trip to Denver in 1869, claims to have seen the arrival by train of the duke and his company; he is mistaken, or he may have confused one of his visits to Denver with another one, because that hunting party arrived in January 1872, not in 1869.

The first group Armstrong escorted in 1871 included Captain Sparks of the White Star Line and a Lord Sanford. A White Star agent, Captain Hyde Sparks arrived in New York from England in July 1871, so it is quite possible that during that summer he made an excursion to the West.[19] Lord Sanford may have been the Lord Sanford with an estate in Shropshire, England. It is inconceivable that Armstrong would have come up with these names if he had not met the men. His disclosure that he was offered a position as a gamekeeper on Sanford's estate is, therefore, quite plausible. These wealthy men travelled with twelve wagons, one of which conveyed nothing but wine, spirits, and other pleasurable goods. After a lazy day at the hunt, the party "sat and yarned over the evening smokes and drinks." Armstrong remarks: "This trip was the swellest trip I ever undertook. I gained twenty pounds in six weeks—high wines and good grub tell the tale." The tourists, evidently, were pleased with their guide as Sparks offered Armstrong first-class return passage to England, and Sanford invited him to work on his estate. Predictably, Armstrong declined the offers, saying, "I figured a game keeper's life in England would be too dull; and then again I might have to shoot the ears off someone and that would be bad form over there even though it was permissible out West."

The second sporting group Armstrong escorted that summer consisted of sixteen college students from New York and their supervising professor. Unlike the first party, with their comfortable tents, these young students spent two weeks sleeping under the stars, worrying about whether the howls they heard came from coyotes or from Indians preparing an attack. Armstrong was bemused when they placed their bedding as close as possible to him, believing that the closer they were, the safer they would be.

Armstrong was still in the Fort Wallace area when, in 1873, a journalist, Amos Jay Cummings, journeyed to the American West and sent stories about his trip to the *New York Sun* and other papers. Surprisingly, Armstrong, or Mudeater, as he was known then, featured in one of Cummings's snapshots of life on the frontier. Armstrong, not without reason, does not mention this episode in his memoir. Cummings writes:

A few days ago two hunters got on a spree in Wallace. One of them was a notorious character known as Mud-Eater. Under the influence of whiskey his bump of self-esteem began to swell, and he had a desire to let the people know who he was. "I'm a coyote! I'm a wolf!" he shouted. One of his comrades said, "Well, I've knowed [sic] you a good many years, an' I've heered [sic] you howl; but I never knowed [sic] you to hurt anybody." Mud-Eater's destructiveness arose. He drew a navy pistol, and shot the speaker dead. After procuring another drink he moosied [sic] off over the plains. A party followed him and returned a day after with his clothes, declaring that they had lynched him. As they were nearly all intimate friends of Mud-Eater, their story is doubted.

Another version of the affair is that one of the crowd shouted, "I'm a wolf!" Mud-Eater replied, "I'm a wolf eater!" and put a bullet through him, making a hole big enough for a rabbit to jump through. He then disappeared, but returned within a half an hour. Lifting the dead body, he tore the shirt away from the breast, and pointing to the hole in the heart, chuckled out, "Popped just whar [sic] I aimed, by—!" He then mounted his horse and left the settlement unmolested. The man's body laid around Wallace for days before it was buried.[20]

If there are two versions, there probably are others. The remark, "I never knowed [sic] you to hurt anybody," however, is revealing as it suggests that the shooting may have been provoked in a more serious way than was reported.

Armstrong continued his hunting in the Fort Wallace area until the winter of 1873 when he moved south to the Texas Panhandle. This move was precipitated by the shrinking buffalo herds in what had been Armstrong's hunting grounds for the past several years. Until 1871 buffalo were killed for meat and for their hides, which were used for coats, rugs, blankets, and other items. However, in 1871, the development of an economical method for tanning the hides and producing a variety of leather goods from them greatly accelerated the killing.[21] John Hanner, in *Government Response to the Buffalo Hide Trade, 1871–1883*, writes, "The commerce in buffalo hides destroyed itself with remarkable speed. The buffalo of western Kansas was destroyed in less than four years (1871–1874), those of western Texas in less than five (1875–1879), and those of eastern Montana in no more than four (1880–1883)."[22] These dates align with Armstrong's movements—he migrated from regions depleted of buffalo to those areas where herds could still be found until, finally, when the Montana herds were nearly extinct, Armstrong's long career as a hunter was over.

At least on one occasion over the course of the year when he hunted in the Texas Panhandle, Armstrong brought his hides to Adobe Walls. This trading post was established in the spring of 1874 by merchants from Dodge City who looked to capitalize from the hide trade when scores of hunters moved to that uninhabited area of Texas that was the hunting ground of several tribes. The tribes that traditionally hunted there viewed the newly arrived white hunters as a threat to their survival and became increasingly hostile toward them. On June 27, 1874, a large combined force of Comanche, Cheyenne, and Kiowa warriors attacked Adobe Walls, but the twenty-eight or so defenders managed to withstand the day-long assault. Armstrong's dubious assertion that he was a participant in that renowned and much-written-about fight is probably the most controversial claim in his memoir. In his recollection of the fight, Billy Dixon, acclaimed buffalo hunter and scout, states that there were twenty-eight men and one woman at the "Walls."[23] He adds that after the fight, hunters in the area headed for safety to the post "like blackbirds from all directions and by the sixth day there were fully a hundred men at the Walls, which may have given rise to the statement so frequently made in after years that all these men were in the fight."[24] Rather than being in the fight, Armstrong may have been one of those blackbirds who flocked to the post for safety.

Armstrong's name does not appear on Dixon's list of participants, nor does it come up in the recollections of any of the other participants. It is also not inscribed on the granite monument erected at Adobe Walls to commemorate the fight. Yet, these are not sufficient reasons to dismiss his claim out of hand, even though his assertion seems tenuous. In *Guns Magazine*, Mike Venturino writes: "In fact, the actual number of white men at Adobe Walls when the Indians struck cannot be ascertained exactly, despite a granite monument in place there with names on it. Some names on the monument should not be there and some not there should be."[25] Indeed, Frank Brown, named by Dixon as a participant, and whose name appears on the monument, stated that he came to Adobe Walls after the fight.[26] Seth Hathaway, whose name is not on any list or on the monument, later declared that he was at the fight, and this was not disputed by some of the participants. He was not included because, as Lindsay Baker and Billy R. Harrison write, "he left the post at ten o'clock on the night after the battle to warn other hunters of the Indian danger. After reaching his own camp on the buffalo range, Hathaway returned directly to Dodge City rather than going back to the trading post. Thus, none of the other hide men who came in from the camps for protection offered by the post saw him there or heard his stories of the fight."[27]

Dixon says that on June 26, the day before the clash, "several hunters had come in."[28] Armstrong may have been one such hide man who arrived that day or evening and left shortly after the fight. He, too, had a camp and crew in the field to which he returned. It is unlikely that Dixon or the others would have known Armstrong's name as introductions then were not always made. Colonel Milton Moore, who was freighting on the same trip as Armstrong when Blanchard was killed, remarked, "The plainsman of that period, like his successor, the cowboy, was not inquisitive. He might ask another where he was from, but rarely his name—never his former business."[29] As a matter of fact, several of the other participants indicated that they did not know the names of some of the people at the trading post, and only later did they learn that Dixon and the famed Bat Masterson were at the fight.[30]

Whether or not Armstrong's name appears on someone else's list of participants, it will not determine if he was one of the defenders at Adobe Walls. The case against Armstrong's claim, rather, is made by his own account of the event, an account that is inaccurate and strangely silent about many of the more unforgettable happenings on that day. Adobe Walls was a tiny place made up of only four buildings from March of 1874 until the place was abandoned soon after the attack. The four buildings were the Rath & Company store, a saloon, a blacksmith's shop, and the Myers & Leonard store, which had a large stockade (corral). Baker's and Harrison's descriptions of the two stores and stockade more or less match the description provided by Armstrong, which suggests that he had been at the trading post at some time before, or shortly after, the fight.

Apart from the shooting of Billy Tyler, Armstrong says very little about the events of June 27, which is uncharacteristic of him. Understandably, memory fades; but also, during those days, the defenders did not know that the fight at Adobe Walls would one day be recorded in American history—for them, it was just one of many hostile engagements they had experienced with the Indians on the frontier. Still, for Armstrong to leave out most of the key incidents casts doubt on him being a participant. For example, Armstrong does not relate the much-talked-about, and controversial, cracking of the saloon's ridgepole in the middle of the night prior to the attack. This kept some of the occupants busy rectifying the apparent problem until dawn, when one of the men spotted the approaching attack, thus preventing a massacre at the post.[31] In addition, Armstrong neither describes nor names a single participant in the fight, save Tyler; he offers no word about the burial of Tyler, whom he says he knew well; he does not mention that there was a woman on site; he says nothing about the death of two brothers at the post; he does not speak of the accidental shooting of an employee of the Rath & Company store on the following day; he says nothing about the hunters decapitating the heads of the killed Indians and impaling them on pickets; and he is silent regarding other incidents that would have provided some credence to his claim of being present at the fight.

The site of Adobe Walls was abandoned after the fight, and the hunters retreated from the area. Armstrong says he returned home to visit his family, but gives no explanation for why he stayed there for seven long months. By 1874 most of the tribes of the Southwest had been subdued and restricted to reservations. However, a large number of Comanche, Kiowa, Cheyenne, and Arapaho still remained free, and after the failure to destroy the defenders at Adobe Walls they unleashed devastating raids in Kansas, Colorado, New Mexico, and Texas: "Parties of hide men were tortured and killed. Men were staked out on the prairie and women raped and murdered in terrible ways. The Indian outbreak that swept the southern plains that summer killed an estimated one hundred ninety white people and wounded many more. Its effects were immediate. Hide hunting stopped all together.

Hunters and settlers and anyone on the edge of the frontier fled to the protection of the federal forts."[32]

The ferocity of these attacks on hunters and others explains why Armstrong retreated to the safety of his parents' home in Oklahoma. Before describing his part in the Adobe Walls attack, he acknowledged the threat hunters faced— "Considerable risk attended the hunting game as Indians were very hostile and continually on the lookout for lonely hunters, setting them afoot by running off their mules, thus rendering them an easy prey to the Indian's rifle and scalping knife."

The vigorous raids brought on military reprisals, beginning in late summer 1874 and lasting until late spring 1875. This campaign terminated the free-roaming life of the Plains tribes in the Southwest and, in a way, the frontier itself. The defeated Comanche, Kiowa, and Cheyenne presented themselves at various forts and eventually joined their tribesmen on the reservations; some groups would escape, only to be captured and forced to return. The last of the destitute Cheyenne and Arapaho gave themselves up at the Darlington Indian Agency beside Fort Reno, Oklahoma. Armstrong admitted the role played by the buffalo hunters in bringing about the privation of these and other tribes: "The majority of these Indians had been driven into the Post by white hunters, who by this time had practically cleared large areas of the country of the buffalo, and the Indians were often in a starving condition."

It is probably not a coincidence that Armstrong left home and went west again, either in late January or February 1875, just about the time that hostilities there were coming to an end. However, he did not return to the Texas Panhandle from whence he had retreated, and neither did he resume hide hunting. Instead, Armstrong headed to Fort Reno, which began as an army camp in 1874 and was established as a fort in 1875.

In his memoir, Armstrong describes his work with the government beef herds at the Darlington Agency and then the time he spent with a survey crew. In all likelihood, the order of these two activities is reversed in Armstrong's story. He recalls two events that can be dated and that argue for the survey work occurring before his work at Fort Reno. He writes, "Shortly after returning to Fort Reno, to which place we returned after completing our [surveying] duties, riders came in with the news that a band of Kiowas had arrived in the vicinity with a couple of white girls whom they had taken prisoners, at the same time murdering their parents." This occurred on March 1, 1875.[33] He also reports working at the Darlington Agency when a clash occurred there between the Cheyenne and the soldiers on April 6, 1875.

Thus, early in 1875, Armstrong left home and joined a survey party whose government surveyor happened to have the name Robert Armstrong. Robert Armstrong and his crew had been on a survey assignment in August of the previous year.[34] The headline "The Armstrong Surveying Party" in the August 4, 1874, issue of the *Leavenworth Daily Commercial* gives the location of his camp as 1.5 miles south of Dodge City. Two weeks later the same newspaper has surveyor Robert Armstrong reporting the death of four men from Indian raids sixty miles west of Dodge, not between the Canadian and Washita Rivers where Armstrong (Mudeater) worked with the crew.[35] However, according to the *Chronicles of Oklahoma*, "all of the lands east of the one Hundredth Meridian in the western half of the present state of Oklahoma were surveyed and the plats for the same were approved between the years 1871 and 1875, inclusive."[36] This would include the region in which Armstrong (Mudeater) worked in 1875, and it is possible that Armstrong (the surveyor) had moved there when his 1874 assignment was completed. The above-mentioned August 4 article hints of this possibility: "Meyers got in here from the Canadian yesterday." It appears that Meyers was a member of Armstrong's survey crew and may have gone to the Canadian River for a preliminary assessment of the work to be contracted in 1875. Though it cannot be said with certainty, Robert Armstrong, the surveyor, may be the man whose name Irvin Mudeater adopted when he moved to Canada.

In his memoir, Armstrong (Mudeater) says, "During this survey we had to be always on our guard against possible attacks from Indians. I had volunteered to act as front sightman, this was the most dangerous position on the survey as the previous [1874] survey had amply proved, for most of the sightmen were killed." The Indians were aware that settlers followed the surveyors, and they were bent on preventing settlement. Earlier in Texas, [Comanches] "were especially worried by surveyors, determined men who practiced a dark and incomprehensible magic intended to deprive the Indians of their land. The Comanche killed them in horrible ways whenever the opportunity arose."[37]

While with the survey party, Armstrong (Mudeater) chanced upon the burial place of Chief Lone Wolf's son, who had been killed by the U.S. Cavalry in December 1873. Grief-stricken, "Lone Wolf cut off his hair, killed his horses, and burned his wagon, lodge, and buffalo robes, and vowed revenge."[38] In May 1874 Lone Wolf led a raiding party to successfully recover his son's body, which he then honoured according to Kiowa traditions. Armstrong, in his memoir, writes:

> I found the last resting place of the son of Lone Wolf, head chief of the Kiowas. He was killed during a war raid into Texas. Around his scaffold in a large circle, two hundred horses were lying dead. Lone Wolf had had these horses killed for the use of his son in the happy hunting grounds. Near his body lay his rifle, bow and arrows, also coffee, etc. I am sorry to say these articles were always looted by the boys to keep for souvenirs or, perhaps, in the case of a rifle or knife, to be used by the finder.

After surrendering at several army posts, the defeated tribes became dependent on provisions supplied by the government. Cattle were made available to the subjugated and demoralized Indians camped beside Fort Reno. Armstrong had hired on with the government and participated in apportioning those herds. When the weekly meat requirement was determined, the requisition was brought to Armstrong; he segregated a part of the herd, weighed the selected animals, and then turned them loose on the open prairie, where the Indians, reportedly, enjoyed hunting them down.

On April 6, 1875, at Fort Reno, those Indians who were involved in the hostilities of 1874 to 1875, others selected for crimes committed, and some innocents chosen to fill an arbitrary quota were being prepared to be sent to a prison in Florida. One of the prisoners escaped and ran to a Cheyenne camp near the fort. Rifle fire from the guards struck the camp, causing the occupants to think they were under attack. A fight lasting most of the day ensued.[39] Armstrong's remark that "every buck dropped his blanket and revealed to the gaze of the astonished soldiers a Winchester" is somewhat sensational and different from other accounts, which have the warriors recovering guns they had buried when they had come to surrender. Armstrong complains that he and his companions had trouble sleeping the following nights when the women "howled and groaned and at times chanted weird songs in mourning for the lost braves. Several times during the night someone would stick his head out of a tent and yell over to the Indian camp telling the squaws to shut up, perhaps following the request by a revolver shot. It was useless to do so as in a few minutes the racket started up again ad infinitum. This was kept up for several nights until they tired themselves out and we had peace."

In 1876 Armstrong, with a partner, Henry Hughes, once again returned to the buffalo range. They journeyed to the headwaters of the Brazos and Concho Rivers in northwest Texas, and from their camp on the Brazos River carted their hides to Fort Griffin. During his time in the area, Armstrong nurtured a baby panther and later a starving eagle, making pets of them. When the panther grew up, it became aggressive and had to be done away with. But before that time, "Nelly" provided plenty of amusement for Armstrong and his crew: "She always slept close to me, her gentle, though at times rather loud, purr indicating how contented she was. We often had much fun watching her feed. Sometimes we would tie a quarter of a buffalo to the hind wheel of one of the wagons and then stand back and watch her attack." It was the eagle, however, that became his confidant:

> She grew and thrived into a beautiful bald headed eagle and I became more attached to her than I had been to the panther. When we moved she would perch herself on top of the load, her huge claws grasping her support with tremendous strength, and there she would sit in solemn majesty ever and anon her beautiful wings outspreading to catch

her balance as the heavy wagon lumbered over the rough trail. Often I would spur my horse alongside the wagon and talk to her and I'll swear she understood almost all I said to her for she would look at me with her great solemn eyes as much as to say, "Yes, pard, I know all about our trials and troubles, but there's a better time coming."

Armstrong's next camp was on the North Concho River, about sixty miles from Fort Concho, Texas. His hides were brought to San Angelo, about one mile from the fort, which he describes as a "tough, little town." It was to become a "center for farmers and settlers in the area, as well as a fairly lawless area filled with brothels, saloons and gambling houses."[40] Armstrong claims he was offered the position of town marshal but declined, "although I several times acted as deputy."[41] His account of driving his horse up to the entrance of the Last Chance Saloon and a typical night in San Angelo is not far-fetched;[42] indeed, such activity was commonplace:

It was nothing thought of to ride one's horse into a saloon or store. In fact, in some places the owner of any place of suchlike business had two wide doors built, one in each opposite wall so that a bunch of horsemen out for a "time" could ride right along through without causing much damage. I have seen a crowd of hunters (and been one of the crowd) march into a saloon in Indian file, each with a Winchester in the crook of his arm pointing at the roof; as each man passed through the door, he would commence pumping the lead through the roof. In a moment the place would fill with smoke, the shingles fly, and the noise would be deafening. After getting that off their chests they would call for drinks for the house, pay for the damage wrought, and promptly forget it.

While still in the same general area, Armstrong relocated his operations to what he calls Double Mountain. Double Mountain was a way marker for travellers and hunters that consisted of two buttes in an otherwise flat landscape. Armstrong, like some others, probably means the Double Mountain Fork of the Brazos River when he uses the term "Double Mountain." The stream has its source in the Llano Estacado (also known as the Staked Plains), and somewhat farther on that high plain are the Double Lakes that Armstrong says were in the vicinity of his camp, whereas Double Mountain was in the opposite direction from Double Lakes, and quite some distance away.

By now this part of Texas was crowded with hunters and their crews: "By late September [1877], perhaps four thousand hunters, skinners, teamsters and others had scattered over the West Texas plains."[43] Bison hunter John Cook indicates that camps used to be separated by a few miles so that they did not interfere with one another. However, when at the Double Mountain Fork of the Brazos River, Cook reports finding camps "from half-mile to a mile and a half apart."[44]

In the early part of 1877, a Comanche band had left the reservation, raided several buffalo hunters' camps, and escaped to the Llano Estacado, a semiarid high plateau in northwest Texas and eastern New Mexico. The commander at Fort Concho, Colonel Grierson, was ordered to find the raiders. However, family issues forced him to leave the area, and Captain Nolan was assigned the mission. The action that followed is referred to as Nolan's Lost Expedition or the Buffalo Soldiers' War. Armstrong relates that while he was at his Double Mountain camp he acted as a guide for the 10th U.S. Cavalry during its four exhausting days without water on the Llano Estacado.

Captain Nolan, Lieutenant Charles Cooper, and sixty troopers of the 10th U.S. Cavalry set out from Fort Concho on July 10. One week later they encountered a group of twenty-eight buffalo hunters, who, after having had their horses and mules stolen, also were searching for the Comanches.[45] The two groups agreed to team up—the hunters would guide and find water while the army would provide the supplies and do the fighting if hostilities should occur. Twenty-two of the twenty-eight buffalo hunters agreed to go along with the army; six did not. José Tafoya, who was with the hunters and also had lost stock to the raiders, was chosen to guide the combined force. A supply camp was organized at Bull Creek, the place where the two groups met. Twenty soldiers remained there, some to guard the supplies, while others returned to Fort Concho for additional supplies.

The combined force of hunters and soldiers picked up a trail that led in the direction of Double Lakes (sometimes called Double Lake). After stopping for water at the lakes, Captain Nolan and most of his men spent four gruelling days in searing heat on the baked plains. The main group would not find water again until they returned to those lakes on the way back. The trail they were following went off in many directions, at times crisscrossing, creating uncertainty about which way they should be heading. Soon the group put aside the pursuit of the Comanches in favour of finding water. Part of the problem was that some of the watering spots that may have provided water at other times proved to be dry that summer.

On July 7 Lieutenant Cooper wrote that the group was lost and ". . . our men were dropping from their horses with exhaustion as we had been two days without water."[46] A decision was made to send Tafoya and eight soldiers with canteens to a possible water source. When the men did not return, Nolan elected to return to Double Lakes, the only place where they knew they would definitely find water—even though it was barely potable. The buffalo hunters disagreed, feeling water could be found in a different direction within a day. The hunters went their separate way and, after extreme trials, found water. After exiting the high plateau and returning to their home base, the hunters chanced upon some surveyors who informed them about the many horses the Comanches had abandoned when they headed back to their reservation. The hunters eventually recovered most of their lost stock without difficulty.

Meanwhile, Tafoya and the soldiers who were sent to find water did so; but then they were unable to locate Nolan and the rest of the force. They returned to the water source, expecting the troopers to make their way there as well. Rather than continuing the search for Nolan and his men, they eventually returned to the supply camp that had been established at Bull Creek.

On July 28 Lieutenant Cooper reported, "Our men had dropped back one by one, unable to keep up with us, their tongues were swollen and they were unable to swallow their saliva—in fact they had no saliva to swallow, that is, if I judge of their condition from my own. . . . During this time while lying on the ground, one of my private horses showed signs of exhaustion, staggered and fell; so, in order to relieve the men, I had his throat cut, and the blood distributed amongst them. The Captain and I drank heartily of the steaming blood . . . ."[47]

On July 29, their fourth day without water, some of the soldiers were missing and others were confused. Cooper wrote, "This, our fourth day without water was dreadful . . . men gasping in death around us; horses falling dead to the right and left . . . instead of having with us the forty rational men who left camp with us, our party now consisted of eighteen madmen."[48] Among the soldiers who had dropped out was Sergeant Umbles; he later claimed he left the command in order to find water. He and three others were successful, but they did not return to Nolan. Instead they headed for the supply camp, where they arrived on August 3 and spread the word that Nolan and his men were either dead or dying. Umbles instructed the men at the base to return to Fort Concho. The man in charge at Bull Creek refused to believe that Nolan had perished and set off with supplies for Double Lakes, where on August 4 he encountered the debilitated men.

In the mean time, in the early hours of July 30, Nolan and his men had stumbled on an old trail that they recognized as one that would get them to Double Lakes. Upon arrival there, canteens of water were sent back to the straggling line of soldiers. Eventually Nolan and his men made it back to Bull Creek, where they recuperated before returning to Fort Concho on August 14.

As Nolan and his men struggled back to Double Lakes and from there to Fort Concho, Sergeant Umbles's report about the likely deaths of the rest of the soldiers was picked up by national newspapers as a great disaster. When a courier brought word that Nolan and his men were not dead, the papers chastised the army for releasing false information: "Although they had very little news to report, and nearly all of it in error," the army released a bulletin stating, "it is ascertained that a disastrous encounter was had on the Staked Plains, in which two officers and twenty-six enlisted soldiers were killed."[49]

Armstrong might have been with Nolan's expedition for a while, but his version of the Llano Estacado catastrophe is most likely a second-hand account of the event, into which he inserted himself as the expedition's scout. In his memoir he says that, while at his hunting camp near Double Mountain, he was visited by some black soldiers from the 10th U.S. Cavalry with a message from "a General Woods" to act as a guide to find hostile Comanches headed to the Llano Estacado. (Black regiments were recruited during the Civil War and later participated in the Indian Wars in the West.) However, Armstrong's claim to have received this letter from "Woods" is not credible. Nolan chose Tafoya as his scout when he met the group of buffalo hunters at Bull Creek. Lieutenant Cooper writes, "Captain Nolan . . . thought it best to establish our supply camp at this place, and go with the hunters . . . they having as a guide a Mexican named José [Tafoya], who had been for years in the habit of trading with these Indians, and had became [sic] thoroughly acquainted with the country, and knew every 'waterhole' and possible camping place where Indians might be found."[50]

There is no evidence that any other scouts were employed when the force first reached Double Lakes. When Tafoya, with several troopers, went off in search of water and then was unable to locate the soldiers, the force was without a guide for the rest of the mission. Lieutenant Cooper, after the departure of Tafoya, states, "having nobody to guide us, being in unknown country, we did not better our condition."[51]

The letter from "General Woods" that Armstrong speaks of may refer to when Nolan read a letter he had received from General Ord to the buffalo hunters at Bull Creek. John Cook, who witnessed the first meeting between Nolan and the hunters, wrote that Nolan addressed the hunters:

"Captain Harvey [appointed leader of the hunters], order your men into line, while I read my orders from General Ord." We were standing and lounging in a group all close enough to hear distinctly. Harvey evaded the order by saying, "Captain, the men will all pay strict attention to the reading of the orders." Captain Nolan had taken the orders from his pocket and stood waiting a moment. Seeing that we made no movement whatever, he said, "Oh, I see; that's all right, men; I have been twenty-five years in the regular army and am used to discipline. I forgot for the instant that I was in the presence of civilians."[52]

Armstrong relates that "about thirty of the men decided to head north where they thought water lay somewhat nearer than my camp. They found it alright but it cost them their lives. A search party three days later found them all dead around the water's edge—they having drunk deeply of the gypsum waters of the lake and so perished." The number thirty, more or less, corresponds with the number of hunters and soldiers who had gone off in a northeasterly direction in the search of water and who did not rejoin Nolan's group. However, not only did they not die, they found water and fared better than Nolan and the soldiers who were still with him. Armstrong's claim that thirty dead men were found is groundless. The official record reveals that only four soldiers and one hunter died. Armstrong may have heard the false report of the deaths of twenty-eight men and believed it, just as Umbles felt that Nolan and his men had perished. Armstrong withdrew from the area soon after the failed expedition and probably did not hear the end of the story, which explains why he perpetuated the rumour of the dead soldiers.

MOVING NORTH

After withdrawing from the Double Mountain area, Armstrong meandered his way to Montana via New Mexico, Colorado, and Wyoming—a pattern followed by other hunters who had decimated the buffalo stock in the Southwest and now moved north to the last surviving herds in Montana. His partner, Hughes, journeyed with him, but Armstrong discloses that on their trip they joined up with another hunter, Jim White, and his crew. Armstrong, at one point, refers to White as his partner. White did travel approximately the same route at about the same time, so the two may have "partnered" from time to time on their trip north, but the two were not business partners:

> White had a reputation in Texas for being a tough character. He operated best alone or with his own men. By late summer, 1878, he had reached the Big Horn Mountains with two big span of mules, two wagons, 700 pounds of lead . . . and an old buffalo skinner named Watson. White soon met Oliver Hanna, who had been a scout with General Crook in 1876, and they soon became partners. During the winter of 1878–79, the two men had a contract to furnish 5000 pounds of game meat to the army at Fort McKinney, near present day Buffalo, Wyoming. The following winter of 1879–80, White and Hanna had a buffalo hunting camp north of the Yellowstone River near Miles City. The two hunters kept six buffalo skinners busy. . . . In the following fall of 1880, White and Hanna came into the Big Horn Basin and set up a hunting camp on Shell Creek, near the Big Horn Mountains.[53]

Armstrong's date of arrival in Trinidad, Colorado, can be determined precisely from his recollection of an event that initially bewildered him and his companions: "I remember being out on the mountain side one day when along about two o'clock in the afternoon it began to grow dark. We wondered what was the cause as it was a clear day when suddenly we remembered it was the foretold eclipse of the sun of 1878. It grew so dark we were obliged to head for camp at Dick Houghton's toll gate." The eclipse occurred on July 29, 1878.

From Trinidad, Armstrong advanced to Las Animas, Greeley, Cheyenne, Fort Fetterman, Fort C. F. Smith, and finally Fort McKinney.[54] At Greeley, the hunting party encountered a "happy colony founded by Horace Greeley who advised the young men of the East to 'Go West and grow up with the country.'"

When Armstrong reached Fort McKinney, he tarried awhile, hunting along Crazy Woman Fork, a creek that ran into the Powder River. August Trabing ("Trabourn" in Armstrong's memoir) had built a store by Crazy Woman Creek in early 1878, but because of numerous robberies he moved to the community of Buffalo in 1879. Armstrong went in to Trabing's trading post to purchase some baking powder, where the "bullwhackers . . . invited me to stay overnight and yarn to them." Armstrong reports that while he was yarning, the store was robbed by Big Nose George and his gang.

Big Nose George and his gang were cattle rustlers and bank robbers who murdered several lawmen in Wyoming in August 1878. They then made an unsuccessful attempt to rob a train in September 1878. The gang murdered two agents who were after them, and during their getaway they robbed Trabing's store. Armstrong's remark that the robbers were after "Trabourn and his goods—he having done them some injury, and they were out for revenge" does not square with a gang that was fleeing after just having killed two men. Wilson, in *Outlaw Tales of Wyoming*, says of these robbers: "needing food, supplies, and money to make their escape, the gang next robbed the Trabing Mercantile on Crazy Woman Creek. They stole the supplies they needed, and Parrott [Big Nose George], who liked his liquor, also stole two barrels of whiskey and a horse to pack it on."[55] Eventually, Big Nose George was arrested, and he was sentenced to hang in 1881, but before that date he attempted an escape and was lynched. Because his body was not claimed, a doctor named Osbourne used the corpse for medical studies. When his studies were completed, the doctor had part of the criminal's skin tanned and made into a medical bag and a pair of shoes. Osbourne later was elected governor of Wyoming and, reportedly, wore those shoes to his inaugural ball.[56]

Although Armstrong says he was present for the Trabing robbery, he was likely remembering a different stick-up. (The post was robbed three times that fall.) His account is a closer match to a holdup performed by robbers who were actually after someone, a man named Tillotson. Burton Hill writes that the Trabing post "was also visited by marauding road agents who robbed him of his best wares" and "on one occasion at Trabing, these robbers laid in wait for a man by the name of Tillotson, who was supposed to have been in possession of twenty-two thousand dollars for the quartermaster at Fort McKinney. . . ."[57]

In the autumn of 1878, leaving the robberies at Crazy Woman Creek behind him, Armstrong set out for Fort Custer, hunting over the grounds where Custer fought his last battle two years earlier. In the following spring, he situated himself in Huntley, Montana, where for a very brief time he joined a spring cattle roundup. His foreman, Sim Roberts, who also came to Montana in the same year, began work with the Montana Cattle Company, whose founder, John T. Murphy, had set up a ranch between the Musselshell and Yellowstone Rivers. Roberts, accused of being a "clever thief," was twice brought to court on charges of shooting someone but was never convicted.[58] Armstrong lasted only several days on this job—instant mutual dislike between himself and a grouchy cowboy resulted in a gunfight. Armstrong told Roberts that he had had his fill of "cow punching" and did not want to deal with any other men on the roundup who might want to take revenge.

Armstrong may have mixed up the order of some of the events he describes during his time in Montana. After that episode on the roundup, he informs that he drove a stagecoach for the Salisbury Stage Company from Huntley to Coulson to Stillwater, a fifty-six-mile route that was part of a longer line running from Bozeman to Miles City.[59] However, unless he worked as a stage driver on more than one occasion, he himself provides compelling evidence that this stagecoach stint occurred in 1881, not 1879, when he declares that "I well remember carrying the news of the death of President Garfield, the first news the people in that part of the country had of the tragedy." President Garfield was shot in July 1881 and died in September of that year.

In the winter of 1879–1880, Armstrong traded with the Peigan (often spelled Piegan in the United States) and Crow peoples in the region of the Musselshell River. Though many of the Plains Indians had occupied different areas in their past, in Armstrong's time the Peigan, part of the Blackfoot Confederacy (called Blackfeet in the United States), lived on both sides of the Alberta–Montana border, while the Crow were located in the region of the Yellowstone, Musselshell, and Judith rivers. The Peigan and Crow belong to different language families; however, many of the Plains tribes were able to communicate by using a sign language.[60] Armstrong had learned the sign language at an early age and "knew practically all the Indian signs, and could speak to any Indian in the sign language." Somewhat later, while in Big Horn City, Armstrong accepted an offer to return the daughter and son of a Peigan chief who had been kidnapped by the Crow, enemies of the Peigan. He does not explain how he accomplished that mission—in all likelihood he only had to pick up the two siblings after an agreement had been reached for their return. As a reward, the father of the pair presented Armstrong with "two pretty good ponies, a beaded jacket, and a pair of moccasins."

In the late 1870s and 1880s, huge cattle and sheep ranches were being established in Montana, providing opportunities for frontiersmen to become cowboys. In Huntley, Tom McGirl and his partner Omar Hoskins owned and operated the Salisbury stage station and post office, which they sold in late 1879 or 1880 in order to take up ranching. The census of 1880 records only thirty-seven people in Huntley at the time, making it very likely that Armstrong would have been acquainted with Hoskins and McGirl. By now Armstrong may have gotten over his first unfortunate experience as a ranch hand and agreed to join a cattle roundup that brought a large herd from near Missoula to the Hoskins and McGirl ranch near Huntley.

For the next two winters (1880–1881, 1881–1882), Armstrong resumed hunting near the Missouri River, selling his hides to buyers who shipped them by steamer to Saint Paul, Minnesota. (The last of the buffalo herds were centred in the region where the Musselshell River joined the Missouri.[61]) In the summer of 1881, he returned to the Yellowstone area to continue the hunt there, and by September he was driving the Salisbury stagecoach.

While hunting in Montana's Judith Basin in 1882, Armstrong tells us he met Louis Riel and that Riel was teaching school at the time. Riel had agreed to teach at the Catholic mission of St. Peter's only in 1883, that is, a year after Armstrong had left for Canada in 1882. Therefore, Armstrong's meeting with Riel could not have taken place while Riel was a teacher.[62] Riel being a teacher probably entered Armstrong's story because during the time Riel was active in Batoche, Saskatchewan, everyone knew he had been a teacher in

Montana. Armstrong must have projected Riel's time as a teacher onto his other memories of the man. Indeed, the two men had plenty of opportunity to meet one another since, before he taught at the mission, Riel had been living in Carroll, Montana, for several years. Carroll is situated about midway between Judith Creek and Musselshell River, the region where Armstrong was present intermittently between 1879 and 1882. While there, Riel "became a woodchopper, a subagent for a trading company, and an unofficial 'fixer'—business interpreter and mediator between Indians, Métis and whites. He also occasionally accompanied the half-breeds on a buffalo hunt, acting as their purchasing agent. . . ."[63]

In the autumn of 1882, Armstrong dismissed his crew, disposed of his hides and wagon, and with some mules and a riding horse made his way to Canada without saying why he did so. One can speculate that the law was finally catching up with him for murdering a man while on a drunken spree in Wallace some nine year earlier. More likely, his move to Canada was prompted by a more recent event in Montana: he admits to shooting and injuring someone near Huntley, Montana, in 1879. Since Armstrong juxtaposes driving a stagecoach with his gunfight while working for Sim Roberts, one can speculate that since the former took place in 1881, rather than 1879 as Armstrong recounts in his memoir, then the gunfight may also have happened in 1881, or perhaps even later. The event was serious enough that repercussions may have followed. Armstrong explains that he quit the roundup "as I figured that having crippled one man I would always have to keep a sharp lookout and it might lead to more trouble of like nature." His granddaughter, Ella Melendrez, learned from her mother that Armstrong crossed the border to avoid capture and adds, "Mother said that he had harmed some man, not sure if he killed him or not, maybe injured him so he was a cripple for life. If I remember correctly it was in a fight."[64]

Saskatchewan writer Frank Anderson learned of this secret but, regrettably, he does not reveal his source nor does he elaborate on the incident. Anderson, who lived in Saskatoon, interviewed many old-timers for his numerous short books on prairie history. He may have spoken with someone in Prince Albert or Rosthern,

Saskatchewan, where Armstrong and his family lived for some time. In his description of Riel's apprehension, Anderson writes: "Constable Armstrong, who with Constable Diehl and Scout Hourie, was carrying dispatches from Colonel Irvine at Prince Albert to General Middleton, may well have found this situation ironical, for it is said that he himself was, at that time, a fugitive from American justice, being wanted for a murder in California—a crime of which he was later acquitted."[65] Commenting on Anderson's remarks, Melendrez writes, "I had heard that Grandpa had killed somebody in the U.S.; but I think it was in Montana, not California. He might have been acquitted, I don't know."[66]

Unfortunately, it is impossible to accurately determine what crime Armstrong may have committed. The county court records at Yellowstone County Court begin only in 1883, a year after Armstrong left for Canada.[67] The records at the sheriff's office in Billings, Montana, also do not go that far back, and the local paper, the *Billings Gazette*, began publication only in 1885. The court and sheriff's records for Judith Basin County also exist only from a more recent period. In all likelihood, Armstrong had been acquitted at some later time, for he returned to Oklahoma in 1904 and remained there for ten years. When he returned to his old home, he took with him his two oldest daughters—an unlikely undertaking if there was still a possibility of being arrested.

TO CANADA

Armstrong and a companion, Lu Mulholland, entered Canada at Fort Walsh, then in the District of Assiniboia (now Saskatchewan). His account of paying duty to the North West Mounted Police (NWMP) when he entered the country agrees with the procedure at the time. Though there were no customs posts as such, "the Department of Inland Revenue prevailed upon the police to establish and operate outposts along the frontier to enforce customs regulations, collect duties owing to the government, and to issue 'let' passes to those individuals wishing to cross from one country into the other."[68] The 1916 Census of Manitoba, Saskatchewan and Alberta records 1880 as Armstrong's year of immigration to Canada; however, this could not be correct. In his memoir, he indicates that he entered Canada in 1882 and that he came to Maple Creek just before the railway reached the site where the town developed. The rail had stopped a few miles east of what would be Maple Creek when construction halted at freeze-up in the fall of 1882.[69]

When the pair, travelling with Mulholland's buckboard and Armstrong's mules and riding horse trailing behind, arrived at the railroad construction camp, they attracted a crowd of curious onlookers. The appearance of the two men, evidently, presented quite a sight—Armstrong says his hair "at this time was rather long, in fact down to my shoulders" and Mulholland was described as "a very dilapidated looking fellow. . . . His face was blackened in spots from frost bites, and his fingers were badly frozen."[70] When someone in the crowd made "insulting remarks" about his hair, Armstrong calmly walked over and flattened him, at the same time expressing his thoughts about local hospitality.

After purchasing supplies, the two proceeded to Moose Jaw, then Regina, doing some work along the way. At Troy (present-day Qu'Appelle, Saskatchewan), Mulholland was contracted by a Mr. Clinkskill to freight supplies to Prince Albert while Armstrong met "Flatboat McLean and agreed to take charge of a stage station for him on the Salt Plains" (west of the Quill Lakes). Flatboat McLean had a mail contract, and according to Hawkes in *The Story of Saskatchewan and Its People*, just as Armstrong indicates, the mail came every three weeks. Stations, located every forty miles, would provide fresh horses when the mail arrived.[71] During the bleak winter months, Armstrong subscribed to various magazines to while away the time, using their illustrations to decorate the walls. Few travellers passed by the station at that time of year, but two notable visitors were Amédée E. Forget, secretary and clerk of council for the North-West Territories (NWT), and his wife, Henriette. Armstrong had baked some pies the previous day and was pleased to hear Mrs. Forget compliment his baking. Years later, Forget would become the lieutenant governor of the North-West Territories and then the first lieutenant governor of the Province of Saskatchewan.

In the spring of 1883, Armstrong, bored at the isolated post, moved on to Prince Albert where he was hired to bring settlers from Qu'Appelle to Prince Albert. (Settlers travelled by train to Qu'Appelle and then by horse and wagon to Prince Albert.) Not long after, in a major changeover from his previous activities, Armstrong opted to apprentice as a painter. While adapting to a more settled life, he entertained his acquaintances with stories of the American West and must have demonstrated his skills with a gun. W. J. Carter, who lived for six years in Prince Albert prior to 1885 and claimed to have known every white man in the town or district, informs that "Armstrong was also an American from Oklahoma and before coming to the West, was employed as a buffalo hunter by the Government of the U.S., and was one of the best shots with a revolver that ever came into Western Canada."[72] When the 1885 conflict began, Armstrong offered his services as a scout and dispatch rider. He could hardly have imagined that he would soon be jolted from anonymity to celebrity.

Chapter Three

1885

THE CONFLICT

Robert Armstrong was living in Prince Albert during the time variously referred to as the Riel Rebellion, Riel Uprising, the North-West Rebellion, the Rebellion of 1885, the North-West Insurrection, the North-West Resistance, or sometimes simply, the Resistance. The genesis of the conflict was the relinquishing of authority over Rupert's Land and the Northwestern Territory by the Hudson's Bay Company to the Crown, followed by that region's transfer, in 1870, to the recently established Dominion of Canada. The imminent extension of Canadian authority to the Northwest without any consultation with the inhabitants of the area and increased settlement by English Protestants alarmed the Métis and French populations in the Red River Settlement in what is now Manitoba. Tension escalated when government surveyors arrived in October of 1869 and were met with armed men who prevented the surveyors from carrying out their assignment. Soon after, Riel and his followers seized Upper Fort Garry and established a provisional government with the purpose of negotiating with the Government of Canada the terms of annexation. Armed confrontation between opposing parties in the Red River Settlement and the order by Riel to execute Thomas Scott, a vocal Protestant settler from Ontario, interrupted the federal government's plans for the takeover of the area, diminished support for the Métis cause, and inflamed the people of Ontario. Nevertheless, in the end, negotiations culminated in the establishment of the Province of Manitoba in 1870, with provisions for a separate (Catholic) school system and French language rights. Riel was elected to Parliament, but, with no amnesty for his part in the death of Scott, he was instead forced to become a fugitive. A general amnesty in 1875 included Riel, with the condition that he go into exile for five years. In 1883 he became an American citizen.

In the following years, a large number of Métis moved westward, establishing communities along the southern branch of the Saskatchewan River. Worried about obtaining title to the lands they were living on, and frustrated by the seeming indifference of the authorities to consider their grievances, a delegation of Métis went to Montana to enlist the support of Louis Riel. Riel arrived in what was then the North-West Territories in the latter part of June 1884. Though his initial strategy was cautious and peaceful, no progress was made, and discontent soon turned to armed conflict.

The first skirmish occurred a short distance west of Batoche, at Duck Lake, on March 26, 1885. Mounting tension in the preceding weeks prompted Major Crozier, superintendent of the NWMP in Battleford, to bring a contingent of his police to Fort Carlton. In Prince Albert, after being sworn in by Lieutenant-Colonel Sproat on March 21, a band of volunteers proceeded to Fort Carlton to provide support for Crozier. At the same time, Colonel Irvine, commissioner of the NWMP, left Regina with reinforcements for Prince Albert. His destination also was Fort Carlton but, before his arrival, Crozier's police and the Prince Albert volunteers stumbled into a deadly clash with the Métis at Duck Lake.

In the years following the signing of treaties, some Indian bands, without buffalo to rely on for food, unprepared for an agricultural life, and with inadequate support from the federal authorities, were experiencing severe hardship and starvation. Shortly after the skirmish at Duck Lake, several Indians raided some stores and farms when their requests for food were ignored. First Nations leaders at this time were in a difficult position—they endeavoured to balance negotiations with the government with restraining the younger men who advocated more aggressive approaches. Despite Cree leader Big Bear's desire to avoid conflict, he could not convince even his son Ayimasis (Imasees) to refrain from militancy.

On April 2 Cree war chief Wandering Spirit and his warriors killed several civilians at Frog Lake and took others hostage. They proceeded to Fort Pitt where the NWMP were allowed to evacuate and civilians joined the detainees from Frog Lake. Though individual Indians joined Riel's forces, most bands were hesitant to become involved in the Métis struggle. The events at Frog Lake and elsewhere, however, were enough for federal officials to interpret the turmoil in the Northwest as a Métis *and* Indian uprising.[1]

In the meantime, Major General Middleton, commander of the North-West Field Force, who was put in charge of suppressing the Resistance, arrived by rail at Qu'Appelle and marched to Fort Qu'Appelle and then on to Humboldt. His advance on Batoche was stalled at Fish Creek when, on April 24, the Métis under the leadership of Gabriel Dumont inflicted heavy casualties on them. Another part of the North-West Field Force, commanded by Lieutenant-Colonel William Otter, travelled by rail to Swift Current and then marched to Battleford. Otter's plan to defeat Chief Poundmaker and his Cree force at Cut Knife Hill on May 2 ended in failure. At the same time, recovering from his setback at Fish Creek, Middleton finally reached Batoche where skirmishes occurred for three days before the Métis were defeated on May 12. After Riel's apprehension on May 15, Middleton and his militia moved on to Prince Albert and, after a brief stay there, took steamers to Battleford where Chief Poundmaker offered to surrender. The last major task for Middleton was to rescue the hostages and capture Big Bear and other Cree leaders.

While these hostilities were taking place, a third column of troops, which included Colonel Steele's scouts, led by Major General Thomas B. Strange, had advanced from Calgary to Fort Edmonton and down the North Saskatchewan River to Fort Pitt where they unsuccessfully engaged Big Bear's band at Frenchman's Butte on May 27–28. Subsequently, Big Bear and his followers, with the hostages, withdrew to the northern muskeg regions. They were pursued by Steele's scouts and were attacked near Loon Lake, the last military engagement of the campaign. The outcome was indecisive, with Steele withdrawing to await reinforcements from Middleton, who had just arrived at Fort Pitt. The hostages were freed by the Cree in three separate groups over the course of the following days. Unable to follow Big Bear's trail in the swampy terrain, Middleton abandoned his plans to capture the chief, who surrendered himself by showing up at Fort Carlton on July 2. Prior to that date, and for some time after, military formations began returning home. Middleton and his troops returned to Prince Albert and then proceeded to Winnipeg for victory celebrations.

WHOSE SCOUT WAS ARMSTRONG?

Among the dead at Duck Lake in March were nine volunteers from Prince Albert, one of them a friend of Robert Armstrong. Armstrong says, "Up to this time I had determined to keep out of the trouble as I felt that I had seen enough fighting in the States; however, after seeing how serious an aspect the situation had assumed, I offered my services as a scout, which were accepted."

The residents of Prince Albert, a small community of only several hundred people at the time, upon learning of the deaths at Duck Lake, grew alarmed and feared an imminent attack, even though there was never a real threat. Women and children were sent to stay in the safety of the Presbyterian Church and its manse, which was surrounded with a hastily constructed stockade. Residents outside the town were urged to leave their homes and come to Prince Albert. On the evening of March 28, Frank Cherry, who was posted as a lookout some distance from Prince Albert, "rode to town with the greatest possible speed and shouting at the top of his voice to everyone he met to get to the Fort with all haste as the rebels and Indians were close behind."[2] In his memoir, Armstrong reports that he rode out of town and found no sign of trouble. That may have been so, but, at least initially, he must have accepted Cherry's story and spread the alarm. Jane Garson, who worked in Prince Albert, had gone to visit her father who lived one mile away from the town. She found her sisters there very scared, saying, "Don't you know the Indians are surrounding us. . . . Then Bob Armstrong arrived and said, 'You people get out of there, and get into town, to the Manse. The Indians will kill you. Move out or they will think you are helping the rebels.'[3] Curiously, Armstrong warned the women of two possibilities—attack by Indians and accusations by the locals if they did not join the panicked crowd in Prince Albert. Thus began Armstrong's participation in the 1885 conflict.

Though Armstrong became one of Middleton's scouts, his scouting and courier activities in the 1885 Resistance did not begin with Middleton. Armstrong has been variously labeled as a Prince Albert volunteer, Irvine's scout, a police scout, a police constable, Boulton's scout, an independent scout, Middleton's scout, and in Armstrong's own words, "Chief Scout NthWest Field Force."

Armstrong was a Prince Albert volunteer in the sense that he was a Prince Albert resident who volunteered his services as a scout, but he would not have been a Prince Albert volunteer in the manner of the other volunteers. The Prince Albert volunteers formed a militia, first to assist the NWMP at Fort Carlton and later to guard the town from any possible attack.

When Armstrong offered his services in Prince Albert, he was accepted into Commissioner Irvine's command. In his diary entry of May 6, 1885, Irvine informs that Armstrong was in his employ:

> Still colder than yesterday, a very raw and chilling wind blowing all day from the north, making it feel very disagreeable. Two scouts, George McLeod and Armstrong, started off about noon with a dispatch from the Commissioner to General Middleton, and a telegram for F. White, the comptroller of the North-West Mounted Police, the latter to be forwarded from Humboldt, for which point the scouts were to make first, before going to the General's camp.[4]

In his report written in 1886, Irvine stated:

> The importance of the work performed by my scouts could not, I think, have been surpassed. These men, all perfectly familiar with the country, were kept constantly employed

Humboldt Telegraph Station, circa 1885. Courtesy Provincial Archives of Saskatchewan, R-B1387.

from the outset, under the direction of a man (Mr. Thomas McKay) well qualified for such work. My scouts at all times labored incessantly, cheerfully, and efficiently. By the employment of these scouts I was enabled not only to keep myself posted as to the movement of General Middleton's column ... Diehl and Armstrong, two of the three men who captured Louis Riel, were police scouts, who had been sent by me with dispatches to General Middleton.[5]

Colonel Steele also associates Armstrong with Commissioner Irvine and the police. Steele, an officer in the NWMP, was made commander of a contingent of mounted scouts accompanying Major General Strange's Alberta Field Force, which made its way from Calgary to Fort Pitt to confront the Cree and later to search for Chief Big Bear. During the campaign and later, the NWMP received bad press and derision from the militia units for not being sufficiently involved in the fighting. Steele attempted to correct the record and wrote of Irvine's scouts:

During the whole of the campaign Colonel Irvine's scouts performed valuable services under the daring and capable leader, Mr. Thomas Mackay. They were constantly in touch with General Middleton's force and repeatedly drove back Riel's scouts. Their presence was so dreaded by Riel that he threw up strong entrenchments on the left bank of the South Saskatchewan opposite Batoche. After the battle at that place Diehl and Armstrong, scouts sent out by Colonel Irvine with dispatches to General Middleton, were two of the three who captured the rebel leader.[6]

In some publications, Armstrong is referred to as Constable Armstrong. The use of the term "constable" seems inappropriate since he never was formally a member of the NWMP. However, Captain Ernest J. Chambers, in his *The North-West Mounted Police*, writes: "Immediately upon arrival at Prince Albert, the Commissioner applied himself to completing as far as possible the defenses of the place, and caused all the able-bodied men who offered their services to be enrolled as special constables."[7] Therefore, to preface the name Armstrong with "constable" or "special constable" at that time would have been correct.

It is surprising, but understandable, to see Armstrong referred to as one of Major Boulton's scouts—this was never the case. Boulton, commander of Boulton's mounted infantry, or Boulton's Scouts, as his force is commonly known, had a score to settle with Riel. In 1870, at the time of the Red River Rebellion, Boulton had been made a prisoner and had been sentenced to death. While Scott, another prisoner, was executed, Boulton's life was spared. In 1885 he was authorized to recruit a force and catch up with Middleton in Fort Qu'Appelle. He and his scouts were part of Middleton's operations at Fish Creek, Batoche, and elsewhere, and they also carried dispatches to the telegraph offices. People likely began associating Armstrong with Boulton after Middleton had sent Boulton's scouts to search for Riel. Armstrong, Diehl, and Hourie were also on the search so many people assumed that the three scouts were members of Boulton's search party and, therefore, that Boulton's scouts were the captors of Riel. The May 18 issue of the *Montreal Gazette* informs, "The capture of Riel, cleverly effected by Boulton's scouts ends the rebellion as far as the half-breeds are concerned." Private Mouat of the 90th Winnipeg Rifles in his May 15 diary entry initially wrote, "Bolton's [sic] scouts caught Riel . . . ," but realizing later that this was not so, crossed out "Bolton."[8] Desmond Morton, in *The Last War Drum*, also mistakenly associates Armstrong and Diehl with Boulton's Scouts and erroneously describes Tom Hourie as Middleton's interpreter, a position held by Tom's father: "As for Riel, on 15 May two of Boulton's scouts, accompanied by Tom Hourie, Middleton's Indian interpreter, found him near the main trail to Guardepuis [Gardepuis'] Crossing."[9]

Armstrong discloses that, in addition to carrying dispatches for Irvine and Middleton, he also delivered messages for newspaper correspondents. A reporter noted for his scoops, George A. Flinn of the *Winnipeg Sun*, was the first to report the victory at Batoche. In acknowledging his debt to the couriers, Flinn writes:

> . . . I cannot monopolize all the credit for getting my dispatches on the wire ahead of my fellow-correspondents. A great deal of the credit must be given to "Bill" [sic] Armstrong and "Bill" Diehl, two of the independent guides and scouts who on two occasions carried my messages. The first day of the Batoche fight I hunted up Gen. Middleton to get his permission to employ Diehl. . . . The second day of the fighting I carried my dispatch myself. Armstrong carried the dispatch on the third day and on the last and final day I carried it myself. . . . My thanks go to Armstrong and Diehl for the valuable help they gave me and while I am under the impression that they both came from Missouri, they were both fine, splendidly reliable gentlemen, and I don't care where they came from.[10]

After the battle at Fish Creek, Armstrong relates that Middleton, after reading a letter from Captain McKay, the man in charge of Irvine's scouts, asked Armstrong to be his chief scout. This designation is one that Armstrong applies to himself in his memoir and appears in some reports written by individuals who interviewed him and repeated his words. Official evidence for the title "chief scout," either for Armstrong or for anyone else, is lacking. Coincidentally, the only other mention of a chief scout refers to Hourie; but that, too, is erroneous. In *Footprints in the Dust*, Douglas Light points out that "General Middleton appointed Lord Melgund as his Chief of Staff and Peter Hourie as his Chief Scout and Interpreter." And in the same book, the caption under a photo of Peter Hourie reads "Peter Houri [sic], 1827–1911. General Middleton's Chief of Scouts."[11] Peter Hourie was Middleton's chief translator/interpreter—he was not a scout—and there is no proof that Middleton referred to anyone as his chief scout. In one of his reports, Middleton did write that Hourie, Diehl, and Armstrong were his courier scouts: "[Riel] was driven into the hands of three of my courier scouts, Hourie, son of the interpreter, Deal [sic], and Armstrong."[12] In a list of individuals on active service in the Northwest in 1885, Armstrong's rank is recorded as "scout."[13]

In summary, Armstrong began his scouting/courier assignments with Commissioner Irvine of the NWMP. At the same time, he acted independently and carried dispatches for several newspaper correspondents. Early in the Resistance, he was asked by Middleton to be his scout; he agreed. Armstrong's stature increased greatly after Riel's capture, and in his eyes, and those of others, he *was* one of Middleton's principal or "chief" scouts.

CAPTURE OR SURRENDER?

Louis Riel had made a decision to surrender himself to General Middleton but was in a fix. He had in his possession a note from the general offering him protection until he was turned over for trial, but he knew he might be shot rather than arrested if he encountered any of Boulton's scouts, who were searching for him. John D. Astley, one of Riel's prisoners, implied that this note was a factor in Riel's decision to surrender. Riel showed it to his captors when they found him; and the note also became a subject of questioning when Middleton testified at Riel's trial.

Riel imparted little about his capture, and it is not known if any of his companions recorded their experiences. Varying accounts record two, three, four, or five men accompanying Riel when he made contact with his captors. Riel, after starting out with two companions, may have encountered others along the way before they were spotted by the scouts. Isabelle Vandal provides the names of the two men who initially set off with Riel, and states that Riel had made the decision to surrender before he was captured:

> While we were there, Riel came to us. All his moccasins were torn, and my sister, Mrs. Joseph Vandal [Julienne Branconnier] gave him a pair of moccasins. Then he took two men, Mr. Modeste Vandal and Mr. Modeste Boyer, and wrote out his surrendrance [sic] papers, and the three went to meet the soldiers to give themselves up. He said he took those two men to prove he was surrendering himself, and [so] that no one would get the reward for his capture. . . .[14]

Riel did say a few words about his apprehension when he was being transported from Middleton's camp to the jail in Regina. His military escort included the Reverend Pitblado, a chaplain with one of Middleton's battalions. He interviewed Riel twice during the trip, and in letters to his wife provides the details of those interviews. When Riel told him, "I surrendered myself to General Middleton," Pitblado asked, "Were you not taken by someone and brought to the General?" Riel answered, "Well, I was on my way to surrender to the General when Hourie, Diehl, and Armstrong met me. I had received this note from General Middleton." Pitblado adds, "he produced a note from the General which read to this effect: To Louis Riel—If you will surrender I promise you protection for yourself and councillors until you are dealt with by civil authorities. . . . He said 'I did not receive this note till the 15th. Whenever I received it I proceeded to surrender myself. There will no doubt be a fair trial.'"[15]

Though Riel had been in hiding, he was cautiously trying to find his way to Middleton, all the while avoiding Boulton's hostile scouts. Even with the note from Middleton, he feared for his safety, especially since Middleton was no longer nearby at Batoche but had moved on to Gardepuis' Crossing. That he made no attempt to flee when he encountered his captors was witnessed by Diehl, who told reporters in Middleton's camp: "No effort was made on his part to escape and after a brief conversation in which they expressed surprise at finding him there, Riel declared that he intended to give himself up. His only fear was that he would be shot by troops, but he was promised safe escort to the General's Headquarters."[16]

Clearly, Riel's plan was to surrender, but at the same time this was unknown to the men searching for him. Since he was still at large and evading Boulton's search party, was accompanied by men with shotguns, and had a concealed weapon, it can be said that he was captured while striving to reach Middleton. In spite of that, the phrase "capture of Riel," used in most of the literature describing the event, overdramatizes the actual encounter.

There is a peculiar footnote to this capture/surrender theme. Riel's eventual execution prompted rallies and political protests in Quebec. Laurier (the future Liberal prime minister) reportedly said, "When Middleton sent that request to Riel did he mean that he intended to protect him only until the Government had had time to erect a scaffold. . . . We are bound to believe that Middleton's letter was simply an ambush on the part of the Government."[17] Possibly in reaction to such views expressed in Quebec and in some English anti-Macdonald newspapers, a few citizens in Prince Albert decided to dispel the notion of Riel's intention to surrender and were able to somehow convince Armstrong and Diehl to sign an affidavit that changed the story of their encounter with Riel.

Their sworn statement, notarized on December 28, 1885, was published in the *Prince Albert Times*. Prefacing the published affidavit is a note: "a third scout named Tom Hourie was present during Riel's capture but our agent in Prince Albert has not been able to find him."[18]

In the affidavit, Diehl and Armstrong declare that they served as scouts for about two months; had seen in the eastern press that Riel had given himself up voluntarily; with Tom Hourie went on the search for and captured Riel; and "at the time we made the capture we believed, and we now affirm, that said Louis Riel had no intention of surrendering himself but was preparing for a hasty flight. . . . The statement, before referred to, that Louis Riel voluntarily gave himself up to us arc [sic] entirely untrue."[19]

It is doubtful that these words belong to Armstrong or Diehl. Most of this declaration would not have posed a problem for the pair—they *were* scouts with the Prince Albert volunteers, they *did* take part in the search for Riel, and, with Tom Hourie, *had* handed Riel over to Middleton. However, that these two scouts had seen the story that Riel had voluntarily given himself up "in portions of the press of eastern Canada" seems improbable. The words, "at the time we made the capture we believed, and we now affirm, that said Louis Riel had no intention of surrendering himself but was preparing for a hasty flight," as well, are very different from what the scouts had reported earlier. At the time of the capture, Diehl reported unambiguously: "No effort was made on his part to escape. . . ." More likely, feeling pressure in the small community that Prince Albert was at the time, they put their signatures to a statement formulated by the owner of the local paper and other individuals in the town.

PRIOR KNOWLEDGE OF RIEL'S LOCATION?

There is no evidence that the three scouts had prior knowledge of where Riel precisely was, yet some people felt that was the case. Harold P. Rusden, a member of French's scouts informs, "On the 15th [May] infantry troops remained in camp while the mounted men were sent out to scour the country in the hope of finding Riel and Dumont, but in the meantime two special scouts, a halfbreed and another man, left camp and somehow or other best known to themselves, rode straight to where Riel was."[20] Alexander Laid-law, attached to an artillery unit, also seemed convinced of the scouts' foreknowledge: "Next day the 15th the mounted men and the Gatling gun detachment went out on the hunt after Riel and Dumont, the former being captured and brought into camp about four o'clock in the afternoon by Howie [sic] and Armstrong, who doubtless had an idea of his whereabouts before hunting him up."[21] Reporter Flinn hints that the three scouts may not have been on a random search when he writes, "When I reached camp at Gardepuis' Crossing, Armstrong confided to me that he was going out with Tom Hourie, the son of the official interpreter, to bring Riel in and that if I happened to be somewhere along the river trail in a few hours, I might see something of them."[22] He adds that ". . . Boulton's Scouts who had individually and collectively sworn to hang Riel on sight were sent out on a wild-goose chase to hunt for Riel where he was not." This may or may not be true—the 150 or so scouts were sent out by Middleton in a very broad sweep so many would have been far from where Riel was spotted, but some of the scouts did come across Riel when he was being escorted by Hourie and Armstrong (Diehl had ridden ahead to inform Middleton that Riel was in custody); therefore, they, at least, were not on a wild goose chase. In conspiracy theories that arose soon after the capture, Middleton had provided Armstrong and his companion scouts some intelligence and had sent Boulton's scouts on a fruitless search to honour his guarantee of safe passage for Riel. The threat from Boulton's troops would thus be removed, dispersed and away from camp.

At the outset, Armstrong, Diehl, and Hourie met up with Boulton's scouts and then turned away from them in a deliberate manner, adding to speculation of prior knowledge. The May 16 issue of the *Toronto Daily Mail*, in an item dated May 15, describes how Dumont and Riel may have been spotted by a scout on the evening prior to Riel's capture. General Middleton "took no stock in his [the scout's] story." Presumably, he changed his mind. After Riel was made a prisoner, Middleton had sent a telegram to Minister of Militia and Defence Adolphe Caron, saying:

> I let it be understood I was going to cross at Batoche by not destroying the ferry and then march off towards Lepine Crossing as I was led to believe that Riel and Dumont were in the district, and [on] my way, hearing they or rather Dumont had been seen near, turned into this landing [Gardepuis' Crossing] which is a good one but disused now. I then sent off a party of mounted men to scour the woods. This was all seen by Riel who slipped behind the mounted party and gave himself up to two of my scouts whom they knew, one scout being a halfbreed himself.[23]

If Middleton changed his mind and believed the scout's story, he would have had a good idea of Riel's location. However, he may not have informed the three scouts since Peter Hourie reported that Middleton did not even send them after Riel. Armstrong, Diehl, and Hourie may have heard the same story, and being familiar with the area, headed off in the right direction. In Armstrong's memoir and interviews, and in the accounts by the other two scouts, the scouts give no hint of having information that would have aided their search. The notion that the men had any prior knowledge of Riel's location seems fanciful.

FAMOUS DEED

Some of the many depictions of Riel's apprehension in telegram dispatches, newspaper reports, diaries and other contemporary personal accounts, reminiscences, and early histories and more recent ones are presented in Appendix 1. In Appendix 2 are the versions presented by the three scouts who found Riel—Robert Armstrong, Tom Hourie, and William Diehl. The conflicting statements and errors in several of these reports are examined in the appendices, as are the incongruities in the stories provided by the three scouts. Here, consideration is given only to the key irreconcilable claims made by Armstrong and Hourie, and to details that might indicate whether or not any one scout actually played a leading role.

In addition to Peter Hourie's account, there are others (see Appendix 1) that name Tom Hourie the hero of the hour. After Riel was brought to camp, Armstrong headed to Clark's Crossing with Middleton's dispatch while William Diehl accompanied reporter Flinn to the telegraph office, thereby leaving Tom Hourie the only captor in Middleton's camp to describe the day's events. This may partially explain the "Tom only" accounts. William E. Young, a soldier in the Midland Battalion, records in his diary, "On Friday evening Riel was brought in to the Generals [sic] quarters, a prisoner. . . . Tom Owrie [sic] a half breed scout made Riel prisoner."[24] Another of Young's entries, written after the Battle of Batoche, illustrates how citing just one captor (Tom Hourie, in this case) may have originated—"Many stories of the fight were told that night in camp, true or not, it matters little, all were received alike."[25] One of the storytellers that night might have been one of Boulton's scouts who had been on the search for Riel. He and some companion scouts encountered Hourie, Armstrong, and Riel, who were then making their way back to Middleton's camp. He had recognized Hourie, exchanged some words with him, and then moved on when he was told that the man with him was Riel's cook, not Riel. Not knowing Armstrong, his description would focus on the only person he knew by name. These stories, repeated by others, would fortify the versions they had heard, "true or not." Armstrong and Hourie certainly spun their stories on the following days and nights. The audience's impression would be that the storyteller (no matter which of the two was recounting his deeds) was the central figure in the capture of Riel, even if that was not the storyteller's intention.

Peter Hourie says, "There was Tom and an American named Armstrong and a man named Deal [sic]. These two were friends of Tom's."[26] Tom Hourie was born on April 30, 1859. His father relates, "Tom was born at the Touchwood Hills at the old Hudson's Bay Post. His mother's name was Sarah Whitford. Her parents were both half-breeds. Her grandfather was an Englishman named Creamer. . . ."[27] Tom lived in Prince Albert before and after 1885, until news of gold in the Klondike took him to the Yukon in 1897. He died in Dawson City in 1908. Tom was of big stature and was often referred to as Big Tom Hourie.[28] William Frederick Diehl, born in Buffalo, New York, in 1850, came to Canada in 1875 and married Martha Musgrove in Prince Albert. The couple ranched and farmed in the Marcelin area for most of their lives. William Diehl died on February 5, 1936.[29]

Hourie and Armstrong both claim to have played the principal role in Riel's capture, relegating the other to the margins. Among the most salient controversies in the story of Riel's arrest are: To whom did Riel hand his note of protection, which he had earlier received from Middleton? Whom did Riel address regarding getting a fair trial? To whom did he give his concealed pistol? On whose horse did he ride, and who introduced him to Middleton?

Tom Hourie, date unknown. Courtesy Provincial Archives of Saskatchewan, R-B688.

William Diehl, later in life. Courtesy Bill Smiley Archives, Prince Albert Historical Society, H-472.

When only Armstrong's and Hourie's accounts are compared, the conflicting views cannot be resolved. Neither provides incontrovertible proof that his story is more accurate than the other's. Since the time of the first newspaper reports on the event to the present, there have been a variety of descriptions of Riel's capture—some favouring one scout, some the other. However, many of these are just repetitions or modifications of what had been published earlier. There are four ultimate arbiters of the truth, namely William Diehl—who was with the other two scouts up until Riel's capture and thus was a witness—and three other men: George H. Ham, reporter George A. Flinn, and an unnamed *Toronto Globe* reporter, all of whom were at Middleton's camp when Riel was brought in.

Diehl's account of the event neither favours Hourie nor Armstrong, and there is no reason to suspect that what he said is false. Diehl's account appeared in a 1919 affidavit and in a newspaper article printed at the time of his death; more valuable, though, is what he said when he galloped to Middleton's camp and reported the news of the capture. Unlike the versions put out decades after the event by Hourie and Armstrong, memory was not an issue for Diehl when he spoke with the reporters right after the capture. He blurted out the news without having had time to reflect on and tailor the facts. Diehl reportedly arrived at Middleton's camp at about 3:30 p.m., perhaps fifteen minutes before Riel and the other two scouts. The reporters wrote up dispatches at that time, thereby recording Diehl's initial words; and then they wrote other dispatches at about 3:45 p.m., when Riel was brought into camp.[30]

It is indisputable and significant that Riel handed his note to Armstrong, not to Hourie, and that Riel also asked Armstrong about the type of trial he could expect. The *Globe* reporter writes: "Diehl says Riel was not in the least agitated when arrested and was willingly made captive. He was assured of a fair trial, which was all he seemed to want. During the interview he handed scout Armstrong a note, the contents of which have not yet been heard, as at the time of writing the party had not arrived in camp."[31]

At 3:45 Flinn reports, "He [Riel] wished for a fair trial. He asked Armstrong if he would get a civil or military trial."[32] These statements address yet another issue raised by Peter Hourie, namely that, of the three scouts, only his son knew Riel. Surely, if only Tom knew Riel, Riel would have handed his note to Hourie rather than to a stranger. Peter Hourie's silence about these two matters— the note and the person addressed regarding a fair trial—further suggest that Riel deferred to Armstrong.[33]

On whose horse did Riel ride? Riel might have ridden on Hourie's horse and on Armstrong's horse. In Peter Hourie's words, "When Tom captured Riel he made Riel get on his horse. He told Riel to get on behind, so they were on the same horse." Roderick George MacBeth, who knew Tom, writes, "The giant [Hourie] lifted the rebel leader up behind him on his horse, and took him to Middleton's tent. . . ."[34] Armstrong claims Riel rode on his horse. It would not make sense to burden one horse all the long way back to camp, so a switch could have been made at some point. In correspondent Howard Angus Kennedy's 1926 interview, Armstrong informs that after encountering Boulton's scouts, "I left Hourie to keep the other scouts talking, while I got Riel up behind me on the pony. . . ."[35] Riel, therefore, may have been on

Hourie's horse initially, but at that time transferred to Armstrong's horse. As a result, it is plausible that Riel rode with both Armstrong and Hourie.

To whom did Riel hand his pistol? We do know that the pistol was in Armstrong's possession before Riel was turned over to Middleton. Peter Hourie purports that Riel surrendered the pistol to Tom but that Armstrong asked for it at some later time, and Tom gave it to him. Armstrong maintains that he received the gun directly from Riel, not from Hourie. Peter Hourie further insists that not only Armstrong but also Diehl asked to see Riel's revolver. Yet, when Diehl arrived at Middleton's camp before the arrival of Riel, he told reporters that Riel's companions had shot guns but Riel was unarmed, which indicates that he knew nothing of the pistol or that Riel had been disarmed.

Some support for Armstrong's position comes from Flinn. Having met Armstrong, Hourie, and Riel just before they entered Middleton's camp, Flinn, thus, was the first to hear about Riel's capture from Hourie and Armstrong. In his reminiscences he recalls, "Riel thereupon prayed a little and then put his hand in a vest pocket and produced a small 22-caliber revolver which he held out to Armstrong. . . ."[36] Another point to consider in Armstrong's case is that both Peter Hourie and one of Boulton's scouts, who had encountered Tom during the search for Riel, spoke of Tom's great desire to get the rumoured reward for Riel's capture. Possessing Riel's pistol would be convincing proof of being "the captor" so it seems unlikely that Tom would casually divest himself of the evidence. As well, since Armstrong, Hourie, and Riel were together when they encountered Flinn, if what Armstrong told Flinn was not factual Hourie could certainly have challenged him, and Flinn would thus have reported something different.

There is no confusion as to who presented Riel to Middleton. Peter Hourie does not single out Tom as the one who informed Middleton about the prisoner's identity, and even Joseph Howard, who casts Hourie as the principal player in *The Strange Empire of Louis Riel*, writes, "When the group entered the tent Armstrong said, 'General, this is Riel.'"[37]

All three scouts participated in finding Riel and bringing him to Middleton. According to Peter Hourie, the three were friends so there would have been no "ranking" among themselves. Nevertheless, the first reports by the scouts as presented in the correspondents' dispatches suggest that Riel deferred to Armstrong and that Armstrong may, indeed, have taken the lead in making Riel a prisoner.

HOW IT HAPPENED

Some details of Riel's surrender and escort to Middleton's camp will always remain indeterminate, but a reasonable reconstruction of the event is possible. The story begins with Middleton sending Boulton's scouts to search for Riel on the morning of May 15, 1885, a very chilly day with a "cold wind from the north-east."[38] Hourie, Diehl, and Armstrong, without instructions from Middleton, rode out together and caught up with Boulton's scouts shortly thereafter. They branched off and came across several Métis groups. One or several Métis pointed in the direction Riel had been seen last. The trio spotted a group of armed men. Hourie shouted in Cree for them to drop their weapons. When the scouts got closer to the group of men, they recognized Riel. He showed Armstrong Middleton's note of protection. Armstrong responded to Riel's concern about a fair trial. Hourie collected the weapons from the others. They prepared to return to Middleton's camp, sixteen miles away, but noticed Boulton's scouts in the distance so, to avoid detection, hid from view in a coulee.

Riel and his companions were on foot so Diehl and one of Riel's companions went off to find stray horses for the captured party. Meanwhile, Riel, Armstrong, Hourie, and Riel's other companion(s) (dismissed soon after) disappeared in the coulee. Riel may have ridden on Hourie's horse for a while, but sometime later, just before running into Boulton's scouts, they dismounted. While Hourie conversed with them, Armstrong and Riel rode on ahead. Riel handed Armstrong his concealed pistol. The pair may have found a stray horse on which Riel rode for some time. Hourie then caught up with them. In the meantime, Diehl, unsuccessful in his search for horses, returned to where he had left the group; when he found they were not there, he rode back to Middleton's camp. He arrived before the others and announced the capture in mid-afternoon. Near their destination, Armstrong, Riel, and Hourie dismounted and began walking, encountering the reporter Flinn along the way. When they reached Middleton's tent sometime before 3:45 p.m., Armstrong remarked to Middleton, "This is Riel."

That, apparently, was not the end of an eventful day for Armstrong. After presenting Riel to Middleton, Armstrong went off to eat: "And they didn't even give me time to eat, and I was hungry. . . . I wasn't through eating before I got another order to ride 55 miles to Clark's Crossing, to send a despatch to Ottawa that Riel was a prisoner. I was [good?] and tired too, so, when I found a brand new phaeton which had been confiscated, and stood in the corral, I just hitched-up to that and made the trip."[39]

REWARD FOR RIEL'S APPREHENSION?

Peter Hourie wrote of his son's disappointment in not getting a reward for Riel's capture: "What did Tom get for capturing Riel? Tom only got payment for himself and his horses. He was rather dissatisfied. He was at Nicholas Floyd [Flood] Davin to get the reward but Davin did not succeed."[40] The other two scouts also must have felt let down. Armstrong told the reporter Howard Angus Kennedy that he "never got a penny."[41] The impression that there was a reward, when there was not, may have begun as a presumption that this would be so. In a telegram to Minister Adolphe Caron on May 14, General Middleton suggests a reward would be a good idea:

> Riel and Gabriel Dumont are in the woods about 80 or 90 miles [probably 8 or 9 miles was meant] from here, with few followers, Indians being with them, on hearing of this I altered my halt to this place [Gardepuis' Crossing] and am going to send out tomorrow the whole of my mounted men about 150 to scout the country and try to catch them. I think [the] Government should offer a reward for them.[42]

The May 19 *Winnipeg Daily Times*, in all probability, is reporting gossip in the following: "It is understood the officers of the brigade privately offered one thousand dollars reward for the capture of Riel and a similar sum for the capture of Dumont." Reporter Kennedy, after visiting Armstrong in the 1920s, looked into the matter. He writes:

Of all the myths and fables embroidering the history of Western Canada, one of the most curiously persistent is the tale of a $5000 reward for the capture of Louis Riel, leader of the Metis revolts on the Red River in 1870, and the Saskatchewan River in 1885. I rode through that last campaign and well remember hearing talk of such a reward. Afterwards, I heard it had been paid, and naturally supposed it [had] been divided among the three scouts who made the capture—Armstrong, Hourie, and Diehl.

The last time I was in Calgary, however, I met Robert Armstrong—I had not seen him since 1885, and he told me he had never got a penny of it. The Ottawa authorities had been written to, but they disclaimed any knowledge of such an offer of reward. I was on the way down to Ottawa myself, and made inquiries there, with a very curious result. A reward of $5000 was actually offered, once upon a time, for the arrest of certain unnamed persons, one of whom was undoubtedly Louis Riel—but the men who eventually captured Riel would not touch a dollar of that, for reasons which I shall have to explain.[43]

Kennedy goes on to say that ten people shared the five-thousand-dollar reward, but the reward was for matters connected to the events of 1870, not 1885—no reward had been offered in 1885.

Peter Hourie, Middleton's interpreter, had arranged for his son Tom to be a courier with Middleton when the general arrived in Qu'Appelle. A report of the expenditures arising from the North-West Resistance lists T. Hourie as having received five hundred dollars for one hundred days as courier with Major General Middleton.[44] There is no record of payment for services specifically to

Diehl or Armstrong, but it may have been included in a general category. In the report to Parliament of Lieutenant-Colonel W. H. Jackson, deputy adjutant-general of expenses, "on matters in connection with the suppression of the rebellion in the North-West Territories, in 1885," there is an entry for nineteen (unnamed) men in the category "Special Constables." The three scouts, along with all military participants in the 1885 conflict, did receive a medal bearing the image of Queen Victoria.[45] Charlotte Gordon, writing in the *Western Home Monthly*, observes that "His [Armstrong's] silver medal, stamped with the head of Queen Victoria, dated 1885, is one of his prized possessions."[46]

AFTER BATOCHE

Armstrong's activities in the 1885 crises after Riel's capture are recorded only in his memoir, but there is no doubt that he and Hourie were with Middleton's forces until the end of the campaign. The absence of Armstrong's name in independent sources makes it impossible to either discount or confirm his accounts of the final events of the conflict. The incidents he depicts are verifiable, and there is a reasonable probability that unnamed individuals in some of these incidents described by others could refer to Armstrong.

Once Batoche had fallen, Armstrong reports that "we collected a quantity of furs belonging to Batoche [the man]."[47] This is confirmed by Lewis Redman Ord, a surveyor and a member of Middleton's Surveyor's Scouts, who wrote sarcastically about Middleton's wish to be the first one at an abandoned Indian camp to spot souvenirs or furs—"Visions of furs better than those he got at Batoche fills his mind's eye. . . ."[48]

After Riel had been made a prisoner, Middleton and his forces proceeded to Prince Albert where a band and a detachment of mounted police under Major Crozier welcomed them at 11:30 a.m. on May 19. Their arrival was on a "fine, warm day [with] a fresh breeze from the south-east."[49] Unfortunately, rain during the next two days created a muddy scene that kept the men resting in their camps. At some point in those three days, Armstrong "indulged in a few sports." The *Prince Albert Times* reports that in the presence of a "large concourse of spectators" were held various games and races, including putting stone, greasy pig, tug of war, and horse races.[50]

Middleton departed for Battleford on May 22 on the steamer *Northwest*. Twenty miles before reaching the community, Armstrong was let off and directed to deliver a dispatch to Lieutenant-Colonel William Otter, which instructed him to send some teams with Armstrong to Fort Pitt. (Wagon teams followed the army with food and military supplies.) His trek to Fort Pitt with the supply wagons would explain why Armstrong does not mention the surrender of Chief Poundmaker to Middleton at Battleford.

Middleton reached Fort Pitt on the morning of June 2. General Strange had arrived there earlier with the Alberta Field Force and skirmished with Big Bear's forces at Frenchman's Butte. Major Steele's scouts (part of the Alberta Field Force) followed the retreating Cree and their hostages to Loon Lake. Unable to force a victory, Steele withdrew to await the arrival of Middleton's forces. Soon after, the Woods Cree, who had separated from the Plains Cree, released their hostages. The hostages had been split up into three groups and were set free at different times. One group was found by General Strange's scouts, the second was located by Steele's scouts, while the third was still making its way south to Fort Pitt from Lac des Isles, where they had been freed.

Middleton left Fort Pitt on June 5 but did not join up with Steele's scouts until several days later, arriving at Loon Lake on June 8. Armstrong was still with the supply teams and only met up with Middleton near Loon Lake. Armstrong reports crossing a narrow channel where he was submerged, spotting a Cree woman who had committed suicide, and that some officers had crossed the channel to study the terrain. Others also have reported these scenes.[51]

Regarding the channel crossings at Loon Lake, Boulton comments, ". . . the General sent on two half-breed scouts to ascertain what difficulties were ahead of us. They had to cross the ford which lay beneath our camp, and after going five miles the trail turned north to another crossing, where the water was too deep to allow them to ford."[52] On the next day, June 9, Middleton and his men crossed the first channel and by noon arrived at the second one, which was, indeed, too deep to cross. It may have been at this point where Armstrong, in an attempt to check the depth of the crossing, took a dip in the channel. Tom Hourie's presence at Loon Lake is confirmed in the June 13 issue of the *Montreal Gazette*: "despatch from Fort Pitt, dated June 11 . . . announces the arrival of Hourie, a scout, with despatches which confirm the reported retirement of Gen. Middleton from the pursuit of Big Bear."

Among those reporting the death of an elderly Cree woman was Major Steele: "The same afternoon two scouts who had crossed the little narrows reported they had seen the dead body of a squaw who had hanged herself on account of being lame and unable to keep up with the rest of the people. They stated that there was muskeg on the far side where she was found, and, as it was important that it should be examined, I crossed the narrows."[53] Armstrong recounts that he and other scouts buried the elderly woman, but this is questionable, or else the burial was so shallow as to expose the body at a later time. Kitty McLean, one of the white hostages who was acquainted with the woman, revealed that, after being freed and retracing their path back to Loon Lake, they found the unfortunate woman: "And so we found her with her little dog dead by her side."[54]

About this time, Armstrong "presented Riel's revolver to the General who thanked me saying he would prize it as a souvenir of the war." It seems suspicious that after holding on to it for nearly a month Armstrong would just hand over the pistol, a prized possession—one can speculate that Middleton may have asked for it. On June 12 Middleton received a telegram from Minister of Militia and Defence Adolphe Caron, stating, "I would like you to bring back some souvenirs of your campaign for Sir John, Sir Hector Langevin and myself. I leave it to you to select what you consider of interest." Several days later, Middleton replied, "Will do what I can to get you souvenirs but it is difficult to get anything as everyone in camp is trying to get souvenirs also."[55]

On their way back to Fort Pitt from Loon Lake, Armstrong was challenged to a race by "Gatling Gun Howard." Nonchalantly, Armstrong divulges that he raced with a horse he had looted—"I was riding a horse I had looted at Batoche." Later, he adds that the horse belonged to Riel, and that some officers named the horse Louis Riel.[56] Tom Hourie also appropriated horses at this time. His father discloses that his son took possession of a horse and buggy at Batoche and brought them to Middleton's camp, and that he saw a photo of Middleton on that horse. Further, he adds that Tom's grandmother "had a lot of fine horses" that Tom came across and moved to the camp as well, where Middleton's transport chief, Bedson, laid claim to them.[57] Tom had no intention of surrendering them and got into an altercation with one of Bedson's men. It was only after Peter Hourie pleaded with his son that Tom relented. Those horses were not returned to his grandmother but ended up in Stony Mountain.

Looting was certainly common during the conflict. Lewis Redman Ord, for example, recalling the day after the fall of Batoche, says he "got one or two hornspoons in the Sioux camp, a new bath towel, and some bars of soap, and these, with a few forks and tin dishes for our mess, made up my booty." He adds that "the general [Middleton] had shut down on looting in the most effective manner by taking charge of a good many of the furs himself, and his zeal in this direction was imitated by so many of the officers that few privates got a share."[58] Douglas Light writes that "he [Middleton] seems to have lost control of his troops, as they proceeded to destroy and loot anything of value that they could lay their hands on. Even the priest's possessions and the Catholic Church's valuables were hauled away as trophies of war.[59] Light says that this looting was recalled years later when "some Indians and mixed-bloods compared the troops to army worms: after the victorious Whites had gone through the camps, there was nothing left but a few bare lodge poles."[60]

After returning to Fort Pitt, Middleton proceeded to Beaver River where he met General Strange. While there, on June 19, news arrived that the final group of hostages had been released and were on their way to Fort Pitt.[61] Middleton rushed back to the fort and ordered teams to go out and meet them. He telegraphed Caron that "—my two Indians [Chippewyan scouts] further informed me that the Woods Cree had gone to Lac des Isles and had all the prisoners and were going to send them at once to Fort Pitt, so we are expecting them at any moment. I am sending out tomorrow carts to meet them and clothes which have been got ready for them. . . ."[62] Armstrong's remarks match those in the telegram: "The General at once ordered me to return to Loon Lake with teams and pick up these people. I did so and found around thirty people encamped there." (The hostages had made their way from Lac des Isles back to Loon Lake and were headed for Fort Pitt.) He noticed that the freed hostages were cooking ox meat. In fact, McLean, one of the hostages, reports that "Stanley Simpson went with a gun to the edge of the lake, where to his surprise he found one of the oxen which had been abandoned earlier. It was shot for food."[63]

Charlotte Gordon writes, "teams with food and clothing were at once sent and Mr. Armstrong, as chief scout, met the prisoners before the wagons arrived."[64] The hostages' descriptions of their initial encounter with Middleton's people and their subsequent escort to the fort do not include any mention of Armstrong. McLean writes:

We were watching the direction from which the uncertain sounds came, when suddenly we saw the heads of two horses showing over the hilltop overlooking our camp, and immediately a man showed himself, and asked in English which was the best way to get down to our camp with his team. . . . He unhitched his horses [Armstrong was not driving a team] and after he had done so, he said he would like to see Mr. McLean. . . . He pointed to a large case and then took it down from the wagon, saying he was instructed by Major Bedson to deliver it to Mr. McLean. Seeing the case was addressed to Major Bedson, Fort Pitt, I asked if Major Bedson was out with the troops, and he answered that he was and that he would be with us in less than half an hour, as he only left him and two other gentlemen about a mile and a half away talking to the scout who had seen us in the early morning without our knowledge of it, and had gone back.[65]

Armstrong, as likely as not, was that scout who had seen them and returned to inform the teamsters who were on the way to pick up the hostages.

Before leaving Fort Pitt, Armstrong speaks of several Indians being put on trial, including a Chief "Low Horn." It is not clear to whom he might be referring as there was no trial at Fort Pitt. He places quotation marks around Low Horn so that name may have been just a byname used by the troops, or he may have been alluding to the time he and Middleton were at Beaver River where General Strange had "ordered a Court of Enquiry on the Chippwayan prisoners." Strange says, "No punishment was awarded by General Middleton, who subsequently held a Pow-Wow."[66]

With the hostages freed, preparations were begun to end the campaign and send the troops home. The various contingents that had come together at Fort Pitt began leaving at different times. Middleton, however, did not depart until July 4. A brief stop was made in Prince Albert where, apparently, Middleton was upset when Armstrong told him that he would like to stay an extra day rather than accompany him to Winnipeg. Middleton may have asked him "whether it was the people or country" that made him want to stay, to which Armstrong replied, "Both." Claiming that Middleton flew "into a rage" is probably Armstrong's way of adding melodrama to his narrative. Prince Albert was home for Armstrong and, after being away for a long time, understandably he would not want to leave immediately. Arrangements had been made for steamers to carry some of the troops to Lake Winnipeg and then on to Winnipeg. Armstrong and others chose to travel overland to Winnipeg where they, in Armstrong's words, "plunged into a round of gaieties."

Armstrong, evidently, caught the attention of the ladies of Winnipeg. Charlotte Gordon describes "riding parties" and the participation in one by Armstrong, whose "reputation as a horseman had gone before him." He was asked to touch a buffalo while pursuing the largest one in a herd at Stony Mountain. As Armstrong raced up to the buffalo, he "caught a bunch of hair from the back of the neck, wheeled and rode back to the ladies with his trophy, one of them rolling the result of his prowess in her handkerchief."[67]

"It almost seems to me the old days were the best." Robert Armstrong, date unknown. Courtesy Eleanor Peppard.

Another time, reminiscent of the similar, more recent, behaviour of rock-star groupies, admiring women waited for him at his hotel: "One morning, when he came down for breakfast in the hotel where he was staying, about a dozen ladies were waiting for him at the foot of the stairs. 'Is this a delegation?' asked Armstrong. 'We want to kiss the man who captured Riel,' was the answer. Startled, he replied, 'Where shall I begin?'"[68]

Chapter Four

1885 TO 1940

PRINCE ALBERT, ROSTHERN, AND RETURN TO ROOTS

At the conclusion of the 1885 campaign, and after several weeks of basking in his newly acquired hero status at the victory celebrations in Winnipeg, Armstrong returned to Prince Albert to many life changes. Prior to 1885, Armstrong had learned the skills of a painter and now he resumed that trade.[1] On July 19, 1887, he became a naturalized citizen of Canada. His naturalization file discloses not only that he was an American born in Kansas and a painter in Prince Albert, but also that his previous identity was "Irvin Mudeter [sic]."[2] About this time, Armstrong had problems with some surveyors who had intruded on his property. Owen E. Hughes, who served as the sheriff for the District of Saskatchewan in 1887–1889, states, "I recall him [Armstrong] calling on me when I was sheriff. He had two revolvers and asked me to go out with him to clean out a survey party that had ilegally [sic] run a survey line through his shack. And . . . I rather felt like doing it, too."[3]

Nearing age forty, Armstrong married Adeline (Adelaide) Burke in 1888. Adeline was born in Westmount, Ontario, in November 1856 (Westmeath in 1855 in other sources)[4] and "came to Prince Albert in 1884, travelling from Winnipeg to Prince Albert by boat via Lake Winnipegosis and the Saskatchewan River."[5] In Prince

Prince Albert, looking west, 1891. Courtesy Bill Smiley Archives, Prince Albert Historical Society.

Albert, she "worked at the hotel close to where the ferry landing was."[6] The 1891 Census of Canada indicates that Adeline's mother was born in Manitoba and her father in Quebec, and that both Armstrong and Adeline were Methodists.[7] Elizabeth E. Wheeler, niece of Julia Wheeler (Armstrong's daughter), describes Mrs. Robert Armstrong as "a real 'granny' and as much a part of the picturesqueness as the cuckoo clock and the banister. She had silver, curly locks and apple-red cheeks, and wore long skirts and an apron. Granny never learned to read or write, but she could count her money, she could count her stitches when knitting, and play cards as well as the next person, all of which never ceased to amaze and impress us."[8]

Robert and Adeline Armstrong had six children: Florence Marie (1889), Cora Susannah (1891), Julia May (1893), Ida (1895), Frank Dawson (1896), and Myrtle Jane (1897).[9] Florence was married first to Ernest Jordison, then to Roy Mumaugh. Cora married Richard Humphrey. Julia was first married to Percy Wheeler. She was widowed twice; her subsequent marriages were to Charlie Wilker and Carl Larson. Ida died at age eight. Dawson remained single all his life, and Myrtle married Frank Kroeker in 1924.

Robert and Adeline Armstrong with daughters Florence (centre bottom) and Cora (centre top). Courtesy Ella Melendrez.

A photograph, taken circa 1893, the only known one where Armstrong and his wife appear together, has an uncanny prophetic quality. Armstrong, no longer with shoulder-length hair but with a trim cut, dressed in a suit and tie, has refashioned himself as a

Adeline Armstrong and daughter Myrtle (Armstrong) Kroeker, 1926. Courtesy Trevor Wheeler.

mainstream family man. He sits beside his two girls, head tilted toward them. His wife turns her head away. The pose had no particular meaning at the time; but with hindsight, it appears as a portent of the couple's eventual estrangement and Armstrong's departure for Oklahoma with those two girls.

The 1901 Census of Canada shows that the family had moved to Rosthern, Saskatchewan, and that Armstrong had immigrated to Canada in 1881 (actually 1882); was naturalized in 1886 (actually 1887); was English, Presbyterian, and a painter. By now Armstrong had been a painter for many years; just how appealing he found this trade is not known. He often left his work and family for long stretches of time to go hunting and trapping, probably yearning for his former exciting days on the American plains. During one of his long absences, to sustain herself and her family, Adeline hired on as a housekeeper and moved with her children to the home of Percy Wheeler, a bachelor farmer residing a short distance east of Rosthern.

When a shocked Armstrong returned to find his wife in another man's home he was furious and threatened Wheeler. Only Adeline's intercession prevented a violent conclusion. (Later, Wheeler would marry Armstrong's daughter, Julia.) Armstrong's agitated state was the beginning of a maelstrom of disturbances and changes. Back in Rosthern, he hired a driver to take him to Duck Lake. While the driver was made to race his horses, Armstrong fired his gun at the insulators on the telegraph poles. Another time, in a hotel, he shot the toe off a man whom he suspected of improper conduct toward his daughter.[10] Soon after, in 1904, Armstrong travelled to Oklahoma to visit his family. Since he did not return to Canada until ten years later, he must have decided to ditch his now strained marital situation and start afresh in the place that a long time ago was home.

Another account of those turbulent days suggests the reason for the trip south may have had a financial motive—"in 1903 or 1904, Bob left his wife and family with Percy Wheeler as housekeeper while he went to the States presumably to dispose of some land grant from the U.S. government, came back in early spring of 1904 or 1905 and was (jailed) for causing a disturbance (in Prince Albert) with a livery driver named H. Hughs who worked for Wetherbys of Rosthern."[11] It is possible that Armstrong went to Oklahoma, returned soon after, and then went back again; but in all likelihood, following his initial outburst, he left in 1904 and never again returned to Rosthern. It is interesting to note that in the 1910 U.S. Federal Census, Armstrong revealed the severed ties with his wife by presenting himself as a widower. (In more recent censuses, he gave his status as "married.")

Though outraged by his wife's move and his subsequent separation from her, his motive for leaving the country may indeed have been partly prompted by "some land grants." When the General Allotment Act of 1887 came into effect, the Wyandotte reservation was partitioned, and land grants were distributed to tribal members. Provisions were also made for individuals who were not living at the reservation to receive allotments.[12] Armstrong, at that time, was in Prince Albert, but his name was on the annual Wyandotte rolls and, therefore, he was assigned some land as shown on an allotment map. One stipulation of the act was that these properties could not be sold for twenty-five years. Perhaps Armstrong wasn't clear on these matters and, therefore, had to wait until 1911 or 1912 before he could dispose of his allotment. There may have been other conditions that allowed for an earlier sale, but likely not, as Armstrong's return to Canada occurred in 1914, soon after the required waiting time.

The allotment map of Wyandotte Township in Ottawa County, Oklahoma, shows properties assigned to Benjamin, Dawson, Irvin (Robert Armstrong), Alfred, and Susan Mudeater (not Susannah, Armstrong's sister, but likely Benjamin's daughter). Curiously, there

Robert and Adeline Armstrong's daughters. Facing page: Florence and Cora. This page: Julia and Myrtle. Another daughter, Ida, died as a child. The couple also had one son, Frank Dawson Armstrong. Courtesy Ella Melendrez and Trevor Wheeler respectively.

is no allotment for Matthew Jr.[13] The bend in the Neosho River in the vicinity of these allotments is aptly called Mudeater Bend.

When Armstrong set off for Oklahoma, either on his first and only trip south or on his second, if there was a second trip, he took with him his two oldest daughters, Florence and Cora.[14] Reportedly, he departed with horse and buggy, but his granddaughter, Ella, felt he travelled with horses and a wagon as he took along a huge quantity of supplies for the trip.[15] The trio headed for the small town of Wyandotte, in the northeast corner of present-day Oklahoma, the place where the Wyandots who left Kansas half a century earlier had settled. At the time of their departure, Florence would have been fifteen and Cora thirteen. It is not known when the girls moved back to Canada, but they did not remain with Armstrong until 1914, the year of his return. In 1910 Armstrong was boarding with the Grun family on Maple Street in Wyandotte without his daughters.[16] By then Florence had returned to Saskatchewan and may have been back as early as 1908 or even sooner. She had married George Ernest Jordison and their first daughter, Rosemary, was born in January 1910 in Regina. In 1912 Cora was married to Richard Henry Humphrey and was residing in Calgary.

Two of Armstrong's brothers were living in Wyandotte during Armstrong's decade-long stay there. Benjamin was a farmer married to a woman from Kentucky. His brother Alfred, as mentioned earlier, was the owner of a grocery store and a hotel (the Mudeater Hotel), and was the mayor of the town (1904–1905) when Armstrong arrived and again in 1906–1908. His sister, Susannah Betton, with her husband and two of their six children, made their home in Wyandotte County, Kansas. She was widowed in 1910 and died in 1912.

Armstrong found employment, possibly as a painter, while in Oklahoma. In the 1910 census, he stated that he was Indian, widowed, a painter, was not out of work, but that he was out of work for twelve weeks in 1909. Armstrong's desire to live the life of his younger days was spent. His reputation, however, impressed the people in Wyandotte and prompted the local authorities to ask him "to take the trail again after a couple of outlaws but [I] declined, not caring to risk my neck at that time in a business that did not concern me one iota."

RETIREMENT IN CALGARY AND DEATH IN CALIFORNIA

After ten years in Oklahoma, Armstrong, for reasons undisclosed, decided to move back to Canada. He was nearly sixty-five years old and may have wanted to be with his family, or perhaps he felt alienated in the Wyandot community, having lived nearly all his life apart from it. Or, maybe echoes of 1885 lured him back to where his fame had not yet faded and he would be able to reminisce with others about those glory days. Apparently the rift in his marriage was final, for he did not return to his wife and children in Rosthern but to his daughter in Calgary. A possible further reason for not returning to Rosthern, though Armstrong may not even have been aware of it, is that in that same year, 1914, his daughter Julia married Percy Wheeler, the man whom Armstrong threatened a decade earlier. He closes his memoir with "I remained in Oklahoma until 1914 when I returned to Calgary, Alberta where I now [1920] reside with my daughter." Except for some years spent in Gleichen, Alberta, he would live with his daughter Cora until his death in 1940.

In 1911 Cora's husband, Richard Humphrey, was an employee with the Brackman-Ker Milling Company. Between 1911 and the early 1950s, he was a foreman, at times with Western Canada Flour Mills, and at other times with the Purity Flour Company.[17] When Armstrong arrived in Calgary in 1914, Cora, her husband, and their two-year-old son, Irven (sometimes, Ervin), who most likely acquired his grandfather's original given name, were living at 2015 Seventh Avenue East. Irven Thomas, the couple's only child, was born in Calgary in March 1912. The numerous photos of Armstrong with his grandson, from when Irven was a small boy to when he was a grown man, hint at close ties between the two. One photo shows Irven, now a young man, with a happy expression, his arm resting on his grandfather's shoulder, suggesting a long, satisfying relationship.

Armstrong, Cora, Richard, and Irven moved eight times between 1914 and 1930, always staying in the same neighbourhood, just southeast of today's downtown Calgary. Some of the residences were rentals, but in late 1933 or early 1934, the Humphreys purchased the house at 1208 Tenth Avenue East, which would be their last place of residence in Calgary.[18] In the 1921 census, Armstrong and Richard Humphrey are listed as lodgers at 1328 Tenth Avenue East but, inexplicably, Cora and Irven are not. The census shows incorrectly that Armstrong immigrated to Canada in 1880, was naturalized in 1891, and that he was a Baptist. Armstrong, in earlier surveys, reported being Methodist in one instance and Presbyterian in another, creating the impression that this subject did not interest him particularly. Unless the enumerator erred, Armstrong may have put down Baptist this time because another lodger in the same house was a Baptist.[19]

The 1920s were memorable years for Armstrong. He completed his memoir in 1920, but it was the celebration of Calgary's fiftieth anniversary and the fortieth anniversary of the 1885 conflict in 1925 that put Armstrong back in the spotlight. Before and after that year, several individuals interviewed him, and he was a guest at the Calgary Exhibition and Stampede. Newspaper man and historian William McCartney Davidson, while working on a biography of Riel, visited Armstrong about that time. Charlotte Gordon relied

Robert Armstrong and grandson Irven Humphrey, 1931. Courtesy Ella Melendrez.

on his memoir to summarize Armstrong's life in an article published in 1923. In that year she attended an event where she met him:

> One of the most picturesque figures in our Dominion to-day is Mr. Robert Armstrong, of Calgary, an outstanding pioneer, in that he was the captor of Riel, the famous rebel of Western Canada. To have taken a part in one of the decisive episodes of the history of the great West as the chief scout of the North-West Field Force of Canada under General Middleton, Mr. Armstrong's experience is a story with which to conjure in the realm of romance and history.[20]

Gordon provides a snapshot of Armstrong as he was honoured by his peers:

> It was during a gathering of the old-timers' association in Calgary that Mr. Armstrong was brought out of his life of retirement. Old time pictures were thrown on the screen as part of the entertainment—one a picture of an eager young scout of pioneer days. Not recognizing himself, Mr. Armstrong waited for the name to be announced when there rang out 'Robert Armstrong, the man who captured Riel'. Then quickly followed the demand: 'Robert Armstrong, stand up.' From his modest corner he was led by interested friends to a place beside his picture, amid the cheers of the audience. And they found that time had dealt kindly with him. It was hard to realize that the upright, benevolent looking man, with slightly greying hair and a very merry twinkle in his eye, had seventy-four years to his credit and years in which waved high the magic wand of adventure.[21]

In her concluding remarks, she writes:

> . . . Mr. Armstrong has retained not only the marvellous memory that enables him to distinguish voices heard fifty years ago but the same quick movements, the same

wonderful gift of sight, of being able to see for two miles across the prairie and excellent health of 75 years young.

He is very fond of picture shows but declares that these Wild West Shows make him 'weary.' There is a lack of speed, movement in the gunmen, there is not true depiction of the real Wild West as he lived it.[22]

In 1925 the city of Calgary invited Armstrong to be a guest of honour during the Stampede. He rode in the parade on float twenty-one, which was followed by veterans and a field gun used in the 1885 campaign.[23] In a photo taken at the exhibition grounds, Armstrong does not give the impression of being out of place with the many other dignitaries.

A year or two later, in conversation with William McCartney Davidson, Armstrong talked in detail about the several-hour-long ride from the time of Riel's apprehension until their arrival at Middleton's tent and volunteered his feelings about Riel:

Armstrong was much charmed with him, had liked him earlier, and became very fond of him during this unique journey. "I don't know whether Riel thought he would be hanged, or not," Armstrong has reported in interviews. "He didn't say anything about it, and I do not think he expected anything like that. I had no thought that he would be hanged. None of us thought of that." Asked if he would have arrested him had he known at that time how it would turn out, Armstrong has replied, "That is a funny question to ask me." Then, after a pause, perhaps a reflection of forty years ago, he added, "I was sorry for Riel. If I had had my way, there would have been no hanging of such a man. But that is a strange question to be asked. My orders were to arrest him."[24]

Howard Angus Kennedy, who met Armstrong while reporting the news in 1885, visited him in 1926 and, like Gordon, wrote a brief synopsis of his life based on his unpublished memoir. He reported that "Bob Armstrong, now in his seventy-seventh year,

"Old-timers" photographed at the Calgary Exhibition and Stampede grounds in 1925. Left to right, back row: Lady Lougheed, Mike Costello, James Linton, Robert Armstrong, J. J. McHugh, R. C. Thomas, R. J. Hutchings, James Muir [?], and unknown. Left to right, front row: Mrs. David McDougall, Mrs. John McDougall (nee Elizabeth Boyd), Mrs. R. C. Thomas, Mrs. Shaw, unknown, and Mrs. Malcolm Millar. Courtesy Glenbow Archives, NB-I6-412.

is not unknown to his fellow citizens in Calgary, though he is unfortunately a poor man and holds only a humble position."[25]

Armstrong may have travelled to Oklahoma in 1929 to attend the funeral of his brother, Alfred, who likely had been Armstrong's last surviving sibling. An announcement in the local paper informs that "funeral arrangements have not been made, awaiting word from his brother in Canada." A later bulletin in the same paper states that Alfred "had no immediate relatives except a brother in Canada. He had several cousins living in other parts of Oklahoma."[26]

By the end of the 1920s, Armstrong had been living with the Humphreys for at least a decade. Before the 1920s were over, however, his circumstances had changed. He appears to have become impoverished, and in 1929, or possibly sooner, was living at the Salvation Army's Eventide Home in Gleichen, Alberta. It is difficult to surmise why he chose to move to Gleichen, approximately eighty kilometres southeast of Calgary. In 1929 he had made an application for an old-age pension, but it appeared unlikely that he would qualify because of the requirement for an applicant to have lived for twenty continuous years in the province. Though eighty-one at the time, and having lived in Canada for nearly four decades, his stay in Oklahoma meant he would probably have to wait another three years to fulfil the twenty years of continuous residency condition.[27]

Armstrong's famous deed was his companion for the remainder of his days. Even fifty years after the event, he was sought out for an interview.[28] In 1935, while still living in Gleichen, Armstrong was eighty-six years old and, reportedly, had difficulty remembering some names and other details. The interviewer notes, "From time-to-time through the recital, Mr. Fraser [a participant in the 1885 conflict present at the interview] prompted the story with names and places which the older man [Armstrong] hesitated upon." Mr. Fraser's memory may not have been much better because some of the names in the article are incorrect. Armstrong, with a "little white goatee and all," and Mr. Fraser were both sipping scotch at the time of the interview and enjoying themselves as they recalled the excitement of days past.

Ever since Armstrong detached himself from his wife, there was little contact until their adult years between Cora and Florence, who had gone with their father to Oklahoma in 1904, and their siblings who were left behind in Saskatchewan. However, in 1937 Cora visited the family at Rosthern, and that summer she and Irven, but not Armstrong, together with her sister Myrtle Kroeker, Myrtle's husband, and their daughter, Ina, journeyed by car to California. On June 27 they crossed into the United States at East Port, Idaho, with the declared intention of visiting until August. Cora and Myrtle stated that they were going to visit their sister Florence in Los Angeles while Frank Kroeker, Myrtle's husband, said he was going to visit his sister Mary, also in Los Angeles. He declared that he was born in Nebraska, came to Canada in 1911, was a farmer, and was of German background. (When he entered the United States again in November 1941, shortly before the United States declared war on Japan and Germany, he prudently changed "German" to "Dutch.")[29] The group visited Frank's relatives in Nebraska before returning home.

The visit to California in 1937 came several years after Florence had moved there with her second husband Roy Mumaugh of Michigan. In 1930 Florence and Roy were in Joplin, Missouri, but by 1934 or sooner, the couple were residing in Los Angeles.[30] The palm trees and the ocean, or a climate without winter, must have greatly impressed the Canadian visitors because they all soon moved to California permanently.

The exact time when Armstrong, Cora, and Irven moved to California cannot be determined precisely, but it most likely was late in the summer of 1939. There is reason to believe that Armstrong had moved back in with the Humphreys by 1938, or possibly sooner. A 1938 photo shows him relaxing in the Humphreys' backyard. Richard Humphrey chose not to join his family when they moved to Los Angeles.[31] Another photograph dated Friday, September 8, 1939, places Armstrong and his grandson, Irven, with Florence and Roy in California. Cora, not in the photo, may have been taking the picture, which also includes "Doris, a full blood Navajo Indian." At any rate, by April 8, 1940, Armstrong, Cora, and Irven were already living in a rented house on 1035 Albany Street in Los Angeles.

The 1940 census, surprisingly, records Robert Armstrong as "Irvin P. Armstrong"—combining his Mudeater first name (Irvin) with his adopted surname (Armstrong). The reason for the "P." is

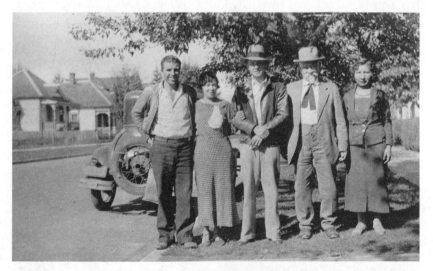

Roy Mumaugh, Florence (Armstrong) Mumaugh, Irven Humphrey, Robert Armstrong, and Doris (last name unknown), in California, September 8, 1939. Courtesy Ella Melendrez.

unclear, but it may not be an error nor just a random choice.[32] Also, without explanation, the annual Wyandotte census in Oklahoma had registered him as Irvin P. Mudeater for the period 1888–1895. In the years prior to and after that time, he is always just Irvin Mudeater. The Mudeaters commonly had two given names, so P. was likely the initial of Irvin's second given name. Bob or Robert, however, had always been wedded to the Armstrong name, so why Armstrong chose to put down Irvin this time is baffling. At this point, he was ninety years old; his memory may have faltered, causing him to lapse momentarily to his childhood name.

The census also reveals that Armstrong was the head of the household and that he was the one who provided the information for that household. Though Cora had indicated a partial Indian background on the 1937 border-crossing form, Armstrong specifies that he, Cora, and Irven were of the white race, all lived in Calgary in 1935, none were looking for work, and that Armstrong and Cora received "income over fifty dollars or more from sources other than money wages or salary." When asked about the birthplace of Cora and Irven, Armstrong provided false answers. He correctly gave Kansas as his birthplace and thus was not required to answer the question about citizenship. Cora was born in Saskatchewan and her son in Calgary. However, Cora was assigned a birthplace of Kansas and Irven, Missouri, thereby also exempting them from the question of their citizenship and, in a way, implying that they were Americans. This calculated answer may have served them usefully in several ways.

When Myrtle and her family entered the United States at Raymond, Montana, on November 12, 1941, with the intention of immigrating, she found herself excluded. Because her husband was an American who had not become a naturalized Canadian, their children also had American citizenship; but, though Armstrong was born in Kansas, Myrtle was not able to claim American citizenship because, unfortunately for her, she showed the immigration official a letter stating that her father, Irvin Mudeter [sic] / Robert Armstrong was granted naturalization in Canada on July 19, 1887, and that his children are "deemed automatically to be British subjects by the father's local naturalization."[33] Her exclusion was appealed but rejected on December 12. She was granted the right to reapply with a passport and immigration visa. Armstrong may have been thinking of such complications befalling Cora and his grandson when he changed their birthplaces.

Shortly before his death, even at an advanced age, Armstrong's frontier habits, seemingly, were still with him. While jay-walking in Los Angeles, he was struck by a car. He beat up the driver, and was arrested and put in jail where he remained until Cora located him. A photo of Armstrong taken two months before his death shows him with a walking stick, which may have been used on the unfortunate man who had bumped Armstrong but obviously had not harmed him. Upon his release from jail, he told Cora, "This is the toughest jail I ever was in."[34] The episode demonstrates that in his nineties, Armstrong was still in good shape, both physically and mentally.

At the age of ninety-one, Robert Armstrong's / Irvin Mudeater's "long, long trail" came to an end on December 22, 1940, in Los Angeles, where he was cremated. Calgary is the place where Armstrong resided the longest so, fittingly, he is memorialized on a plaque listing early southern Alberta pioneers at the Centennial Gate to the Memorial Building of the Southern Alberta Pioneers and Their Descendants.[35]

Armstrong communicates abundant details about his activities but little about himself. Today, nobody with personal experience with the man can provide us with insights into what sort of person Armstrong was. His character, therefore, has to be inferred from his actions, his dialogue, the words of those who knew him a long time ago, or from what might be divined from photographs of him.

There is no question that Armstrong was a colourful figure. It was inevitable that the many years spent on the frontier, where violence and danger were routine, would shape his character. When Armstrong, in his memoir, talks of the tough individuals in the Old West, he may well be offering an explanation for his own behaviour: "their other traits may well be overlooked because as the environment, so the man." Whether he was fighting for his life with the Native Americans of the Southwest or responding to provocations and threats from crooked or bad characters, Armstrong's survival called for swift, vigorous reactions. That this combative or gruff behaviour became entrenched is demonstrated long after those early years. Practically his first action upon arrival in Canada was to use his fist on the fellow taunting him about the length of his hair. Later, his fighting spirit was displayed when he met his wife's employer, and even in his final year when he attacked a fellow who had bumped into him.

This violent aspect of his character, however, manifested typically only when he found himself in menacing situations. In his memoir, there are far more examples of a different side of Armstrong. He appears as a cheerful, talkative fellow who enjoyed the company of others. He reveals his pleasure in "yarning," and, as shown in the episode with the touring groups he escorted, others found him entertaining.

When Armstrong left his wife, it would have made things easier for him to abandon his entire family, but by taking his two daughters with him, he demonstrated milder, more caring feelings, which he also showed in his relationship with his grandson, Irven. That he was his own man, independent and not a sycophant, was demonstrated when he said "no" to Middleton when the general asked him to accompany him to Winnipeg. Two photographs convey additional traits of the man. In a photo taken during Armstrong's middle age, he radiates confident self-assurance, seemingly proud of having played a role in the history of western Canada. Another shows an aged hunter in modern dress, alert eyes staring directly at the viewer with a semi-smile whispering, "the stories I could tell you."

What did the people who knew Armstrong have to say about him? The young university students on tour in the West who had Armstrong as their guide dubbed him "a peculiar specimen." General Middleton said Armstrong and his companion scouts were "all good men and true."[36] Commissioner Irvine similarly praised him as one who "labored incessantly, cheerfully, and efficiently."[37] Reporter Flinn called Armstrong and Diehl "fine, splendidly reliable gentlemen."[38] Correspondent Kennedy recognized Armstrong's adventurous spirit, saying, "that man's adventures, if thrown on the movie screen, would hold a crowded house thrilled and breathless

Robert Armstrong in middle age, radiating confident self-assurance, seemingly proud of having played a role in the history of western Canada. Courtesy Bill Smiley Archives, Prince Albert Historical Society, H-472.

"The stories I could tell you." Robert Armstrong, circa 1925. Courtesy Glenbow Archives, NB-16-552.

through a hundred reels."[39] Further, Kennedy provides us with an "auditory" impression of what Armstrong might have sounded like when he spoke. He records Armstrong's words while being told about a gunman who was about to be hanged: "a sure 'nough bad hombre, who wore out the patience of a sure 'nough tough town."[40] Charlotte Gordon summed up her impression of Armstrong in his seventy-fourth year as an "upright benevolent looking man, with slightly graying hair and a very merry twinkle in his eye," who was "straightforward, rugged and humorous."[41]

Taking Riel into custody marked the climax of the most serious crisis western Canada had faced until that point. That event thrust Armstrong into the ranks of celebrity; it was an event almost without

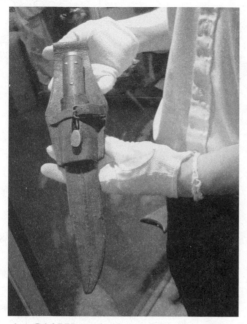

Robert Armstrong's hunting knife and sheath, which are on display at the Batoche National Historic Site Exhibit Hall. Author photograph.

drama in its execution and brief in its duration, but one that made national headlines. Armstrong had many more harrowing experiences than the apprehension of Riel. Maybe because they were the carefree times of his youth, Armstrong appears to have loved his days in the Old West the best. His nostalgic departing words to us suggest so: "I often look back down the long, long trail, sometimes wishing for the old days of camp and trail, wondering if the men with whom I hunted and fought and shared the hardships of frontier life are still living . . . here I will close, having talked long enough, as the campfire is dying low, knock the ashes out of my pipe, roll into my blankets, and sleep contented, so au revoir."

Part Two

ROBERT ARMSTRONG'S MEMOIR

PREFACE TO ARMSTRONG'S MEMOIR

A rmstrong's manuscript, written in 1920, consists of seventy-three handwritten pages, with pages three and six missing. It is reproduced here entirely with only some slight editing for clarity. The memoir opens with "The writer of this story had the facts presented to him by the lips of the old hunter and scout whose life the story depicts from boyhood until the ending of the Canadian North-West Rebellion of 1885." The writer who put Armstrong's words to paper most likely was the old hunter's son-in-law, Richard (Harry) Humphrey, the husband of Armstrong's daughter, Cora, with whom Armstrong lived for many years from 1914 until his death in 1940. The language of this chronicle confers a credible picture of Armstrong recounting his life story, but often the scribe's contribution is sensed when a contrived manner occasionally intrudes on Armstrong's chatty style. After Cora's death, the manuscript was passed to her sister Myrtle, who in turn gave it to her daughter, Ella Melendrez. Two journalists viewed the manuscript in the 1920s, and both published articles summarizing Armstrong's life with copious quotations from it but without any investigation into his stories.[1]

Armstrong was one of hundreds of hunters who participated in the slaughter of buffalo on the U.S. plains. Except for those few who became legends, they did not leave a paper trail, thus making it difficult, and in most cases impossible, to verify many of the

Richard Humphrey and Cora, 1948. Courtesy Ella Melendrez.

events and details in Armstrong's narrative. The experiences he relates range from the incidental to those linking him to historical events. When he talks, for example, about his pets, he contributes to the picture of a buffalo hunter's daily life, and there is little reason to doubt what he says. In his portrayal of some other events, Armstrong does not explicitly declare that he was a participant in those events, though the implication might be there. For instance, his description of the 1868 killing of William Comstock, chief scout at Fort Wallace, gives the impression of being a first-hand account even though Armstrong does not make that claim—he was not there until some later time. This does not invalidate his story as he is merely passing on what he had learned about the incident after coming to Fort Wallace. And then there are some stories that are doubtful, such as his participation in the fight at Adobe Walls and in Nolan's Lost Expedition.

Armstrong makes some errors in chronology. For example, he places his school days in Ohio before his employment with Andrew Blanchard. Both events are documented and prove that his Blanchard trip came before his time at school. Some episodes recollected by Armstrong in his Calgary home had occurred fifty years earlier so it is inevitable that not all of them would be presented sequentially. Strict chronological order is not a necessary condition when stories from a distant time are recalled. Missteps in order do not negate the events. This memoir was not written in a day—it is conceivable that Armstrong, while describing one event, may have had a flashback of another event that he then narrated before continuing the story, leaving it to Humphrey to put it in its right place.

In an era before television, even radio, storytelling was a common pastime, and adding flourishes was not an attempt to mislead but was simply a method for holding the interest of an audience. Further, it is common for men reminiscing about their youth to see their activities in a manner more triumphant than they may have been. Armstrong describes an occasion when he met some bullwhackers who invited him to stay the night and yarn to them, a situation ripe for exaggeration and invention to impress an audience. No doubt, over the years, Armstrong had many occasions to entertain others with his feats. With each telling, embellishments seeped into his accounts so that decades later these embroidered versions of reality may have become indistinguishable from his initial experience.

Therefore, Armstrong's portrayal of events is factual in many cases, exaggerated in others, and occasionally inaccurate. When doubts arise about his claims, they are sometimes dispelled by his attention to incidental matters, to minute details that one would not expect if his descriptions were fabrications. For example, one might wonder whether the account of his experiences at Loon Lake is a restating of what he learned from others or the result of personal involvement. When he speaks of the suicide of an elderly Indian woman (described also by others who were there), he notices that "a good sized tree lay fallen, broken off about six feet or so from the ground still holding to the butt by a huge sliver." This sort of description throughout the memoir adds credibility to his accounts where evidence to the contrary is lacking.

Be that as it may, after the 1885 conflict was over, when Armstrong, with some companions, travelled from Prince Albert to Winnipeg to partake in victory celebrations, Armstrong, unwittingly, cautions the reader of his memoir when he says, "we had considerable fun with farmers along our route, representing ourselves to be somebody far-fetched, causing many of them to open their eyes in astonishment at our wild stories."

Armstrong was born in 1849. The territories west of the Missouri had not yet become states of the Union, and lawless frontier towns were populated by notorious outlaws and lawmen. His formative years were spent in that chaotic world. He hired on the wagon trains heading from Kansas to Denver and Santa Fe, fought off Indian attacks, was caught up in the Civil War, spent some time with a crew building the Kansas Pacific Railroad, scouted for a survey crew, drove a stagecoach, but, most of all, he was a buffalo hunter. By the time he arrived in Canada in 1882, the buffalo herds were decimated, lawlessness had been curtailed, the Indians were subdued, the railway replaced the wagon trains and stagecoach—in short, the Old West had nearly vanished. The defeat of the Métis and the final settlement of the Cree on reserves set the stage for transforming the Canadian Prairies. Quite appropriately, Armstrong ends his memoir with an account of his activities in the 1885 conflict—for by then the world had changed, and the unruly ways of his former life were no longer possible.

Written a century ago, Armstrong's memoir draws a lively picture of an era even more distant, allowing us to hear "from the

Descendants of Robert Armstrong: Ella Melendrez, granddaughter (daughter of Myrtle Armstrong), and Trevor Wheeler, great-grandson (grandson of Julia Armstrong). This book could not have been written if they had not shared their stories about Armstrong and if Ella had not preserved his memoir. Author photograph.

lips of the old hunter and scout" stories about the conflict between the Indians and the hunters, the unrestrained nature of life in the American Old West, and the events of 1885. As has been pointed out in the introduction, some of the words Armstrong uses are derogatory and racist and unacceptable by today's standards. It is not possible to know if he was aware of the dehumanizing nature of those expressions, but it is probably true that his vocabulary says as much, or more, about the society he was part of than it does about the man. It was tempting to delete some of these offensive words, but I could not avoid feeling that this would be an act of vandalism. Changing or deleting Armstrong's words would not undo the past. Biting as those harsh words will be to present day readers, it is more informative to hear the authentic voices of the past rather than some ersatz version. His memoir, not unlike an old photograph, can be viewed as an archeological find, a source that reveals the character and bigotry of Armstrong's world.

In the closing lines of his memoir, Armstrong imagines himself back on the frontier and talks about "the campfire lying low" and rolling into the blankets for a good night's sleep. A fitting image for understanding his memoir—Armstrong at a campfire, yarning to listeners eager to hear thrilling stories.

ROBERT ARMSTRONG'S MEMOIR

The writer of the following remarkable story had the facts presented to him from the lips of the old hunter and scout whose life the story depicts from boyhood until the ending of the Canadian North West Rebellion of 1885. Robert Armstrong or "Bob" as he is known to many old timers of the Canadian West, or as "Muddy" to the hunters and plainsmen of the great South West, is a Westerner of the Westerners. Born and raised there before the advent of the Railroad when the long trains of bull wagons, prairie schooners, stage coach or saddle were the only means of travel the West knew. When large tracts of the West were unexplored and looked upon as desert, where the noble Redman held sway over an empire full of mystery and romance, a wonderful country into which a few intrepid men penetrated bringing back news of wonderful gold discoveries, huge herds of game and hair breadth escapes from the savages who inhabited these wonder regions; such was the West of his youth and there his story begins:

I was born and raised in Kansas about two miles west of Kansas City, Wyandotte County, in the year 1849. I resided with my parents on their ranch until I began to feel that I had arrived at manhood's estate, which in my case and in the case of most boys with an adventurous spirit is about the fourteenth or fifteenth year of their lives. Owing to the circumstances surrounding my youth, I came into close contact with real adventure at an early age. I was able to ride and shoot from the time I was old enough to "fork" a horse; at fourteen years I considered myself quite capable of taking care of anything placed under my charge in any and all circumstances. When I first learned to rope a steer I don't remember so I must have been quite juvenile—I imagine it was just plain natural that I should be able to do so about the time I learned to walk.

During the period of the Civil War my Father suffered heavy losses as we were situated, so to speak, between the "devil and the deep." The troops of both sides raided the old homestead right frequent, commandeering horses and stock to their heart's content. We received the worst treatment from Jennison's Red Legs and Quantrill's men, the latter, by the way, sacked Lawrence, Kansas, murdering many of its inhabitants; both outfits were filled with hard men who rarely showed much mercy. With my boyish eyes I have seen these fellows raid our home while my sister Sue, whose fighting spirit was second to none, has stood in the doorway defying the men to set foot inside. Even with a saber pointing at her breast she refused to give ground until dragged indoors by my mother to avoid possible bloodshed.

Previous to the war, it was my custom to accompany my Father on buffalo hunting expeditions for our meat supply and robes, etc. We penetrated as far west from my home as the district surrounding Fort Riley, also hunting along the Republican River, sometimes 150 miles from home. I can remember when quite small my Father taking me along with him on his hunting expeditions. At first I was almost scared stiff when we rode into the thick of a stampeding herd, Father shooting with all possible speed to down as many as he could before they got out of range. It was some experience for a ten-year-old boy but I was learning to take care of myself, gaining confidence and much hunting knowledge that stood me in good stead in later years. Few boys my age, even in those days, were enabled to hunt big game so far away from home.

I soon became expert on the trail, learning all the tricks in regard to approaching game without disturbing them; how, in the case of buffalo, to get them going in a circle, always downing the leader first or any particular animal who first became restless; the best method of handling skins during the process of curing them; and skill in the use of the skinning knife as well as the rifle and pistol—in fact, these weapons were my daily companions and very often my only protectors at night time. I learned during all this time to beat the Indian in craftiness on the war path or during the hunt, knew practically all the Indian signs, and could speak to any Indian in the sign language; in fact, at the age of fifteen years, I had a man's experience and I had almost said a man's strength.

At fifteen years of age I enlisted in the [missing page]. . . . per sack for a short time. At the end of our two-weeks camp we pulled into Denver, delivered our goods, and turned the cattle onto the range on the Platte River. The men were mostly returned to Leavenworth by wagon and four-mule team. On our trip out we were fortunate in not being attacked by Indians; the main reason for this was the fact that it was winter weather and this northern route was fairly well supplied with soldiers and Forts. I returned to Leavenworth via stage coach, which accomplished the trip in seven days of almost continuous travel. The wagon teams took nearly a month to make the trip, against almost three months on the outward trip.

A short time after arriving home my brother and I with a small party of friends left to attend school at the Baldwin University in Berea, Cuyahoga County, Ohio. The ground the University stood on was donated by a gentleman whose name the University adopted. This old gentleman and his wife resided near the school and were very kindly and highly thought of by the students. We spent many happy times at their home where we were always welcome. My life up to this time had been decidedly lively to say the least and in the course of time school life began to pall and I soon began to turn my eyes westward again. At last my brother and I resolved to return home and go out west once more. To enable us to return home with the least trouble we used the money Father had sent to cover the expenses of our schooling. We first were forced to obtain the consent of the Principal, President Wheeler, and agree to forward our tuition fees, etc. as soon as we arrived home. In those days we traveled by rail to St. Louis and from there to Kansas City by water.

I stayed around home a month or six weeks and then hired out with the Blanchard outfit, which was about to start for Santa Fe. The trip turned out very unlucky—Blanchard lost his life along with several others in a fight with Redskins at Big Bend, or as it is now called, Great Bend, on the Arkansas River. There were several other outfits preparing for the train, which puts me in mind of one small outfit owned by an old man who was of a religious turn of mind. Drivers were scarce and one day, whilst his outfit was loading up, a certain man passed him heading for some other outfit. The old man called out to him, "Hello there, can you drive bulls?" The man turned and replied, "Yes, I can drive 'em to hell and back." The old man returned, "I'm not freighting there this year, you can go on."

Our outfit loaded up in about a week and, by the way, we loaded on the very ground Leavenworth Penitentiary is built on. It is great fun to watch the teamsters getting their outfits together. Some, more expert than others, quickly get hitched up, while others have no end of trouble; probably with so many green bulls to handle, they are all over the place. The main thing is to get two old timers in the lead and the rest will usually follow. It is often amusing to notice how slow and pokey some teams are until we are attacked by Indians when quite often the slowest teams will quickly get out of hand and start out across the Plains in every direction at a dead run, with their tails in the air, the heavy wagons going bangah, bang, bang, bang in their wake. I guess the bulls could scent the Reds because they were sure afraid of them and would become terrified and commence bawling and milling around. To scare them as much as possible and cause a stampede, the Indians would go to shaking their blankets or robes and whooping, when away the teams would go as I have described.

Our first drive took us out to Salt Creek where we camped for the night. After leaving Salt Creek we pulled out onto the Plains. Up to about fifty miles from Fort Leavenworth there were scattered a few farms and ranches, after that there was nothing till the small settlement of Marysville, where we met the first Indians on our trip. They were Caw Indians; though these Indians were not really savages, they dressed wild enough to look decidedly interesting. Their heads were shaved with the exception of a strip down the centre from forehead to neck, each side of the roach the head was painted red or yellow or green, a different colour at each side. Their dress consisted of little else but a loin cloth or g-string, as we called it. These Indians were in the habit of tying a rawhide rope around the neck of their ponies, allowing the loose end to trail along on the ground behind them; this was for the purpose of tanning the rope. Then at night the rope would be greased to take the glue out of it and allowed to drag along again until it was in proper shape. I myself have dragged a rope for miles, day after day for the same purpose.

Whilst at Maryville we had a little fun one day at the expense of one of our teamsters. He possessed a fine whip with a sixteen-foot lash and, when talking to some Indians, one of the boys tied the lash to one of the Indian's rope. When an Indian gets ready to go he usually goes "sudden" and on the jump. Of course, when this particular Red started to leave, the rope with the whip tied to it was bound to follow. The teamster hung on with all his strength, yelling to the Indian to stop; the latter calmly smiled at him and increased the speed of his pony. When the teamster was forced to let go he never recovered his whip and of course never discovered who the culprit was that tied it up—the result was a mad bull whacker and a laughing crowd.

As Marysville was the last outpost of civilization and on the borders of the Indian country, we were each served out with a rifle and bayonet and twenty rounds of ammunition, the latter being the old-fashioned paper cartridge. Before inserting it into the breach of the rifle it was necessary to bite off the paper end. We teamsters carried our rifles strapped in a convenient manner to the side of the wagon box so that a man walking alongside could at once reach his rifle in case of trouble, and trouble came right often as we were fired upon almost every day; occasionally a man would be hurt or perhaps some of the bulls.

Upon our arrival in the vicinity of Cow Creek we [missing page]. . . . them off, a proceeding they never failed to attempt doing as nothing pleased an Indian better than to set a man afoot. The ends of the corrals were closed, the small or narrow end by means of yokes and chains and the other, or wider, end by the use of rope.

Shortly after leaving Walnut Creek, trouble aplenty overtook us at Big Bend on the Arkansas River. Up to this time three other trains were traveling West with us, one a Mexican outfit. We had all just nicely made camp with the stock turned out to graze when we were attacked by a large force of Comanches and Kiowas, as near as we could judge around three hundred in number, while others attacked the remaining three trains who were camped on our flank. When the attack commenced I and a companion named Dyster were out on herd but had been bathing in the river. The first thing we heard was the whoops of the savages who were then charging down on the corral. I had not had time to secure my boots properly and in making a break out of the willows for camp, I lost them in the mud and was obliged to run for it in my bare feet; the ground being covered with prickly pear, I suffered somewhat in consequence. Three or four Indians saw me and came at me with a rush. I was, however, between them and camp and, my life depending upon my speed, I sure split the wind. A cousin of mine, Si Armstrong, came out of camp to meet me and opened fire on the Indians, bringing down three of them and causing the other fellow to retreat right pronto, thus saving my life. My feet were in bad shape being full of spikes from the prickly pear with the result I was laid up several weeks as my feet festered.

In the meantime, Blanchard, our Boss, became rather excited at the first attack and rode out among the cattle in an attempt to drive them inside the corral. It cost him his life as the Indians were amongst them almost as quickly as he was. Shaking their blankets at the Indians, the boys unfortunately hit Blanchard in the stomach; at about the same moment an Indian dragged him from his mule, immediately shooting him through the breast with an arrow. When picked up, the head of the arrow protruded away out in front of his body. He died the same evening. The Indians failed to get his scalp as the fire from the corral was too hot and they were driven off.

The main force continued to attack the corral, riding their ponies at a dead run around the camp, firing arrows and rifles as they did so; we kept up a steady fire from every point of vantage, especially from between the spokes of the wagon wheels. The Indians presented a decidedly hair-raising appearance—they were naked with the exception of the usual g-string, their bodies being painted in several colours with hideous designs drawn down and across the face and other parts of their bodies. Sometimes one or more would be seen riding over the off side of his pony entirely out of sight with the exception of one foot; or again, riding upright, their heels drumming a tattoo on the ribs of their ponies making them grunt so that we could hear them when the shooting and whooping eased up for a moment or two. It was surprising with what force the arrows arrived in our midst, with a sharp hissing sound, often quivering in the woodwork of the wagons and at times penetrating through into the freight. Things looked bad for a while but after some pretty stiff fighting we at last drove them off.

They had, however, run off all our cattle and mules with the exception of one blind mule. As they left several dead near the corral we decided to try our hand at scalping, which, by the way, was considered quite legitimate in those days and thought nothing of; anyway, I took my first scalp at the Big Bend of the Arkansas River. As night came on we could see the fires of the Indians—they were using this means to signal to each other. At this time a good many of the men began to fear a night attack, but the old timers in the outfit who had [illegible] the uneasy ones by imparting to them the fact that an Indian will not make a night attack as he fears that in case he gets himself killed his chances of entering the "Happy Hunting Grounds" are decidedly slim—dawn is the time to look out for trouble. The Redskin loves to creep up to a camp at the hour when nature is the quietest and man is sound in slumber. The hour just before dawn or just as dawn is breaking is the time for the sentinels to be very wide awake and on the alert because the Redskin can creep upon a camp as noiseless as a snake until, with a yell of hate and triumph, he springs to the attack; woe betide the sleepers if they are caught off their guard through the carelessness of a sleeping sentry. However, in this particular instance we were attacked no more.

The same night two men left camp with the blind mule to obtain assistance from Fort Leonard [Larned]. It was a risky trip as the country swarmed with the red devils. They, however, made the trip in safety by alternately riding and walking. On the third day they returned accompanied by an escort of fifty soldiers and about one hundred teams. During the time we had to wait, the Indians refrained from attacking again as they knew what kind of a reception they would get if they made the attempt. The teams hauled off all the wagons they could handle and proceeded up the river under escort for Fort Lyons [Lyon], Colorado, whilst we, under escort also, headed back for Marysville and Leavenworth, our trip to Santa Fe being called off. Our losses in the fight amounted to Blanchard and seven other men killed. We had not traveled more than a distance of five or six miles from the scene of our late troubles when upon looking back we saw the remainder of the wagons going up in smoke.

After arriving back to Fort Leavenworth I returned home and stayed there until my Father moved south into Oklahoma. In '68 I went out over the plains with the Railroad, then pushing out towards Denver. The end of the track was having considerable trouble with Indians who continually attacked the grading gangs and anyone else who happened to run afoul of them. In June of '68 the Indians were extra troublesome. On one occasion they made a simultaneous attack upon sixty miles of track in one hour. Delivering the attack when the sun was just past noon, they caught the teams and men at work in the cuts and owing to having no escort of soldiers they soon scattered the whole outfit, running the teams out on to the prairie and killing the teamsters, some of whom attempted to escape by hanging onto the hames between the mules with the scrapers banging along behind.

I was rather fortunate that day, having been hauling out bridge carpenters to work. I was returning with my team to camp when I was met by a man riding a mule, and he warned me to go no further east as the track had been attacked and the Indians would be here any moment. Sure enough, I had barely got my team unhitched (thinking my chance of escape would be better if I abandoned my wagon) when a number of Indians on ponies came up over the skyline. I quickly turned my mules loose and made a run for a small camp occupied by some men building culverts. It was about three hundred yards away and I soon saw I should be unable to make the grade so turned for the dry bed of Sand Creek whose banks were around fifteen feet high. By this time, I was sure "splitting the wind." As I reached the top or edge of the bank, I jumped and landed safely on my feet, at once ducking under the overhanging bank. As I did so, I heard the Indian ponies running overhead; I, however, fooled them. Shortly after they were driven off by rifle fire directed at them from the camp I had hoped to reach. On my way up the hill I noticed a man walking ahead of my team and wagon—the Indians got him and in the slight delay caused by them stopping to kill him, I obtained a sufficient lead to save my life.

A rather tragic incident occurred in connection with the boss of the bridge gang who was a rather peculiar old man from Ohio and who always maintained that if you treated an Indian right he would not attack you. We advised him to keep them at a respectable distance and not to try making friends with them as they were only looking for scalps and would not hesitate to lift his if they got the chance. He replied that he knew better, so on this particular occasion he attempted to prove his argument by going out to meet the braves. Extending his hand in welcome, one of the latter grasped it whilst another one shot the old man through the head killing him instantly, taking his scalp. There was no mistake about their intentions; they were out to kill and scalp the hated white man and drive him off the plains—was he not taking the Redman's hunting grounds from him, sufficient reason.

The end of track stopped in the Smoky Hill Country for about a year and here the frontier town of Sheridan grew up, only to be deserted when the track moved on. However, for some time Sheridan was certainly a lively place with its saloons, gambling halls, and dance halls running full blast. The town was full of hard men, many of whom died suddenly and in their boots; gun play being right frequent and deadly. From here bull trains freighted west and south to Denver, Mexico, and waypoints bringing in large quantities of wool from the latter country to be sent east by Rail.

About this time, I became acquainted with Buffalo Bill or Bison Bill, as the boys call him. He was killing meat for the Railroad gangs. I hired out to him with my team and wagon to haul his supplies. I was with him about six weeks; during that time, we were out on several trips. Upon one occasion, sixteen Indians made a show of attacking us. Bill was riding ahead about a quarter of a mile when suddenly I saw him stop and wave to me to do like-wise. He galloped back to me telling me he had seen Indians and they him. To see what I was made of, he asked, "Bud, what'll we do?" I replied, "fight." He then said, "that's the way I like to hear you talk, unhitch your mules and tie them behind the wagon." I did so immediately, afterwards taking my rifle and joining Bill in preparation to resist the oncoming Indians who were by this time in plain sight urging their ponies at a run in our direction, thinking we were their meat. They got a nasty surprise for Bill's first shot broke one of the pony's forelegs bringing the rider with a crash to the ground. I at once opened fire with the result that we soon had several horses and men out of action. The remainder soon saw it was unwise to advance and at once turned tail for cover. They made no further attempt to attack us so we soon lost sight of them.

After quitting Buffalo Bill, I commenced killing for myself, making it a regular business. I can well remember boarding at the hotel in Sheridan late in the fall of '68. At this time the herds were traveling south in such numbers I could get up in the morning, take my telescope and locate a large herd, ride quietly out and kill from sixty to one hundred head so that by early afternoon I was back in town again, leaving my skinners to take off the hides and haul them in. I killed large numbers of buffalo around Cheyenne Wells, which at that time was nothing more than a water hole and accounted for the large numbers of game in the vicinity. Consid-erable risk attended the hunting game as Indians were very hostile and continually on the lookout for lonely hunters, setting them afoot by running off their mules, thus rendering them an easy prey to the Indian's rifle and scalping knife.

Sometime about the year 1870 the Federal Government placed a ban upon the wholesale slaughter of buffalo. The restriction remained in force for only a very short period as the Government soon found that just so long as the buffalo was allowed to roam at will in such large numbers it would be a very difficult task to subdue the Indians as the buffalo was the Indian's chief source of food. Hides were worth from $2.75 to $3.50 each, although I sold one batch of extra fine quality at $3.80 each. Completing my kill around Sheridan, I moved westward to Fort Wallace and Kit Carson. I had a crew of six men in my camp who did most of the skinning, and as it was necessary to kill from seventy to eighty or one hundred head per day to keep them going, I was kept pretty busy.

My hunting outfit consisted of mules and wagons and riding horses or mules, food, and supplies for six or seven men sufficient to last us several weeks. We usually took along a keg of "fire water", often very poor dope too; but as everybody was strong and healthy through living outdoors and eating nothing but plain coarse food, the after-effects of its use were seldom alarming. We mostly slept on the ground with robes for bed and cover so that we were warm and comfortable.

My rifles were of special make, made expressly to my order at Sharps' Hartford, Connecticut, factory. Most of them were single-shot weapons and of 45 caliber, the gun weighing from 14 to 16 and 18 lbs. I also had rifles of 40 caliber, but I found these were not quite as satisfactory those days as the larger caliber. The shell of the latter contains 120 grains powder to 550 grains of lead. We tried out mixing a small quantity of tin with the lead but soon abandoned the practice because we found that it made the balls too hard, which often was the cause of them going right through a buffalo at 100 or 500 yards' range, often failing to cripple them. The only time they were of any advantage was in trailing up a herd, then in raking a buffalo from stern to stem, they would plow forward the entire length of the animal's body and strike a vital spot, causing death. I remember upon one occasion killing two bulls with one shot-tinned ball. I was certainly surprised. The animals in question were grazing side by side and I, of course, aimed for the one nearest to me. When upon firing I saw the one farthest away drop in his tracks, I could hardly believe my eyes, whilst the one I shot at stood right up though I knew he was hit by the way he switched his tail; however, he also soon keeled over and upon examination I found the ball had gone right through the first fellow, mushrooming as it did so or directly after striking the second buffalo, causing a bad wound in a vital spot.

The reason we used single-shot rifles was because there was less likelihood of them becoming too hot to shoot effectively; also a magazine rifle would give all kinds of trouble besides the important tendency to waste ammunition. I always found that I could load my rifle quickly enough for almost any purpose whether it was hunting or Indian fighting. Some of my rifles were equipped with two triggers, one to set the hammer and the other to pull off the shot; the latter trigger I had set very fine, so fine in fact that I could blow the hammer down. I always detested a "creeping" trigger as it is sure to spoil your aim. Although the trigger was set so fine, I can honestly say that in all my years of hunting, often going over tough ground after dark, crossing prairie dog holes, etc., I never once fired my rifle accidentally. I used the same system in my old single action 45 Colts, favorites with me to this day in spite of all the new fangled automatic pistols now in use. I think I can still fan my old single action gun about as fast as the automatics. My rifles were often equipped with a telescopic sight but I rarely made use of them as the open sights were quite effective for all ordinary work.

Besides rifles, we were, of course, armed with six-shooters and knives. Most everybody packed a full outfit of arms; or at least one six gun, as in those days they mostly constituted the law. Whether right or wrong, it was the man who could "get there first" and fan his gun the quickest whom the "law" usually favored, although quite often a double killing was the sequel to an argument. I have seen men fatally shot "get" the other fellow as they were falling dead, by sheer determination of will. I have seen many, many gun fights and taken part in some few myself, not always coming out of them unscathed, as old wounds or scars will show.

We manufactured all our own ammunition in camp; the powder came in kegs and the lead in bars. The cook was mainly responsible for this work as well as pegging out hides to cure in the sun. The shell cases were brass, enabling us to make use of them two or three times, though they often expanded, giving us more or less trouble. I remember upon one occasion I almost lost my eyesight through that very cause. I was trailing up a herd on foot having left my horse back a short distance. I was watching the herd ahead of me, at the same time loading my rifle as I walked along. However, the cartridge, being a second-hand one, was sticking in the breech of the rifle, refusing to be pushed home. I began to tap it with the wiping stick, not taking particular notice where I hit it. Suddenly it exploded, the stick having hit the cap with sufficient force to cause this; the powder flared up into my face, blinding me and badly burning my face and hand. I thought for a time that I had completely lost my sight, the blood streamed down my face as I dropped my rifle and turned in the direction of camp. Having shot some buffalo as I trailed along, I feared perhaps one of them might be only wounded and charge me; however, the boys noticed my predicament and quickly came to the rescue, taking me into camp. I doctored myself with raw meat but was forced to stay in camp several days before I was able to hunt again. I carry powder marks on my face to this day to remind me of the incident.

My best day's killing amounted to one hundred twenty-six head of buffalo. Many times have I had four or five animals staggering around at one time, often falling in a heap, necessitating the use of the teams to drag the bodies apart so the skinners could go to work. I well remember about this time killing a number of calves to fill a contract for Christmas meat and show window purposes in Chicago. After sighting a bunch of cows with calves, I dismounted and crawled to the top of a knoll so that I could get a shot at the calves without disturbing the cows too much. Sighting at the nearest calf I fired, the heavy ball struck it over the heart but instead of dropping in its tracks as I expected, the calf turned and ran in my direction practically on its last breath. In a moment or two it reached my position falling almost at the end of my rifle barrel as I lay full length on the ground. The mother had followed her youngster wondering what was wrong and no doubt ready to give battle at once to her enemies. She reached me about the same time as her calf, stopping at once when the calf fell. Not noticing me in her anxiety for her calf, she began smelling around and licking it. During this process I remained perfectly quiet, well knowing if she caught sight of me she would trample me into the ground. I however attempted to push home a shell with my thumb. Slight as the movement was, she saw it. I scarcely breathed. At that moment, the calf gave a last convulsive kick; this at once drew the cow's attention away from me. I at once pushed home the shell, firing immediately. The rifle being only a few inches from her head, the blast parted the hair on her forehead as the ball ranged plum through the skull. She fell dead in her tracks; the whole incident didn't take longer than a couple of minutes to happen, but it seemed almost an hour to me. I killed about two hundred head of calves to fill the contract, receiving eight dollars per head for them.

Numerous bands of wild horses roamed the plains, some of them containing fine Kentucky-bred horses, also heavier breeds that had broken away from emigrant trains crossing the plains. I once saw seven stallions being unloaded from a railroad car in Kit Carson and driven downtown to a livery barn. Five of them broke loose and that was the last we saw of them. One day I ran across three stallions fighting. They had over an acre of ground soaked in blood, one of them was down and almost torn to pieces. I shot the three of them.

I caught a wild pony stallion in a rather peculiar manner. I was riding out ahead of my outfit towards a herd of buffalo when I noticed a pony get up and start limping away. He only traveled a short distance and fell again. I spurred my horse over to him and found he had one of his hind legs entangled in his long mane which swept the ground in a tangle. No doubt he had been scratching his neck and got himself mixed up in the process; he was very nicely hobbled. I dismounted and got a robe over his head and a couple of half hitches over his nose, he biting at me in a savage manner during the process. I then mounted my horse, taking a turn around the horn of the saddle with my rope, and had the boys drive a wagon alongside of him. We tied him securely to the axle and cut his foot free. Right there the show commenced—he kicked, reared, squealed, and bit the tires of the wagon wheels and wagon box, making the sparks fly in his wild efforts to free himself. However, we had him secure and a day or so later we hit for town.

I had an adobe stable wherein we fed him. The roof beams being rather low, we soon saw more fun, for that pony stood right up on his front legs and kicked holes through the roof like he was a Gatling gun. This all happened in Fort Wallace, and just at this time a large number of people were snowbound there and they got up a purse for any man who would ride him. I loaned the man a pair of extra thick chaps or the pony would have chewed the legs off of him. He wasn't much to buck, but he sure did some tall chewing and squealing for a spell.

Wallace at this time had a considerable garrison of soldiers stationed there, and the incident I am about to describe came about over so simple a matter as cord wood. A man named White [Wyatt] had a contract to supply the Fort with cord wood, and on account of the fact that trees were a scarce article on the Plains the wood had to be brought overland from eastern Kansas and at considerable expense. The chief scout at this time was Comstock, a part-Cherokee and a fine man. About the best scout on the Plains, he knew more about that country than anyone else. Incidentally, he knew of a patch of timber about forty or fifty miles from the Fort and he asked White [Wyatt] how he would like to cut his timber within a day's ride of the Fort. White [Wyatt] of course grasped at the opportunity and an agreement was entered into, whereby Comstock was to receive five thousand dollars for the information.

Comstock then guided White [Wyatt] and his outfit with a strong escort (Indians were very troublesome around Wallace at this time; in fact, a man leaving the Fort alone and going out to hunt, say only a mile or so, was in constant danger of being cut off; many men, particularly soldiers, met their fate in this manner) to the bush, receiving $1200 on account—he was to receive the balance upon completion of the contract. However, White [Wyatt] acted like he intended to double-cross Comstock as upon completing the contract he failed to come through with the balance of the money.

Comstock discovered at the Quarter-master's office that the contract was complete and fully settled for; also learning that White [Wyatt] was preparing to leave the country, he at once began to hunt for him and, finding him in the Pool Room, he walked up to White [Wyatt] saying, "Say, White [Wyatt], I understand you have received full settlement for the contract so you can pay me the balance owing me." White [Wyatt] replied, "I have already paid you $1200 and that is sufficient." "But," said Comstock, "the contract calls for $5000." White [Wyatt] again replied, "You have already received $1200 and that is all you will get and that is too much." Comstock then drew his gun and said, "Why, damn you White [Wyatt], I'll kill you if you don't come through." White [Wyatt], at this, made a jump for the door and the scout immediately fired. White [Wyatt] then called, "I'll pay, I'll pay," but it was too late for he pitched forward dead. Comstock got his horse and rode out of camp. As he knew the country so well it was a simple matter for him to evade capture. The troops attempted to get him but failed. About this time Gen. Sheridan arrived at the Fort to commence active operations against the Indians, and as Comstock was a valuable man and badly needed for scouting work, the Gen. pardoned him and he returned to the Fort.

Comstock, however, got his from a man named Sharp [Abner "Sharp" Grover], another scout who later became chief of scouts at Wallace. Sharp was killed by another scout named Mooney [Moody] who coveted his job. This man killed Sharp in a treacherous manner by inducing a woman to disarm Sharp while he was drunk and asleep. Sharp knew Mooney [Moody] was laying for him and as soon as Mooney [Moody] woke him up Sharp went after his guns, which were gone. Mooney [Moody] just laughed at him and shot him dead as he sat in his chair. Mooney [Moody] in turn was killed by a young scout named Langford whom he had abused by tongue and action, having slapped Langford's face. Langford got "fed up" with the treatment so he threw down his gun on Mooney [Moody] and calmly riddled him. Langford in turn was hanged by a bunch of gamblers and saloon keepers who formed a so-called vigilance committee and who were afraid to run afoul of him because he was some expert with a six gun.

However, they encompassed his ruin by catching him drunk or asleep. He was made of stern stuff and scorned to be pulled up by a rope in their hands so deliberately climbed a tree, tied the rope to a branch, took off his high-top boots and with an oath flung them into the crowd, jumped off the tree dying at once. Such was the end of a bunch of hard men, fine fellows in a sense, fearless as a rule, quick with gun or knife, plainsmen all, living in hard stern times, when law was but a myth or a story told but rarely enforced. With all their bad traits they helped to bring the Great West under the control of stable Government, and for that alone their other traits may well be overlooked because as the environment, so the man.

I was on the force of scouts for some little time with Sharp as chief. I remember one day whilst out with the command, Sharp and I were riding along early in the morning, the command being a mile or more away, when suddenly Sharp espied two Indians crouching over a fire with their blankets completely covering them so as to shut out any possibility of the fire being seen. There was no smoke as it was red coals, or rather buffalo chips. We dismounted without being seen and crawled up to within sixty yards of them when Sharp said to me, "You take the nearest one and I will take the other fellow." I then threw my rifle forward and fired, killing my man. Sharp missed his and turned on me with, "Kid you must have hoodooed me as I can't see how I missed at that range." The buck at once ran for it and threw himself down in the long grass where we couldn't see him. Sharp then ordered me to go back to the mules and ride my mule around the Indian's flank, and when he signaled me, to stop and turn towards him, put spurs to my mule and ride close past the Indian at a dead run. I did as directed, and as I came within range of our man he raised up out of the grass to give me an unpleasant surprise with bow and arrow. As he did so, Sharp got him between the shoulders. When we examined him we found three revolvers but only one round in the three guns. Sharp remarked, "he's meat for the buzzards."

A party of us were one day heading towards Wallace when we were jumped by Indians in the hills near Cheyenne Wells. Our party consisted of about one hundred soldiers and forty wagons. A lively fight ensued, but we were too strong for the war party who attacked us and drove them off with loss. After the fight some of the boys were looting any trinket they could see on the bodies of the dead when I saw a buck sitting on the ground with a broken hip raise his bow and put an arrow into the thighs of one of the soldiers as he was running around, completely hobbling him; he turned a complete somersault when he fell. We later gathered around this particular Indian who looked his defiance at us. Suddenly he put out his hand to the Dr. who was standing near, at the same time saying, "How." The Dr. grasped the extended hand which was covered with gore. The Indian gave a derisive laugh as he did so, intending it for an insult. As he was bleeding profusely, he soon weakened; just before he died he began to chant his death song, striking the ground with one hand as he did so. As he gasped his last, he said, "Goo'-bye," and died.

After the fight I was sent with dispatch, but shortly after starting out I ran into a herd of buffalo and was just preparing to shoot from the saddle when my horse stepped into a prairie dog hole, turning a complete somersault. When I came to, I was laying across one of his hind legs while the other leg was across my neck, when he jumped up he raked me under the jaw with his shoe cutting me pretty bad. We fell right in the middle of the herd and it was lucky I didn't get a shot at one as I might only have wounded him in which case he would have made short work of both of us. After getting up, my horse became scared and lit out for the outfit with all my ammunition excepting the pistol ammunition I carried in my belt. A rescue party soon appeared bringing along the Dr. who stitched up a bad scalp wound, and we then returned to camp. Before we struck Wallace, we were again attacked but drove them off.

After leaving the scouts I got my outfit together and went out hunting again and filled a contract with the Railroad for two hundred buffalo heads. The Company sent out a taxidermist to cure and mount them. He remained in my camp until the contract was filled. I then pulled back to Fort Wallace. In '69 I pulled out for Denver, taking with me a carload of buffalo meat for sale. It was A1 cow meat; however, I was out of luck as just about the same time Buffalo Bill and a special train with Grand Duke Alexis of Russia pulled into Denver. They brought along a few old bulls that the Duke had killed, the meat selling as high as twenty-five cents per lb, which in those days was quite a price. What meat I had left by this time went a-begging.

After a short stay in Denver I returned to the buffalo range near Fort Wallace, where I hunted for hides. I made camp about thirty-five miles from the Railroad in a waterless country with the exception of a lake. I killed over seven hundred head at this place. During the summer of 1871 I killed over sixteen hundred buffalo and piled the hides at Wallace for shipment East. One night when

I was camped near the Railroad, all the boys were in town and only myself and a boy about fifteen years of age were in camp. I later went over to the depot to see the agent on some business when upon returning to camp, after hearing some shots fired, I found the boy in my absence had got hold of one of my rifles and riddled several of my pots and pans. Naturally I was some riled and proceeded to take measures to punish the rascal. He, however, stood by and laughed at me saying I would have to catch him first, at the same time sticking his fingers to his nose. I said, "Well, I am not going to run after you but I'm going to get you just the same." At the same time, I was coiling a rope ready to throw. I made a quick jump throwing the rope as I did so and got him before he had time to turn and run. I then dragged him over towards me, picked him up and threw him two or three times pretty heavily. I got rid of him the same night by passing him along to the conductor of a passenger train whom I knew; he took him along to Denver.

During this same summer I acted as guide to two parties of tourists, one party being from England and the other from New York City. The English party was composed of several naval officers, also Capt. Sparks of the White Star Line and Lord Sanford. They had a large outfit, consisting of every imaginable convenience; for instance, one main item consisted of a large marquee divided into several apartments, including dining room which also acted as smoking room, etc. where we sat and yarned over the evening smokes and drinks. They also had a four-mule team wagon load of nothing but wines, spirits, etc. and smokes. The outfit altogether consisted of twelve wagons and a complete outfit of horses and mules loaned by the U.S. Government; also a company of soldiers as escort in case of our being jumped by Indians. They also had a staff of their own servants, cooks, waiters, etc. I left my hunting to take charge of their outfit at a salary of thirty-five dollars per day. I could make more hunting, but the officers at the Post kindly recommended me to the outfit so I signed on with them, turning my horses out to pasture. Some of my men went along with us to drive team, etc.

This trip was the swellest trip I ever undertook. I gained twenty pounds in six weeks—high wines and good grub tell the tale; more wines than grub at that. It was some amusing to see the crowd the day they killed their first buffalo, they spent the best part of half a day around his old carcass making speeches and drinking champagne. They were a jolly bunch of fellows and we, one and all, had a first-rate time. Nothing alarming happened during the trip. Upon leaving Wallace they turned over to me their surplus supplies, also each making me a present of a sum of money. Capt. Sparks also presented me with a first-class return passage to England and an invitation to visit him there. Lord Sanford intimated that he would like to have me in his services as head gamekeeper of his estate in England. I, however, declined the offer as I figured a gamekeeper's life in England would be too dull; and then again, I might have to shoot the ears off someone and that would be bad form over there, even though it was permissible out West.

My second party consisted of New York college youths under the care of Prof. Fairrens of Fairrens College, if I remember the name correctly. There being sixteen students and the Prof in the crowd, we made a nice little lively party. I well remember the name of one young man of the party on account of his father, Prof. Morse of telegraph fame. We were out about two weeks or so and several of the boys proved themselves good shots, killing quite a few buffalo. It was amusing to watch the boys when we made our first camp. They were all keyed up to a high pitch of healthy excitement at the novelty of being out on the Plains, and enquired eagerly as to the prospects of fighting Indians. They arranged their beds around mine as closely as possible, thinking the closer they were to me, the safer they would be in case of an attack. After darkness came on, the coyotes and buffalo wolves began to howl and bark, and many were the conjectures as to whether the noises they heard were all from animals, or from Indians calling to each other in preparation for an attack upon us. I reassured them and told them there was small chance of us being attacked at night, the time to keep a sharp lookout being just as dawn is breaking.

I found Prof. Fairrens a very agreeable man, who handled his charges with a degree of sagacity wonderful to behold and who was like a father to them. The boys thought I was a peculiar specimen as I told them several tall stories of my travels. I also told them I had never tasted any kind of cake, only sponge cake, and that only on one occasion, and had lived on nothing but wild meat for months at a time. They opened their eyes and wondered what manner of man I was. If I would only visit them in New York City, they promised me all [illegible], also they would drive me around town and show me the sights, introduce me to their sisters and in general give me a good time. They were delighted with their trip and frequently expressed the wish to become hunters and scouts.

During this summer I met up with a remarkable character in the shape of an old man as tough as hickory. He was out after wild horses and had the most remarkable method of rounding them up I ever saw—he literally walked them off their feet. When I first became acquainted with him and listened to his ideas as to how to catch wild horses, I thought he was sure locoed. However, I hauled him out about forty miles and set him afoot with his little old Mex mule which had a cow bell tied to its neck. The old man's method consisted of turning loose the mule after locating a bunch of horses. She would at once join the bunch and away they would go with the old man trailing up behind. The bell would direct him and he would keep them moving practically all the time, allowing them no rest. In this manner he alone, in two weeks, had sixty head of horses inside the corrals at Wallace where he sold them, making himself quite a stake for two weeks' work.

A week or so after my short trip with the "horse hunter" I commenced killing buffalo again. I took out five men and three wagons with teams, making a good kill though hides in the Fall of '72 fell away in value to almost nothing and I was obliged to "treat" them with a poison and store them until the following spring when the price recovered. During this last trip I hunted over the ground of the Sand Creek massacre of '64 where Col. Shillington and his outfit cleaned up a large band of Indians, killing "papooses" and all, as the Col. in referring to the youngsters said "nits make lice."

In the fall of '72, a man came up north from Texas, driving about two thousand head of cattle. He struck the Arkansas River at Bent's Ford and there lost his outfit of horses. Indians ran them off. Nothing daunted, he struck out for Fort Wallace to obtain another outfit of horses. He was afoot, which means some trip through Indian country, a distance of close to two hundred miles. However, he made the trip though he suffered some hard luck. He struck the Railroad twenty miles east of Wallace. In the meantime, a very bad snowstorm overtook him and, overcome by the cold, he lay down exhausted on the track in a cut. Shortly after, a train came along and threw him out of the snow drift; how he escaped death is a mystery. He was badly frozen and lost both his feet and ears. He recovered and arranged with me to go down to the Arkansas and recover his herd. I got together twenty-eight head of horses and a number of men, and struck south for Bent's Ford. It was a two-hundred-mile trip through a wild country which speaks something of the grit of the owner of the cattle. We struck the river within four miles of the Ford and rounded up the cattle, only a small number of which were lost. I left the outfit to come along behind whilst I headed back for Wallace to go hunting again.

During my stay in Wallace I had several tilts with bad men who attempted to round me up, but as I crippled several of them they began to think I was a tough customer to handle and so steered clear of me. One man I shot through the lungs, partially destroying his talking apparatus. He, however, recovered and later I met him in Trinidad, Colorado, where he surprised me by his welcome, saying the shot I put into him cured him of his wildness and he had married and settled down and had a nice business. He could scarcely speak but was making good and invited me to his place where I stayed about a week.

During the winter of '73 I struck South towards the Texas Panhandle where I engaged in hunting, hauling fourteen hundred hides into Adobe Walls on the Canadian River in the Panhandle country. There being no railroad in this country, we were forced to do business with the local traders who, after collecting a large number of hides, would then ship them north to Kansas City. Adobe Walls was named after the first trading post established there, it having been built of adobe, the Mexican style of building composed of straw and mud baked in the sun. These buildings are very cool and very satisfactory in a hot climate. Adobe Walls in its early history was a renegade post where rustlers and men of that ilk collected stolen cattle, disposing of them from that point.

During my stay in Adobe Walls the Indians made a determined attack upon the place. The Adobe Walls fight is well remembered by old timers. A large party of Cheyennes attacked the town and a stiff fight followed. I never saw them so impudent, with the exception of one or two other occasions elsewhere. During their advance on the Post they had surprised numerous hunters and taken their scalps as well as their horses and rifles, etc. The latter fact accounted for the reason they were able to open fire on us at a range of upwards of eight hundred yards. The heavy balls came plunging into town in a rather disconcerting manner, causing us to hide out right pronto. Most of us gathered inside an adobe warehouse as it seemed about the strongest position we could take up. It, however, had one very weak point and that was the fact that there was only one window facing the direction in which the attack was developing. One other building built of logs with a fairly high and powerful stockade around it afforded a pretty good vantage point to resist an attack, the greatest danger being fire as the wood was very dry and once it was fired it would be some interesting to put the fire out.

The action became very stubborn as the Redskins showed lots of sand, advancing right into town and engaging us at close quarters. The Indians fought from behind their ponies and we very soon had a number of these out of action. Before we succeeded in driving them off, we inflicted upon them a loss of a dozen killed and the wounded were quite numerous, but they managed to carry them off so we never knew their exact number. The raid cost the white men about fifteen lives, including the hunters killed outside of town.

I well remember the case of two hunters who were "jumped" by the Redskins. These men quickly mounted their horses and streaked for town; however, one of them who had by far the best horse lost his head and ran his mount, a fine well-bred mare, so severe a pace that in two miles she was run to a standstill. Of course the bucks caught up with him, and the day following the fight we found [R?]osburg with a bayonet through him from the right breast to the left shoulder. He was lying there with his right hand clutching the point of the bayonet and minus his scalp. His partner who escaped had been contented to maintain a certain distance between himself and the savages and thus had escaped.

The bayonet had, no doubt, been taken from some soldier in a fight in which the soldiers got the worst of the deal.

One man I knew well named Billy Tyler met his end in a peculiar manner. He was inside the stockade and with drawn pistols was looking through a crack between the posts to get a shot when a buck rode up alongside the stockade, stood upon his pony's back and looked over into the area. As luck had it, Tyler's back was turned and the buck got him square between the shoulders. He died some time later with a death clinch on his guns, hoping to the very last to get a shot in before he "crossed the divide."

Shortly after this I went down into Oklahoma to visit my people where in the meantime they had moved. I stayed home about seven months and then headed West once more for Fort Reno, also known as the Cheyenne Arapaho Agency, on the north fork of the Canadian River. The Fort at this time was in process of building. I worked for the Government there in charge of the beef herd. This herd provided beef for the Indians whom the soldiers had rounded up or who had come into the Post on their own account because they were starving. The soldiers disarmed and set them afoot as they arrived. The tribes represented were the Arapahos and Cheyennes, and they numbered no less than ten to twelve thousand souls.

It required over one thousand head of Texas steers per week to keep the Post going. The system in vogue at the Post in regards to the serving out of the beef ration was as follows: the head Chiefs and under-Chiefs of the tribes would put in their application for so many pounds of beef to the quarter-master's office. They would then bring to me their requisitions, I would then order so many head of beef to be cut out of the herd and run onto the scales. After they were weighed, they were run out onto the open prairie where a number of bucks were in readiness to take up the chase. The bucks imagined they were buffalo hunting and would shoot the steers down with great gusto, enjoying the fun immensely. The carcasses were left where they fell for the squaws whose duty it was to skin and cut them up. The whooping and shooting would at times make one think a battle was going on. The system was pleasing to the Indians and saved work which might otherwise have had to be performed by white men at the Post. The majority of these Indians had been driven into the Post by white hunters who by this time had practically cleared large areas of country of the buffalo, and the Indians were often in starving condition.

At this time the soldiers were after a certain number of extra bad Indians who were known to have committed certain crimes that the authorities were anxious to see them punished for. They eventually rounded up over seventy of them and sent them to prison on some island off the Florida coast. These men were lined up and the blacksmith with his helper went down the line and riveted iron shackles onto the legs of each man. When he reached the end of the line he checked up his men and found he was two short. There being a number of Indians standing around, the officer in charge ordered the soldiers to seize the first two Indians they came to "as they couldn't go very far wrong," most of them being bad ones anyway.

The moment the soldiers attempted to do as they were ordered, every buck dropped his blanket and revealed to the gaze of the astonished soldiers a Winchester, which they promptly brought into action, at the same time scattering in every direction. A running fight followed which lasted the greater part of the day with losses on both sides. The bucks were, however, mostly all rounded up and disarmed. That night the squaws made things interesting as they howled and groaned and at times chanted weird songs in mourning for the lost braves. Several times during the night someone would stick his head out of a tent and yell over to the Indian camp, telling the squaws to shut up, perhaps following the request by a revolver shot. It was useless to do so as in a few minutes the racket started up again ad infinitum. This was kept up for several nights until they tired themselves out and we had peace.

In the spring of '75 I went out on a survey as hunter for the party. The survey was conducted in the country between the Wachita [Washita] and Canadian Rivers. This section of country had witnessed a previous attempt to subdivide it but the Indians ran the surveyors off, killing a number of cartmen and sighters. One man had quite an experience—the Indians rode on each side of him and lashed him with their quirts, almost blinding him. They did not kill him, being content to whip him good and hard.

One day during our trip we were honored or otherwise by a visit from "Big Bow" and his band of three hundred braves. Things looked squally for awhile. The Kiowas demanded two pack loads of flour, sugar, and tobacco. I happened to be standing near the chief with my rifle in my hand when "Big Bow" suddenly took a fancy to it and laid hold of the barrel. I, however, hung on to it as he attempted to wrench it away from me. He was a fat, bowlegged sample of an Indian and pretty heavy. Some of our fellows began to fear a general mix-up as the bucks were beginning to look kind of hostile and shouted to me to let him have it or "there'll be hell apopping in a minute." I, however, understood the Indian nature better than they and so hung grimly on and suddenly got in a blow with my knee in the region of the chief's bread basket that made him let go with a grunt. I immediately threw my rifle down on his old stomach, full cock, and gave him to understand if one of his band made a false move I would put a kink in his back bone that would make him meat for the buzzards. He stood there looking kind of foolish for a moment; suddenly he turned, leaped upon his pony, gave an order, and the whole band dusted out of camp in short order. No doubt if I had given way to him as some of the boys wished me to do, his demands would not have been satisfied until he had about cleaned us out and we might possibly have lost our "hair" in the bargain. To show any kind of weakness to an Indian is fatal, especially in a case like the above where they are in strong force.

The country we were in proved to be one of the richest game countries I ever saw; there being lots of water, it was a perfect paradise for game. I never saw so many wild turkeys as I did there; they swarmed in thousands. All one had to do to get a mess of turkey was to take a pole, and after they had gone to roost on the low trees in the vicinity, knock them off the branches by the dozen. We sure got fed up with turkey. Deer, antelope, buffalo, bear, and wild horses were plentiful.

During this survey we had to be always on our guard against possible attacks from Indians. I had volunteered to act as front sightman. This was the most dangerous position on the survey, as the previous survey had amply proved, for most of the sightmen were killed. My method of advance was very cautious—upon reaching the top of a knoll or any high ground, I always took a careful look around as far as I could see ahead for Indian signs, and I remember one day a few minutes after gaining the top of some rising ground I was taking a careful survey ahead when suddenly a brilliant light flashed in my face. It proved to be a lucky flash for me as it warned me that Indians were in the vicinity. In signaling to each other, Indians quite often resorted to the use of a mirror or any piece of one they manage to pick up. By flashing it in the sun they quickly found it a useful means whereby they could signal to each other. This time, however, I imagine the buck made a mistake as I am sure he took me for one of his band or it is a certainty he would not have betrayed himself. Anyway, it probably saved my life because I waited for the main body of our outfit to reach me before proceeding ahead and, as we were fairly numerous, the Indians no doubt decided not to attack.

I quite often came across Indian burial grounds. However, instead of being buried, the bodies were wrapped in rawhide and securely fastened by rawhide rope to scaffolds erected on the plains or maybe resting between the forks of some tree. Near the body would be placed the usual implements of war and chase, perhaps a little coffee and other food would be there for the use of the brave in crossing the divide into the happy hunting grounds. I found the last resting place of the son of Lone Wolf, head chief of the Kiowas. He was killed during a war raid into Texas. Around his scaffold in a large circle, two hundred horses were lying dead. Lone Wolf had had these horses killed for the use of his son in the happy hunting grounds. Near his body lay his rifle, bow and arrows, also coffee, etc. I am sorry to say these articles were always looted by the boys to keep for souvenirs or, perhaps, in the case of a rifle or knife, to be used by the finder.

Shortly after returning to Fort Reno, to which place we returned after completing our duties, riders came in with the news that a band of Kiowas had arrived in the vicinity with a couple of white girls whom they had taken prisoners, at the same time murdering their parents. These Indians had previously been warned to give them up and had decided to do so. One of the girls, the eldest, had been forced to become the wife of the chief of the band and had lived under those conditions for six or seven months. It was truly pitiable to see the condition they were in. They were made as comfortable as possible after their hard experience. Some of the Indians felt sympathy for them and showed their feelings in a very practical way as, for instance, Little Raven, chief of the Arapahos, presented the girls with four hundred beautiful robes.

In the year '76 my partner Henry Hughes and I started southwest towards the Llano Estacado or Stake [Staked] Plains, in those days an absolute desert. We penetrated into the country containing the head waters of the Paladora [Palo Duro], Red, Colorado, Concho, Brazos, Double Mtn., and Blanco Canyon Rivers and Creeks. At a camp we made on the Brazos River northwest of Fort Griffin we killed over four hundred head of buffalo, hauling their hides into Griffin.

During our hunt along the Brazos River we one day came upon a small animal that at first puzzled us. It was almost dead from starvation. It being too young to hunt its own food, we decided the mother must have been killed and so we adopted it. After awhile we decided it was a panther and so it proved to be as she later grew to be a lovely animal measuring eleven feet from tip to tip with a black coat just like silk. We all became much attached to her and she to us. She always slept close to me, her gentle, though at times rather loud, purr indicating how contented she was. We often had much fun watching her feed. Sometimes we would tie a quarter of a buffalo to the hind wheel of one of the wagons and then stand back and watch her attack. She usually played with it for awhile, making the quarter spin around with the heavy blows of her paws. After tiring of the play she would then proceed to tear it asunder, her antics affording us much amusement.

At times we would be camped near other hunters, and their dogs wandering over our way would get the surprise of their lives. Nelly loved to lay low with her tail stuck out at right angles to her body. Laying perfectly still, she would allow the dogs to come pretty close; sometimes they would fail to notice her when she would attract their attention by moving the tip of her tail. As quickly as the dog's eyes were drawn to the movement, she sprang out towards it, and the dog, turning with howls of terror, would streak for home and usually stay there. Nelly, being hitched to a rawhide rope, could not follow very far but it afforded her supreme satisfaction to put the fear into them. As she grew older she began to show signs of being cross and in the end I was obliged to shoot her.

I later acquired another wild pet during a hunt south of Fort Griffin, where I had gone to the assistance of a rancher near Phantom Hill or Fort Phantom. His cattle were being lured away by the herds of buffalo and he desired to see the latter driven off. One day whilst riding over the mesa we saw standing in solitary state a large tree and near the top a nest of rather huge dimensions composed of sticks as large as a man's arm. That same evening, we had a severe storm accompanied by very heavy wind, and upon riding past the tree next morning we noticed the nest was gone. I rode up to the tree and there stood a comical looking bird—naked, lost and forlorn with a few pin feathers sticking out at the end of its wings and tail. As I dismounted and approached, it opened its huge mouth for food. It sure looked funny standing there so big and naked; however, I signaled the wagons and we picked up our find, placing it in one of the wagons as the most suitable place for it to travel. We soon killed some meat and cutting off a strip about a yard long and half an inch thick we presented it to our baby who gulped it down so quick she almost choked. However, she grew and thrived into a beautiful bald-headed eagle and I became more attached to her than I had been to the panther.

When we moved she would perch herself on top of the load, her huge claws grasping her support with tremendous strength, and there she would sit in solemn majesty ever and anon, her beautiful wings outspreading to catch her balance as the heavy wagon lumbered over the rough trail. Often I would spur my horse alongside the wagon and talk to her and I'll swear she understood almost all I said to her for she would look at me with her great solemn eyes as much as to say, "Yes, pard, I know all about our trials and troubles, but there's a better time coming." If I ever had any reason to scold her she would hang her head like a child. Unlike the panther, she refused to obey anybody but me and would at once show fight if the boys attempted to interfere with her in any way.

I later presented her to a friend in Fort Griffin who kept her as long as I was in that country. I remember calling to see this friend after being away about eight months, and as I rode down the trail the eagle saw me and at once recognized me for she came towards me screeching and flying in huge bounds up the trail, a distance of two or three hundred yards, and as I stopped my horse and spoke to her she became silent and hung her head in the same old way. As we moved towards the house she hopped ahead once in awhile uttering her welcome, delighted to see me once again. When I left Fort Griffin she would not be consoled; however, I never saw her again so do not know what became of her. They kept her wings cut short so she was unable to fly.

After completing our hunt around Fort Griffin we struck south towards the Concho, making camp about sixty miles from Fort Concho on the North Concho River. In this district I discovered a very fine spring about twenty feet across. It afterwards [was] named Muddy Springs although its waters were clear as crystal; old timers who knew me in those days will know the reason for its peculiar name. At this spring I made my record kill—one hundred and twenty-six buffalo falling to my rifle in five hours. The herd was very large in this district and were more determined than usual to get to water. I was obliged to shout at them to scare them off to shooting distance as, in case of wounding only, they are liable to charge a person with disastrous results to the person involved. I have shot them so close that the blast of the discharge parted the hair in the middle of the forehead and they have actually fallen with their head and shoulders brushing my legs. The buffalo have a keen sense of smell but very poor eyesight. They travel in a determined manner, but should they smell anything strange such as a man, for instance, they would not charge or stampede over him as wild cattle would be likely to do but would split their ranks and pass by on both sides strictly attending to their own business unless interfered with in some way or hurt—then a person would have to look out for trouble swift and immediate.

It's very amusing to see a herd crossing the Railroad. If a train happens along they don't want to stop and be forced to cross the track behind the train but will run at top speed alongside the train with their tongues hanging out like they were almost done for in the endeavour to get around in front of it. This habit was the cause of many a buffalo being killed by passengers shooting from the moving train. They were oftentimes destructive of the right of way, especially at a fill, as they would pull down the ballast until for a stretch of perhaps fifty yards the track would be in the air without any support. The Railroads were obliged to employ hunters to more or less patrol the right of way and drive off the herds.

In the country around the Paladores [Palo Duro] River we met with a strange experience. One day about noon we struck a huge sunflower forest, miles in extent. As we could not see any end to it, we plunged into the thick of it. Following buffalo paths, we could hear these animals crashing through ahead and on both our flanks. The sunflowers were fifteen feet and more in height and the dust was stifling. We rode along for three hours not knowing what might happen as we couldn't see any distance ahead. We, however, finally emerged onto a mesa whereon countless buffalo were feeding. After looking around we turned to await the wagons, and upon looking towards the herd once more we found to our surprise they had vanished as though the earth had opened and swallowed them.

We promptly investigated and found a deep depression almost like a huge canyon only pretty wide and several hundred feet deep. It looked as if the ground all around had suddenly collapsed through some convulsion of nature. Anyway, at the bottom of the depression and ranging down the sides were our buffalo. They looked like black ants at the bottom of the valley. A stream ran down the middle of it and there appeared to be lots of feed. My attention was directed to one of the numerous projections of earth and rock sticking out from the sides of the canyon. Laying at full length upon one of these was a young bull buffalo who had wandered or been driven out there by an older bull; he looked gaunt and his eyes were sore from the wind blowing the dust into them. The ledge was so narrow he couldn't turn round and retreat. I remarked to Hughes, "watch me make that fellow jump." I then fired and he leaped out into space like a bird and went crashing down to the foot of the break, no doubt most every bone in his body being broken in the fall. We also caught four head of workhorses with shoes on, showing they had recently broken loose from some outfit. We utilized them to change off on our wagons and so rest our teams. They were fairly well bred heavy types of horses.

After completing this trip, we went over to Double Mtn. on the Stake[d] Plains where we made camp close to two lakes. There we killed five hundred head and hauled the hides to San Angelo, a tough little town situated about one mile from Fort Concho. An exchange of marshals was right frequent at this place, owing to demise of said marshals, usually quickly and with their boots on. I myself was once offered the post but declined with thanks, although I several times acted as deputy. On one occasion we trailed up a bad Mexican for some considerable distance, in fact, to the Pecos River, where we got him ok and handed him over to justice. On his next trip, the marshal bit the dust and I was elected in his place, but as I said, I wanted none of it.

The first night we hit San Angelo we entered the "Last Chance" saloon, bellied up to the bar and called for drinks when suddenly I found two six-guns pointing in the general direction of my stomach. I stepped back, whipping out my gun as I did so, when the crowd began to shout, "don't shoot, don't shoot, he can't hurt you." I thought all the time there was something wrong as the man didn't look like a killer nor even dangerous. I could also tell by his eyes that he had no intention of shooting. It developed that the crowd had fixed this stunt up for a little fun. I told them that there came near being a funeral as I wasn't in the habit of allowing men to poke a gun in my direction without taking prompt measures to head off such like demonstrations, sometimes to the serious inconvenience of the party or parties demonstrating. The man was a middle-aged Dutchman on his monthly "bender" and the boys had reversed the cylinders in two six-guns so they wouldn't shoot, put them in the hands of Dutch John, and persuaded him to stage a comic hold-up. Dutch John made and repaired boots and was the butt of many jokes got up by the cowpunchers of that region. His sign hung out over the sidewalk and was barely hanging together owing to the fact that the boys considered it to be a public target for revolver practice as they galloped up and down the street; it was riddled with bullet holes.

San Angelo in those days was a sure enough tough town. I found it necessary to cripple several of its rambunctious citizens and casual visitors who attempted to make things disagreeable for me. Upon one occasion I had trouble with a man who had always professed to be a friend of mine but who proved himself to be something entirely different. It appears that he had been working over in his mind the idea of "getting" me; anyway, he took occasion to get the drop on me in a peculiar manner.

One day I was challenged, for a joke, to ride my mare into this man's saloon. Being quite willing to have a little fun, I rode the mare at the door; just as she placed her front feet inside the door, I saw my friend. He held a gun in his hand pointing in my direction and warned me to back out as he wouldn't allow anybody to ride into his place. I said, "why, it's only a joke." At the same time, I saw by the look in his eyes that he intended to cut loose. I barely had time to jerk the mare's head back when he fired and the ball intended for me struck her square between the eyes; she dropped in her tracks. I was so surprised at his action that I made no attempt to draw my gun but left my horse where she lay and went to my camp. I brooded over the incident all evening and decided on my course of action.

Next morning, I got up bright and early and headed for the scene of my troubles. As I approached the place my man stepped out of the door and headed for the opposite side of the street. I called out, "Say there, are you heeled?" His hand at once began to move towards his gun. I then said, "Don't draw if you care anything for your life." He at once arrested the movement of his hand as he well knew I was quick on the draw and could quite easily beat him to it. I then walked over to him, informing him that in my opinion he was a coward and a flee-bitten coyote. Drawing my gun as I informed him of the above, I hauled off and introduced him to the weight of it on top of his skull. He promptly went to dreamland and the boys who had been standing out of the line of fire, expecting to smell powder, gathered him inside of his place of business to administer first aid. During the remainder of my stay in San Angelo he found it convenient to avoid my company.

It was nothing thought of to ride one's horse into a saloon or store. In fact, in some places the owner of any place of suchlike business had two wide doors built, one in each opposite wall so that a bunch of horsemen out for a "time" could ride right along through without causing much damage. I have seen a crowd of hunters (and been one of the crowd) march into a saloon in Indian file, each with a Winchester in the crook of his arm pointing at the roof; as each man passed through the door, he would commence pumping the lead through the roof. In a moment the place would fill with smoke, the shingles fly, and the noise would be deafening. After getting that off their chests they would call for drinks for the house, pay for the damage wrought, and promptly forget it. I have known a crowd of us to ride our horses into a saloon, oblige the bar keep to step out from behind his bar, and buy his own fire water.

After being engaged for a short time on the Pecos River in a cattle war, I returned to my camp at Double Mtn. to continue hunting. Shortly after my arrival there a company of negro troops of the Tenth U.S. Cavalry arrived at my camp. They carried a letter from Gen. Woods at Fort Concho to me, requesting my assistance as guide in following up a band of Indians who had committed acts of violence upon settlers in the Pan Handle [sic] country and who were known to have headed out over the Llana Estacada. The force had brought along water tanks, canteens, skins, etc. to carry the water supply. After filling these at the lake we struck out for the sand.

We found the going terribly hard; the wheels sank [fallow?] deep in the loose sand, which at once ran back into the tracks as quickly as the wagons passed through it. The mules, also, and horses found poor footing and the heat was severe. When we lay down in our blankets at night the sand drifted over us so that in the morning we were weighted down by the sand on top of our blankets. We penetrated into the desert about sixty miles and then found our water supply dangerously low even after very careful rationing. A counsel was held as to the advisability of pushing on or retreating. After some talk, the latter plan was decided on. It was a wise one as things turned out.

Our water gave out completely before we reached the edge of the desert. The horses were dropping and the troopers' tongues turned black and swollen, even protruding from their mouths in some cases. These fellows at last got out of hand and refused to obey their officers. Upon clearing the sand, the outfit began shooting their mounts and drinking the blood from the wounds. In a few minutes the situation was hair-raising. A light breeze blew the sand like fine dust through the air and, the mules bespattering the men with blood, the sand stuck to them also forming a combination that reminded one of the descriptions of some infernal region or other. We managed to get one man headed for the lakes with mules and water bottles, etc. Sometime later the remainder of the outfit decided to hit the trail likewise and so we started for Double Mtn. lakes. However, about thirty of the men decided to head north where they thought water lay somewhat nearer than my camp. They found it alright, but it cost them their lives. A search party three days later found them all dead around the water's edge—they having drunk deeply of the gypsum waters of the lake and so perished. It was a gypsum lake and unfit for either man or beast. In driving cattle near water of that kind a cow outfit would have the time of their lives keeping the cattle from stampeding into the water and perishing. About ten miles from the edge of the desert we met our man returning with water, which relieved the outfit, enabling us to push onward to safety. So ended one of the hardest trips I ever undertook. The outfit lost both men and horses, and the Indians were never in sight.

I remember one trip carrying dispatches for Gen. Sheridan out of Fort Wallace when I was obliged to shoot the mule I was riding, which of course set me afoot in a bad Indian country. I was soon "up against it" for food and water. After awhile I began to "see things"; at times I was certain I could see water, or again I saw food aplenty spread out before me. I was afraid to use my gun for fear of attracting attention as Indians were numerous. At last I sank down exhausted beneath a low bush and slept quite a long time. When I awoke the first thing I saw over my head was a crow perched upon a branch regarding me with interest, no doubt expecting me to cash in and provide him with a meal. However, I turned the tables by drawing my gun and knocking him off his perch, Indians or no Indians. I ate him raw and he surely tasted good, reviving my strength enabling me to proceed.

Shortly after my desert trip I broke camp, and along with another outfit belonging to Jim White, one of the most expert hunters on the plains, we headed for Montana via New Mexico and Colorado. Our party consisted of fifteen men. We had a lively time passing through certain small Mexican villages in New Mexico; the boys were having an easy time and were plum full of devilment. Several times they had the Mexicans dusting for cover or the open prairie to avoid the shots that were flying around in all directions. At one of our stopping places we were obliged to salve the old Alcaldes [sic] troubles with a few good American dollars as in our promiscuous shooting some of the village bake ovens were rather badly riddled. These ovens were always built clear of the huts the people lived in, and built of adobe.

We traveled north as far as Trinidad, Colorado, before striking the Railroad. At this place the boys took the teams to make a few dollars for themselves, taking out ties in the Ratone [Raton] Mtns. White, Hughes, and I went out after bear. I remember being out on the mountain side one day when along about two o'clock in the afternoon it began to grow dark. We wondered what was the cause as it was a clear day, when suddenly we remembered it was the foretold eclipse of the sun of 1878. It grew so dark we were obliged to head for camp at Dick Houghton's toll gate. The latter place was located near the entrance to a tunnel that was in process of building through the Mtns. for the Railroad. Houghton was quite an old timer in this district, having maintained a roadway over the Mtns. for years, charging toll to travelers who desired to use the same. He also owned large herds of cattle and sheep as well as the inevitable saloon. At this time the track's end was located at El Moro, a tough little town east of Trinidad. It was at Trinidad I renewed acquaintance with my former enemy of a gun fight which cost him his voice; nevertheless, he welcomed me right heartily to stay at his place.

From here we proceeded down the line to Las Animas on the Arkansas River, then north to Greeley on the South Platte. Here we found a happy colony founded by the well-known Horace Greeley who advised the young men of the East to go West and grow up with the country—truly a land flowing in milk and honey, a well-watered land that produced great crops. Of course everything was cheap for a dollar went a long way in those days unless it happened to be under some abnormal condition such as in a newly formed mining camp. However, at Greeley eggs were only five cents per dozen; watermelons five cents each; and butter five cents per pound.

During our stay there we sure lived on the fat of the land and thoroughly enjoyed ourselves in every way. After leaving Greeley we visited Cheyenne where we had a wild time for a week or so. Crossing the U P [Upper Platte River?] we journeyed north to Fort Fetterman, Wyoming; then to Fort C.F. Smith where a few years previous to this a number of soldiers were massacred. Our next stopping place was Fort McKinney. We stayed here for quite a little while. I hunted meat up to thirty miles north of the Fort on the Crazy Woman Fork, where I killed eleven mountain sheep at one setting. We saw to the north-east of us Wolf Mtn., at which place we had great hunting. Deer were there in large numbers as I shot fifty-two head in one day's hunting. During our trip over to the Mtns. my partner White killed a very large Cinnamon Bear. We rendered over five gallons of the finest lard from his old carcass. It made fine shortening for our biscuits. There was also large numbers of beaver in the small streams at the foot of the hills.

After leaving Fort McKinney we struck a trading post owned by a man named Trabourn [Trabing] and named after him. Here we bought supplies and went on. However, we found the cook had forgot to get baking powder and so I rode the back trail to procure some. This was about sundown and in the meantime a bunch of bullwhackers had arrived at the store. They all eyed me up with some considerable interest as I was heavily armed and the size of my ammunition excited their curiosity. They enquired as to where I came from. I replied, "Texas." "Oh," said they, "you are one of those buffalo hunters we have heard so much about." They invited me to stay overnight and yarn to them.

However, along about eight or nine o'clock the store was held up by Big Nose George and his gang of road agents. At the first intimation of trouble the bullwhackers closed and bolted the heavy doors upon which the agents rained thunderous blows, at the same time demanding that the doors should be opened at once.

Growing impatient, they began to fire through the door, which soon caused the bullwhackers to comply with the order. The gang at once marched in, and a formidable looking crowd they were. Everybody was lined up against the wall and disarmed. When they reached me they saw at once that I didn't belong in that part of the West and after asking me a few questions were soon satisfied that they need not worry about me as all this was none of my business, they being after Trabourn and his goods—he having done them some injury, and they were out for revenge. However, the latter happened to be away so all they could do was help themselves to clothing and grub. The clerks and bullwhackers standing along the wall were forced to keep their hands raised; one smart Alec however grew tired and lowed he "didn't have to hold 'em up nohow." He quickly found out his mistake as one of the gang brought his heavy six-shooter down crashing on top of his skull cutting a huge gash, knocking him cold for a spell. After obtaining all they required they disappeared into the night, still vowing vengeance upon Trabourn [Trabing] should they meet him.

In the morning I caught up with my outfit and we commenced to hunt along the Big Horn. We killed numerous bear here. One day about sundown I was riding towards camp when I noticed something moving in the tall grass and bushes of a coulee. I shouted and at once up stood two large grizzlies. I at once threw my rifle forward and shot one of them through the heart; the other fellow made tracks up the side of the mountain. I at once dismounted, taking a rest with my heavy buffalo rifle, I broke his back over the loins. I then rode my horse over to him, dismounting once more. I rolled rocks toward the bear whose rage was frenzied; the rocks he sent spinning with his huge paws forcing me to step lively to avoid being hit. Young trees were torn to shreds or uprooted before I gave him his quietus. Taking the fat out of both bears, I made camp a little late for supper.

During the Fall of '78 I struck north to Fort Custer, supplying the Fort and numerous woodcutters in the vicinity with meat. I hunted over Custer's battleground on the Little Big Horn, often coming across grim relics of the tragedy such as boots with the bones of a foot in them. In the Spring of '79 I went over to the

Yellowstone for some time, making Huntley my headquarters. From this town I went to work for the Montana Stock Company. The day before I left town I had a rather amusing experience with a cowboy in one of the saloons. This fellow walked in elbowing his way through the crowd, telling everyone what he could do. He suddenly took special notice of me and asked me to allow him to show me a pass with his hands that might possibly be of use to me some day. I at first wanted nothing to do with him, but so persistent was he that I finally consented to be shown. We squared up to each other and before I knew what was coming, he handed me a dandy over the eye that knocked me backward about ten feet. I gathered myself up, coming back at him with my hand on my gun. Disarming him, I threw his gun over the counter, after which I showed him a trick I knew, knocking him out.

Next morning, I rode out of town for the range with a lovely black eye. Arriving there, I reported to Sims Roberts who at that time was foreman for the Company and captain of the round-up. He sent me over to another outfit working on the same range in the spring round-up. This proved rather unfortunate for me as one of the punchers who happened to be a grouch took a dislike to me right at the start and began to show his disposition before I had been with them half a day. We had a round of words on the third day, and I warned him to step easy and put a bridle on his tongue or I would be liable to show him something and make him eat his words. At that he drew in his horns a little. However, next day he must have been feeling punk for he emphasized his animosity by taking a shot at me from a point to the side of me and slightly in the rear. He, however, made a poor shot as he missed me though I heard the whiz of the bullet as it passed my ear. I instantly drew and put a 45 through his right shoulder. He immediately fell off his horse.

Sims Roberts, the foreman, soon heard of it and galloped over to find out what was wrong. I then explained the whole case to him, telling him at the same time that I was through punching cows as there was getting to be too many ornery coyotes like the one I had crippled in the business. He was some riled at the turn of events, especially seeing that he had loaned me to the other fellows. In the meantime, they had carried the wounded man to the tent and Sims dusted over there on a dead run, jumped of [sic] his horse, drawing his guns as he did so, ran into the tent and asked them what they meant by treating "his man that a-way" and informed them also that in case they didn't like the way he did business "to come a shooting" as he was waiting for them; not a man moved as he had the drop on them anyway. After a few more choice epithets he returned to me and said he guessed he had fixed that crowd and that next time he sent a man over to help them out they would at least be civil. He asked me to reconsider my intention of quitting. I, however, was determined to quit as I figured that having crippled one man I would always have to keep a sharp lookout and it might lead to more trouble of like nature.

I then returned to Huntley and drove stage for Salisbury up the Yellowstone from Huntley, through Colson [Coulson] (now Billings), passing the old Crow Agency to Stillwater. I well remember carrying the news of the death of President Garfield, the first news the people in that part of the country had of the tragedy. The following winter found me on the Musselshell River, where I traded with the Piegans and Crows. We had some amusing experiences amongst these tribes.

In the summer of '80 I went over to the Bitter Root near Missoula to round up a herd of eleven hundred head of cattle for a rancher named Hoskins. He had started a ranch near Huntley, to which place we herded the cattle. Upon the completion of this trip I got together my outfit and started north to the Missouri River where I hunted for buffalo once more. I hunted in this district for two winters. We sold our hides to buyers who shipped them by steamer to St. Paul for disposal.

During my stay here I had considerable trouble with a small war party of Sioux from the Poplar Creek Agency—they were rustling horses and making things generally lively. They got into one of my hide yards and cut up quite a few of my hides. Other hunters also had trouble with them and were breathing vengeance against them. I determined to put a stop to the capers of these fellows as I was sure riled. So with two of my boys I hit the trail on foot for the place I thought they had made camp. Sure enough, we soon smelled smoke up a small canyon. I sent the two men up one side of the Canyon whilst I took the other. On account of a light fall of snow lying crusted on the ground, the Sioux heard the two men approaching and came up the opposite side of the Canyon where I was stationed. Upon reaching the top I could see them outlined against the sky (this being during the night) and immediately fired, bringing one of them down. They could not see me but fired a fusillade in the general direction of the flash seen from my rifle. There being about fifteen men in the party, I split right pronto for the bottom of my side of the hill, heading for a dry creek bed. The country here was bad lands covered with a kind of ash, and as I streaked down the hill side I sank over the ankles every step, taking pretty big jumps. I began to fear for the safety of the other fellows; however, they also had made for the creek and we soon joined forces.

When daylight broke the Indians knew our position and at once commenced sniping at us. We returned the fire. They were shooting high, though, from the top of the hill, and failed to do us any injury. After awhile one of the bucks pulled off a little stunt that came near costing him his life. To show his derision of us he suddenly jumped into full view with his blanket spread out behind him and danced a jig for our edification. Just at the moment I was in the act of reloading my rifle and I stayed the operation to watch him. In a moment he dropped out of sight; his very audacity saved him. After it was over I was some annoyed to think I allowed him to get away with it. A short time later we were reinforced by other hunters who had heard the firing and made a determined attack against the bucks, driving them off with some loss. They carried off their wounded and, as they had ponies, got clear away.

I afterwards met the agent from Poplar Creek at Norris's Trading Post down the river. He enquired for the hunter who had taught his bucks a lesson. Upon making myself known he thanked me for helping him out as he had been having considerable trouble with those same bucks for some time. They had been in the habit of leaving the agency, taking French leave. He said we had done them a heap of good as one of their number was killed and they had had a time getting their wounded into the agency in time to save their lives.

I next moved over towards the Yellowstone, where I hunted, hauling my hides to a river landing—I have forgotten the name of the only building there, being a store and post office combined with a stable attached. During one of my trips in with hides I had all my horses and mules (eleven head) run off by Indians. This was done during the night. We followed their trail the following day and caught up with them about ten miles from our late camp. They, however, had a man posted as lookout. He saw us and at once dropped out of sight to the bottom of a coulee where their camp was spread out. I rushed to the brow of the hill in time to see them mounting. I immediately opened fire at about six hundred yards' range, hitting one of the mules on the nose. I got in three or four more shots but only managed to kill a horse and two mules. I failed to recover a single hoof, and with chagrin saw the Indians escape.

We walked to the Yellowstone and procured horses to haul in our loads. After arriving at the landing, I stabled the horses, locking the stable door with chain and padlock. In spite of these precautions, that very night Indians broke into the stable and ran off with the whole outfit. When in the morning we found the stable empty, our rage knew no bounds. We at once organized a posse to give chase. However, everything seemed to go against us. We followed the trail for three days, during which time the weather broke; a severe snowstorm raged, which forced us to abandon the trip. I wished to press on but the majority of the boys decided to take the back trail, which we then proceeded to do. On our way back we had an amusing and at the same time annoying experience. We had made camp in one of the breaks in the vicinity of the river; this particular break had very steep sides and end. We camped at the open end in a pothole and turned the horses out to graze up the canyon. I put one man out to herd telling him to come in and awaken one of the boys about midnight to relieve him.

At the appointed time he came in for his relief. He then proceeded back up the canyon to keep his eye on the herd until his relief was ready. In a few minutes the relief man followed up the canyon and as quickly returned. I shall never forget the look upon the man's face as he stood at the edge of the pothole with the light from the fire streaming up towards him—he appeared like a demon from the nether regions. He commenced to shout in a doleful tone of voice, "My God! My God! My God!" I replied rather testily, being nettled at the loss of my horses, "Speak up, what in hell is wrong?" He then told us (we being all awake by this time) that the horses were no place in sight, neither could he see the herder; also, he thought he could make out moccasin tracks up the sides of the canyon. "Well," said I, "this is a hell of a note, this finishes us, we shall never hear the last of it—to go out after Indians and then to be set afoot by them, that's a good one alright." However, I ordered each man to follow me and I started at a toot up the canyon. I could hardly credit the fact that the horses had been able to climb the canyon side. After examining as well as I could the tracks, I decided there were no moccasin tracks there. We met our lost comrade at the top of the canyon, who informed us that during the time he was away after his relief, the herd had vanished. We started out over the prairie and, as I thought, soon came upon a couple of the horses. I was then sure there were no Indians around. We found them all with the exception of two; these we ran across next day on our way down the river. So we managed to arrive back home without being made the laughing stock of the whole country, for to be set afoot in the West in those days always meant uncomfortable enquiries and caused a man to look very foolish indeed.

One morning shortly after sunup I was fixing around my hides when a small herd of buffalo appeared on the opposite side of the Yellowstone River. They swam across, climbed the bank and proceeded to graze along the Government road upon one side of which was a fence enclosing a field of wheat. Suddenly one of them got too close to the fence and a barb pricked him. This surprised him but he didn't back up on that account; instead of that he calmly walked through the fence like it was built of twine, the others following. They walked across the field without seeming to care much for the wheat and walked through the fence on the opposite side. I thought to myself they don't take to either civilized fences or food.

At Big Horn City I had a little experience with the daughter of a Piegan chief whom the Crows had captured. Certain parties wished to see the girl restored to her people and offered certain inducements to anyone who would undertake to take her home.

Nobody seemed to care to tackle the proposition as the Crows kept a sharp lookout and no doubt meant mischief in case any attempt was made to do so. I felt sorry for the girl and her fifteen-year-old brother and so decided to accept the offer. One thing in my favor was the fact that I had the Crows afraid of me. I had on one occasion stood off over thirty bucks and forced them to hit the trail away from my vicinity. Whether they imagined I was crazy or not, I don't know; anyway, the fact remains, they steered clear of me. I might mention that a crazy man from an Indian's point of view is something to be let alone, he is taboo, they will not harm him.

The trip was made without encountering any resistance though I noticed several bands of Redskins on the skyline in the distance. During the trip I killed several buffalo and to show the inherent cruelty of the Indian nature, I will here mention an incident that took place on the trip. I had shot down a young cow buffalo, breaking her back; she however managed to crawl along on her forefeet, dragging her hind quarters on the ground. The Indian boy dismounted from his pony and ran over to the cow, stood on her hind legs, and as she attempted to hook him by throwing back her head, he deliberately took his knife and stabbed out her eyes, his sister laughing all the time thinking it was a great joke. The father of these two young savages presented me with two pretty good ponies, a beaded jacket, and a pair of moccasins.

After returning from this trip I moved over to the Missouri to hunt, and whilst there saw an Indian buffalo hunt, one of the last to ever take place. This hunt was carried out on the Sioux Agency. Twelve hundred Indians took part in it. I watched them through my glasses and in about three hours they killed fifteen hundred head. This feat was not so very difficult as the buffalo were very numerous on the reserve. It was quite a sight to see the squaws swarming like bees around the fallen animals, skinning and cutting them up.

In the year '82, I first became acquainted with Louis Riel, whom I was destined to meet again under very different circumstances. I met him whilst hunting in the Judith Basin; he was teaching at the Catholic School there. In 1882 I disposed of most of my outfit, sold all my hides, and headed north into Canada. I struck Fort Assiniboia [Assiniboine] on the Milk River, a fine Fort in those days. The Bear Paw Mtns. are near here and one day a trapper arrived at the Post and walked into the store where a number of us were yarning. He was wearing skins and had on his head a skin cap with a long tail hanging down his back. He, to attract our attention, began to get the following off his chest, "I'm the bright barrel of the Bear Paw, I'm the son of a she-wolf and it's my night to howl," at the same time letting out a whoop and then saying he could eat poison. One fool in the crowd immediately gave him some strychnine, which he quickly swallowed. In a moment he came to his senses and realized what he had done, saying, "My God, what have I done!" He fell to the floor in a terrible convulsion and, in spite of all we could do, expired.

In a short time, I continued my trip north and entered Canada near the Cypress Hills at Fort Walsh, Sask., or Assiniboia, as it was then called. Here I made my first acquaintance with the R.N.W.M. Police, paid twenty percent duty on my outfit and, in company with a fellow traveler, moved on towards Maple Creek where we struck the CPR Railroad. [Note: the police force was known as the RNWMP (Royal North West Mounted Police) at the time Armstrong narrated his memoir, but it would have been the NWMP (North West Mounted Police) at the time he entered Canada.] The steel had not arrived there as yet. My companion, Lu Mullholand, [Mulholland] and I then moved East towards the end of steel.

I rode along with him in his buckboard with my mules and riding horse tied behind. We stayed at the camp near the end of steel to replenish our stores. Right here I had a rather disagreeable dispute with a teamster. Mullholand [Mulholland] went over to the Company store to buy supplies while I remained with the outfit. My hair at this time was rather long, in fact down to my shoulders. One of the teamsters, of whom [sic] there was quite a crowd hanging around, took exception to it using some pretty insulting remarks in doing so. I said nothing but quietly got out of the rig, walked around behind and planted one with all the strength that was in me square over his eyes. He fell back amongst the crowd. I then quickly stepped to the back of the rig and grabbed my Winchester, throwing it down on the crowd. I told them that the first man that crooked a finger would precipitate a killing right there. I then asked them if that was the way they treated strangers in Canada and that I had just come from a country where milder remarks than those just recently addressed to me would mean that one or the other would be very likely to have a hole drilled through him with a 45 Colts [sic]. The crowd, however, proved they were not all boors as they agreed that he had got what was coming to him, as he was of a bullying disposition and not much of a favorite with the boys.

Mullholland [Mulholland] and I then moved down the track towards Moose Jaw. Upon arriving there, we contracted to do a little freighting for the Railroad. We only made a couple of trips and then moved down to Regina and from there to Qu'Appelle. Here I met Flatboat McLean and engaged to take charge of a stage station for him on the Salt Plains. It was a dismal place, and being winter time I had few visitors. The stage called but once every three weeks. I constructed a dugout, fixing it up as comfortable as possible with burlap sacks and pictures from the illustrated papers I had sent to me to help while away the hours. I remember two Catholic Priests staying with me overnight on their way from Duck Lake to Qu'Appelle. They were traveling by dog train. Here, also, I entertained Madame and Mon. Forget, afterwards Lieut. Governor of the North West Territories. I found them very nice visitors indeed. I had baked some pies the previous day and Madame congratulated me on their excellence. They agreed, after much joking, to sleep in my bunk, the only bed in the dugout, whilst I took the floor. In the morning, after eating breakfast, they continued their journey towards Regina, the new capital—the Government having changed over from the old capital, Battleford.

In the spring of '83 I boarded the stage and traveled north to Prince Albert. After looking around awhile I made two trips to Qu'Appelle with horses, bringing back settlers to Prince Albert. After returning to Prince Albert on my last trip an absolutely new phase of life opened up before me. After all my long years of hunting, scouting, Indian fighting, and ranching, I actually settled down to learn the trade of painter. Just at this time Prince Albert was enjoying a building boom and the demand for tradesmen was keen, each master tradesman being anxious to teach green men his own particular line of work and pay good wages whilst he did the teaching. One could choose any line one took a fancy to. I chose painting and stayed right with it until I had mastered the art of mixing all colors as well as the use of the brush, etc. I continued painting in Prince Albert until the year '85 when the Riel rebellion broke out.

Trouble had been brewing for some time in connection with the half-breeds and Government over the administration of lands. Riel had been induced to come north from the Judith Basin in Montana in the fall of '84. I met him again in Prince Albert and also heard him speak in support of the half-breeds' demands. He was a man of fair education and a good speaker. He, however, had got in wrong once before with the Canadian Government and he was now heading for more trouble. Among the first steps taken by the breeds to attempt to enforce their demands was the confiscation of supplies en route from Qu'Appelle to Prince Albert. Riel dispatched runners into the north to solicit the aid of the tribes in those regions, instructing them to seize all rifles and ammunition at the Hudson's Bay Co. Posts, several of which were raided and the above articles taken by force.

The first serious fighting in the impending struggle took place at Duck Lake on the 26th day of March 1885. A small force of Mounted Police and Militia, the latter mostly composed of Prince Albert boys, started out from Prince Albert for Carlton to protect the Hudson's Bay Post there. They were under the command of Major Crozier. A small seven-pound brass field piece was taken along and, owing to the fact that in loading the third round the ball was inadvertently rammed home before the powder was put in, which rendered the gun useless, the fight was lost.

The small force was conveyed in sleighs from Carlton towards Duck Lake to meet Dumont, Riel's right-hand man. The parties met at the latter place and began to parley. They had barely commenced to talk when an old Sioux, almost blind, stepped up behind Police Interpreter McKay, attempting to grab his revolver. McKay quickly turned, snatched the gun from the Indian, and shot him dead. Right there the fight commenced. The Indians threw down their blankets onto the snow which was over a foot deep, and cut loose with all the weapons they had. The boys returned the fire but were seriously outnumbered and were forced to retreat with a loss of several dead and many wounded. They managed to get the teams heading for Carlton and, piling into the sleighs, away they went, leaving the dead where they lay but taking the wounded with them. A man by the name of Newart had a nasty experience. He was badly wounded and crawled into some willows, when an Indian found him and was in the act of smashing in his face with the butt of his rifle when a breed interfered and saved his life.

A friend of mine was one of the first to fall with a bullet through his heart. Before he left Prince Albert, we were joking about the business, never for a moment thinking it would really develop into anything very serious; however, Fate ordered otherwise and a good many fine Prince Albert boys lost their lives. Capt. Moore and R. A. Markley were among the wounded, though happily not very seriously. Dumont had the bodies placed in a deserted house and a few days later arrangements were made to go after them. Wm. Drain took teams and sleighs to bring in the bodies of the slain. Sanderson, who had been Riel's prisoner, assisted Drain to collect the bodies and bring them in. They were frozen as hard as flint for the weather during this period was intensely cold, the temperature registering around forty degrees below zero. We had some interesting time thawing them out for burial as they were in all kinds of shapes having frozen as they fell in the snow.

Up to this time I had determined to keep out of the trouble as I felt that I had seen enough fighting in the States; however, after seeing how serious an aspect the situation had assumed I offered my services as scout, which were accepted. During this time many well-known citizens of Prince Albert rendered valuable assistance to the authorities, prominent amongst whom was the late Col. Alexander Sproat who worked in an indefatigable manner, organizing the Prince Albert Volunteers. Col. Sproat had previously seen service as Col. of the Bruce Battalion (32nd) in the Fenian Raid of 1866. He was also a member of Parliament at Confederation in 1867 and held a post as Civil Engineer on the Grand Trunk Railway when it was being built. At the time of his death in 1890 he had held the post of Registrar for North East Saskatchewan from 1881. Mrs. Sproat was also prominent amongst the ladies of

Prince Albert who worked hard for the sick and wounded soldiers during the war.

One night about the time of the Duck Lake fight, Prince Albert experienced a rather disagreeable experience—a man rode into town shouting that the Indians were advancing on the place. Great excitement prevailed, the women and children were taken from their homes and lodged in the Presbyterian Church, which was barricaded with sacks of flour, cases of goods, and cordwood. During the transference some of the young ones were frozen more or less and several women fainted. Altogether it was a decidedly anxious time. Later in the evening I rode out of town to try and locate the force that was supposed to be heading our way. I soon found that it was a false alarm as the country was quiet, and I saw only one man whom I later turned over to the authorities. My report greatly relieved the people and things gradually quieted down.

A day or so later three of us were sent out towards Duck Lake to report on the likelihood of our being able to capture the place. Wm. Diehl and a Frenchman, whose name I have forgotten, and myself started out. Our trip turned out a hard one. On our way back to report to Col. Irvine at Prince Albert, we were fired on by Indians just as we struck the Carlton Road. It was snowing a little at the time and suddenly right ahead of us we saw fresh moccasin tracks. As we were then approaching the firs we decided our best policy would be to retreat, as I knew there was every possibility of our being ambushed. Sure enough, we had barely turned our horses when bang! bang! bang! and a number of balls whistled passed our heads. We put spurs to our horses and managed to escape without being hit. We then dropped down over the ridge towards the lake. There being a couple of inches of water on top of the ice, we splashed our way across, heading for McKiever's Farm, which was deserted and where we expected to find grub. We were lucky in finding a tub of dandy frozen sausages which we soon had frying and they sure tasted good as we were pretty hungry, having been without food for over a day.

Next day we once more headed for town, meeting Col. Irvine's force of Police at the Ridge about eight miles out of Prince Albert. Here we all made camp. Early in the morning Col. Irvine and his outfit returned to Prince Albert, at the same time ordering me to take a few men (not of the Police Force) and return to McKiever's Farm, holding the place as an outpost to guard the main road. About two miles from our post, Bill Tait and a party of men were stationed at Cameron's Farm. We later visited them and found them in clover with all kinds of grub there—poultry and bacon galore on [sic] the place. We lost no time in rendering valuable assistance to reduce the visible supply. I remember one witty Irishman remarking when he saw the spread, "If this is war, may we never have peace."

A few days later I was ordered to return to Prince Albert to carry a dispatch to the telegraph office at Humboldt; this line was one of the first to be run through the country. Col. Irvine had been without news from the outside for about three weeks on account of the men sent out with messages falling into Riel's hands or being driven back. I received a new rifle and revolver (the latter being a new issue) from the Police, also one hundred rounds of ammunition, which was at first refused because they were afraid I might be captured and the whole outfit I carried become rebel property. I, however, informed the Col. I had never yet experienced the sensation of being a prisoner of war and had not the slightest intention of becoming one in this instance. Eventually the Col. decided I could take care of it as the desired quantity was forthcoming.

I then headed for the south fork of the Saskatchewan and upon my arrival there I was ferried across by the Mounted Police. On the other side I met my friend, Drain, who informed me the trail was clear as far as Clark's Crossing. Although I was obliged to pass pretty close to Riel's camp at Batoche, I struck out for the Crossing as it was much nearer than Humboldt. On arriving at Fish Creek, I passed through the recent battle ground that had been fought over a few days previously; strewed around on the ground were about sixty head of dead ponies killed by Capt. Howard's Gatling gun. At Dumont's Ferry, I passed Gen. Middleton's camp. Upon my arrival at the Crossing, I fired a fusillade of shots from my six-gun to attract attention. In a few moments I espied a boat heading my way. After reaching the shore the man in charge asked me where the others were. I replied there was [sic] no others. "Well," said he, "the shots sounded like there was [sic] two or three of you." I fired so fast he was sure there was a party of us.

I crossed over and delivered my dispatches, receiving others in return, and at once started back for Gen. Middleton's camp. I reached the outskirts of camp during darkness, but was quickly halted by a sentry who after satisfying himself as to my identity turned me over to a sergeant who in turn conducted me to the General's tent. The Gen. received me in a friendly manner and, after reading a letter from Capt. McKay, requested that I stay with his command as chief scout. He then ordered his cook to prepare supper for me, after which I retired to a tent and "hit the hay."

Next morning an attack was delivered upon Batoche from the river as well as from the land side. A river steamer was prepared and strengthened by raising a bulwark of bags, mostly kit bags at that, about four feet high. The pilot was protected at the wheel by a sheet of boiler iron around his post. The boat was then manned by soldiers and casting loose from her moorings; she drifted downstream as directed, and upon arriving opposite the rebel position opened fire. In return a heavy fire was concentrated upon the boat, so heavy in fact the soldiers were forced to find more substantial cover than the kit bags afforded. In the meantime, the hail of bullets beat a lively tattoo on the boiler iron and so alarmed the pilot that he allowed the vessel to broach and she was swept downstream in the swift current towards the Ferry. Here the heavy cable suspended in mid-air across the river caught the boat's tophamper [sic], sweeping smoke stack and wheelhouse over the side, completely dismantling her. She then continued to drift with the current until at last she grounded on a sand bar and came to rest.

In the meantime, the command with Gen. Middleton, instead of approaching Batoche on the regular Government road, struck out across the Prairie and circled to approach the town from the East on the Hoodoo Road. During the advance two rebel horsemen, advancing from Batoche towards the command, opened fire upon the advancing troops but failed to do any damage. This caused some merriment among the boys at the idea of two men attempting to halt the Column. We advanced as far as a small church situated about one mile from Batoche, when suddenly we came under a rather hot fire directed at us from some bushes in the vicinity. In the meantime, the one field piece we had with us opened fire on some log stores and Indian lodges or teepees across the river. The shells set fire to the stores, also killing some of the Indians in the vicinity, unfortunately killing a couple of squaws. Riel sent word that unless the fire ceased he would at once execute the prisoners he held in the dungeon, a horrible place, of which more anon. It was interesting to watch the men bringing up ammunition for the field piece. On the way up they came under the fire of the men in the bushes; some of the men would duck and run for it, but the majority proceeded forward at a disdainful walk, standing erect as they did so. The casualties were, however, light. The gun continued firing on Batoche but the advance stopped in the vicinity of the church and threw up light defenses.

The following Saturday night I left for Clark's Crossing with dispatches from the General, also carrying dispatches from the correspondents. I followed the Government road against the advice of outposts who reported having seen Indians cross the river in the direction I was about to go. However, I felt that I could avoid trouble, and this proved to be the case. I remember overtaking a rider at a farm house where he stopped to rest and eat. He had started out several hours before, but on account of having made a wide detour he lost considerable time. I received a bonus from the members of the Press, one of whom was George Ham of the *Manitoba Free Press*, to get my dispatches through first, which I succeeded in doing.

On Sunday evening the other rider and I returned to camp. It was quite dark when we arrived in the vicinity of the place we thought the camp lay—we were by no means sure that the camp had not been moved during our absence. Rumors had been going around that the rebels were contemplating a flanking movement in an attempt to drive us back and so relieve the pressure on Batoche. With these thoughts in our minds, we advanced very cautiously. Soon we espied a solitary light which later proved to be the only visible light in camp, it being at the hospital. Suddenly, almost without warning, a line of men sprang up in our front and the challenge, "Halt, who comes there?" was thrown out to us. We replied, "friends." We could not give the countersign but the sergeant in charge flashed a light in our faces and, recognizing me at once, he detailed a corporal to direct us through the defenses. Just as we passed through, Capt. French, a fine soldier and man, greeted us with, "Hello Bob! you're just the man I am looking for, come right along, I have got a dandy pot of beans cooking and nobody to help me eat it." My old friend, Drain, arrived just at that moment with his team. We stopped to talk with him and whilst standing near his team I had my hand on the rump of one of his horses. Suddenly, bang! bang! bang! went some rifle shots and a ball struck the horse within two inches of my hand, just missing my head as it passed, or so it seemed for I distinctly heard the hum of the ball. I said, "Captain, what in hell have you got us into?" "Oh," he replied, "that's nothing, sniping has been going on all evening." However, we moved away, unsaddled our horses and repaired to the bean pot. After our feed, we retired, but had barely composed ourselves when someone aroused us with the news that the breeds were going to charge. I knew the Indian character better than that, and at once told the man to beat it as I wanted to sleep.

On awaking in the morning, the first thing that greeted my ears was somebody shouting one, two, three, four, etc. I looked around and saw a company of men numbering off for duty in the rifle pits. I watched them awhile, and presently the officer in charge detailed certain men for duty in the cookhouse, etc. These men were very much annoyed at this order and tried to persuade the officer to allow them to go to the pits. He, however, refused to change his plans or orders and they were forced to stay in camp. After the others had marched away, I approached these men and remarked, "Say! You fellows don't know when you are well off, here you are kicking because they won't allow you to go and get your heads shot off." "Oh," replied one, "Heads shot off be damned, I'd rather get my head shot off than stay around here doing cookhouse duty, there's no glory in that." I laughed and replied, "Well, you're some boys, I'll say that." This was typical of the whole force: they would stop at nothing. The men were well protected on their way to the firing line as Capt. Howard, or Gatling Gun Howard, as he was familiarly known, sprayed the enemy rifle pits with a steady stream of bullets from his Gatling gun. He was very popular with the men and he and I, being Yankees, had much in common, having both been through the mill on the frontier.

On Tuesday, about noon, the infantry under Col. Williams made a charge on the enemy breastworks and carried them with ease, the rebels skipping out across the river. Just before the attack took place the Gen., with his staff and myself, were [sic] riding around when suddenly we all heard a yell. The Gen. remarked, "That sounds like a charge; Armstrong, just ride over there and see what is going on." I did so and found it was as the Gen. supposed: the yell we heard was that of the troops storming the enemy position. I reported to the Gen. and then rode into Batoche, heading for Batoche's house.

I entered through the window. I had only been in the house a few moments when Capt. French and some men came rushing in. The Captain shouted, "First in." I replied, "Different here." When he saw who was speaking, he laughed, ran upstairs, looked out of the window, and was immediately shot dead, a bullet piercing his heart. So died a soldier and a gentleman, a fine fearless specimen of a man. I could scarcely believe my own eyes, it was all over quickly, and not expecting anything of the kind. An old breed named Ross was lying on the ground, wounded, a short distance from the house and upon seeing the Captain stick his head out of the window, the old fellow "threw down" on him and killed him.

After this incident I stepped over to the famous dungeon where Riel kept his prisoners. It was a horrible hole, dark and filthy—the men had been confined in the place for a long time without any sanitary conveniences whatever. When we hauled them out they could barely stand upright and had to be placed under medical care. My companion Diehl and I then began to look around for possible wounded breeds or men desirous of giving themselves up. We discovered a bunch of breeds in the bush near town and brought them in prisoners. One old breed named Pronto showed fight, threatening to shoot us; however, we calmed him down and brought him in along with the others. The following day we collected a quantity of furs belonging to Batoche, who later collected a considerable sum of money from the Government for them. These and numerous other articles were placed aboard the steamers Northcote and Blatchford [Marquis?]. We later headed for Prince Albert. However, after going about twelve miles down the river to Gertepees [Gardepuis'] Ferry, we camped there and then began our search for Riel as he had escaped from the scene of our late fighting.

Quite a number of men scattered over the country in the hope of rounding him up. Diehl, Hourie, and I struck out together and headed for the Menichinas [Minichinas] Hills; these hills were more or less covered with bush. We struck several breed and Indian camps, who directed us more or less in the direction we wanted to go. Finally, we hit a camp where we received the information that Riel and four men with him had been seen heading west afoot. After resuming the trail, we overtook them about eight miles further along. Shortly after we sighted them, they passed from our sight behind a patch of bush near the river. We galloped up to the point we last saw them. I then dismounted and cautiously advanced until I saw them not over twenty yards away. I then returned to Diehl and Hourie, and we held a short council to agree as to our best mode of attack.

We decided to rush them, which we promptly carried out, ordering them to throw up their hands. I knew Riel and saw him at once begin to move away from his companions. I at once followed him and ordered him to surrender. In complying, he at once fell forward on his knees and began to pray—he thought it was my intention to kill him. I, however, ordered him to stand up, which he did, at the same time handing me a note he had received from Gen. Middleton at Batoche, requesting Riel's surrender.

In the meantime, Diehl took care of the other four men while Hourie went to look for horses. Riel and I then started for camp. I instructed him if we met anybody to keep his mouth shut, as some of Boulton's scouts had sworn to shoot him on sight. Shortly after starting, Riel, who was riding behind me on my horse, drew a small 32 derringer pistol out of his breast pocket, saying as he handed it to me over my shoulder, "Here, Mr. Armstrong, I'll give you this." I had overlooked it when I searched him for weapons. I thought to myself, how easy it would have been for Riel to put me out of business and make a break for liberty on my horse. When I passed a remark to that effect, he said he could not kill a man in cold blood, especially as he had known me down in Montana. He then told me how that during the war his orders had been to capture me if possible but not to kill me; and on at least one occasion I had been in some danger as I and a companion or two were riding along by some dense willows when, all unknown to us, a dozen rifles were pointing our way and within a very few feet of us at that, Riel's orders being the only thing that saved our lives. They made no attempt to stop us, fearing a killing would result, and this they wished to avoid.

In a little while we met some of Boulton's scouts who enquired as to who the man was I had with me. I told them he was Riel's cook. "Why don't you shoot him," said they and moved on. Hourie now joined us and the three of us headed for camp afoot. Upon arriving there we found everybody confined to their tents on account of the fact that the Gen. feared somebody might take a shot at Riel if he was brought in. As we proceeded down the lines, several men stuck their heads out of the tents enquiring as to the identity of the person I had brought in a prisoner. As before, I replied, "Riel's cook." At this answer the men with snorts of disgust withdrew into their respective tents to await Riel's hoped-for capture. After arriving at the General's tent I reported at once to General Middleton in person, turning Louis Riel over to him as his prisoner. Certain other persons have at different times laid claim to Riel's capture and right here I wish to say that Louis Riel surrendered himself to me personally, and further, that he rode behind me on my horse for some few miles, after which we walked the remainder of the distance to Gen. Middleton's camp at Gertepess' [Gardepuis'] Ferry, and that upon arriving at said camp, I personally delivered Riel a prisoner to General Middleton.

The next day Riel was put aboard the boat and sent to Saskatoon, from which place he was forwarded under guard in charge of Capt. Young to Regina, Sask., where he was incarcerated in the jail at the R.N.W. Mtd. Police [NWMP] barracks, and there tried and hanged. After Riel departed south for Regina, the force proceeded to Prince Albert where we rested up and indulged in a few sports.

After a short stay in Prince Albert, we boarded the steamers and sailed up the river to Battleford and from thence to Fort Pitt after Big Bear and his outfit, who had struck into the timber country north of that place. At Fort Pitt, Big Bear captured the family of Chief Factor McLean of the Hudson's Bay Co.; these he held as hostages. About twenty miles down the river from Battleford, I was ordered ashore by Gen. Middleton with instructions to proceed to Battleford and deliver a dispatch to Col. Otter. The boat pulled alongside the river bank, which at this point was well timbered. I drove my way through this and headed for Battleford.

Upon my arrival there, Col. Otter, acting under instructions from the Gen., turned over to me about fifty teams. With these and the necessary men to drive them, I was ferried across the river and headed out northwest for Frenchman's Hill, at which place a skirmish had taken place a few days previous. On our way up we sighted horsemen ahead, and not being at all sure as to who they might be, I rode out ahead of the outfit to investigate. I found them to be a party of scouts who had been sent down to meet me. In a little while we passed over the battleground and found several Indian graves, open to the view of anyone who cared to look into them. As the teams drove up, the teamsters were curious to look into the graves when my attention was called to one of the teamsters who had been investigating rather closely. He jumped down into one of the graves and calmly hacked the finger off of the corpse simply to gain possession of a cheap ring. I at once told him what in my opinion he was for his ghoulish action, at the same time adding that if that same Indian was alive he would doubtless make him (the teamster) climb a tree. He moved away considerably crestfallen. Here I took leave of the outfit and moved forward to Loon Lake to join the General and his command.

At Loon Lake Col. Steele's force attacked the rearguard of Big Bear's outfit, inflicting upon them some losses in killed and wounded; the main body, however, escaped, owing to the fact that the country was pretty much muskeg. At this point were two lakes joined together by a narrow strip of water about thirty or forty yards wide. The Gen. ordered me to cross and investigate the ground on the other side. I accordingly jumped my horse into the water, little thinking it was so deep; however, horse and I disappeared plum overhead, my hat alone remaining on the surface. Everybody who saw me make the dive had a hearty laugh at my expense. However, we scrambled out at the far side and commenced to look around.

Near the river or lake shore, a good-sized tree lay fallen, broken off about six feet or so from the ground, still holding to the butt by a huge sliver. From behind this tree, suddenly a dog ran out at me barking savagely. Upon investigating, I discovered an old squaw hanging from the fallen tree by a thin piece of rawhide tied around her neck. She was in a sitting posture, her legs on the ground but her body about six inches above ground. She was quite dead. Some of the breeds with the command knew her—it seems she was from Frog Lake, at which place the Indians massacred several people, including two Roman Catholic Priests. Seemingly, the old squaw was forced to accompany the women whom Big Bear carried off and, being crippled, she found it impossible to keep up with Big Bear's outfit and, being left behind, had decided to end her misery. Several scouts swam across and we then buried her. A raft was then constructed and several officers came across and attempted to walk out over the muskeg but only mired down, and so returned to the command, reporting it would be impossible to continue the pursuit.

The command then commenced its return march to Fort Pitt. On our way back, we crossed a very narrow creek only a few feet wide and about three feet deep; it was literally packed with jackfish, one could scoop them out in wagon loads. We all enjoyed a fine feed of fried fish that day at noon.

During our stay at Loon Lake I rode back to Fort Pitt with a dispatch from the General. On my way in, I discovered an old Hudson's Bay Co. cart trail. It was grown up with grass until it was almost invisible; however, as it seemed to head in the general direction of the Fort, I decided to follow it. Luck was with me as I arrived at Fort Pitt, saving a considerable amount of time. In fact, I made the trip in over four hours, less time than the trail we followed going out. During the time we camped at the creek I overheard the General enquiring of a man who had resided in the Fort Pitt country for about thirty years how far did he think it was to the Fort. He replied "about sixty miles, General." The Gen.

then called me over and asked me what time I had left the Fort to return. I told him, and also informed him that in my opinion the distance from the spot we then stood on to the Fort was from twenty-eight to thirty miles. The Gen. then gave the order to mount, at the same time directing me to lead the way, which I did with the three companies of mounted troops trailing along behind.

We rode briskly along until we arrived at the old Hudson's Bay trail; here we turned in off our late trail, proceeding along at a trot until we arrived at a spring where we dismounted for water. Here the General again enquired as to the distance into Fort Pitt. I replied, "About seven and one-half miles," putting in the half-mile more for devilment than anything else. The Gen., looking at me said, "Well, you are sure getting it down fine when you mention half a mile." "I won't take it back, General, and we will see how my estimate comes out." After mounting again, I presented Riel's pistol to the General, who thanked me saying he would prize it as a souvenir of the war. A short distance ahead we could see open Prairie and I soon espied horsemen riding towards us. I at once called the Gen.'s attention to them. We soon met them, and the Gen. asked how far it was to Pitt. They told him about six miles. "Well," said he, "Armstrong was about right when he said seven and a half miles." We had then ridden a little over a mile.

As we rode along, Gatling Gun Howard and I fell back about a quarter of a mile when suddenly Howard challenged me to race him to the General at the head of the Column; the winner was to take the other's horse. It happened I was riding a horse I had looted at Batoche, which I discovered to be some racer. Howard didn't know this so I accepted the challenge and away we streaked. I soon drew ahead of Howard; as I did so, I called out for him to pass his rope and I would give him a tow. My horse beat his quite easily, which caused Gatling Gun's lip to hang down at the thought of being set afoot before the whole outfit. I, however, saved him from that disgrace and then told him all about the horse, saying he had formerly been the property of Louis Riel. The officers, who in the meantime had crowded round to hear the talk, named the horse "Louis Riel." He afterwards ran and won many races under that name, turning out to be one of the best in the country. After the war he was sent down to Winnipeg where hundreds of people visited the livery barn to get a look at the horse that had once belonged to Riel and was now the property of his captor. I kept him in my service for quite a while but eventually sold him before I struck West again.

Shortly after our arrival at Fort Pitt an Indian runner came in with the news that Big Bear had turned his prisoners loose and they were then at Loon Lake. The General at once ordered me to return to Loon Lake with teams and pick up these people. I did so and found around thirty people encamped there. There were both whites and Indians in the party, mostly women and children. They were suffering more or less from exposure and the hardships of the trail, Big Bear not having provided them with many comforts to ease their path. As a matter of fact, they had been obliged to "hike it" afoot, and as several of the party were ladies of refinement, they were pretty well "all in." When I arrived they were busy drying meat which they had procured from an old ox who was mired down in the muskeg. The women managed to kill him and so obtain some food as they were on the verge of starvation. They made enough soup from the carcass of a jack rabbit to do thirty people for breakfast, so it will be seen that even though they were women and in a difficult position, they were full of grit, the stuff that never says die. We got them all to Pitt, where they were furnished with new outfits of clothing and made quite comfortable.

From Fort Pitt the command struck out for Beaver River via Frog Lake. We, however, failed to head off Big Bear and his band as we found later he had turned and headed in the direction of Carlton, at which place the Mounted Police effected his capture. Before the troops left Beaver River I carried a dispatch to Pitt a distance of one hundred miles, which I made in less than ten hours, excepting a short stop at Frog Lake on my horse Louis Riel. Col. Williams was stationed at Frog Lake with his "Midlanders" and, whilst there, was unfortunately taken down with fever; although he was removed aboard the steamer North West and everything possible done for him, he died before she had made twenty miles down the river. The troops returned once more to Pitt, where we met Gen. Strange and his outfit. They, however, moved West again whilst we headed for Prince Albert.

Several Indians were tried prior to our departure from the Fort. The Indians were under chief "Low Horn." They were accused by Gen. Middleton of the crime of assisting Riel and heading people off at certain places causing bodily injury, etc. "Low Horn" instructed Peter Hourie, the interpreter, to inform the General that he spoke with a forked tongue as he had not rendered assistance to Riel or, in fact, injured anyone. It was amusing to hear the chief as good as tell the General he was a liar; he would not back down either but stuck to his guns. However, the Indians who took part in the Frog Lake massacre were found guilty and hanged.

The war was practically at an end by this time and the command now headed for Prince Albert, at which place we stopped for a day or so. Here the General and I for the first time crossed swords—he wished me to travel with him on the boat to Winnipeg, but as the boat was leaving at once I informed him I could not go with him as I had business to transact that required my staying over another day. He at once flew into a rage, asking me whether it was the people or the country I liked the best. I replied, "They both suit me, General." "Well," said he, "I don't admire your choice," at the same time closing the interview. I later travelled overland to Winnipeg with a party of friends, my horse being sent down there by rail in company with a number of officer's chargers. They were afterwards turned out to pasture at Stony Mountain along with a herd of buffalo. Our overland trip to the 'Peg was a lively one as our party was composed of a congenial crowd. We had considerable fun with farmers along our route, representing ourselves to be somebody far-fetched, causing many of them to open their eyes in astonishment at our wild stories. Upon our arrival in Winnipeg, we plunged into a round of gaieties that were being indulged in by the troops. For several weeks I wasn't allowed to spend hardly any money at all and I sure had a great time. I met Gen. Middleton once more and he invited me to accompany him East. I, however, had already decided to return West and so refused his invitation. I never saw him again.

I later returned to Prince Albert, where I resided for some years. In 1904 I headed south for my old home in Oklahoma, visiting my relatives who had lost sight of me for over thirty years and indeed heard that I had "cashed in" years ago in a pistol fight out West.

However, I proved to them that I was very much alive, and was invited to take the trail again after a couple of outlaws but declined, not caring to risk my neck at that time in a business that did not concern me one iota. I remained in Oklahoma until 1914 when I returned to Calgary, Alberta, where I now reside with my daughter.

There I often look back down the long, long trail, sometimes wishing for the old days of camp and trail, wondering if the men with whom I hunted and fought and shared the hardships of frontier life are still living in this year of grace 1920. I am well satisfied knowing that I have lived through scenes and times that can never be duplicated because they are gone. They belong to a past age when the West was truly wild, the home, and when I say home, I mean the free, wide, boundless prairie home of the Indian, once lord of the West, the bold and fearless warrior of a hundred fights who sang the song of his deeds around many a victorious camp fire; the West wherein lived and roamed a hardy race of pioneers, the forerunners of the civilization which we have to-day, though I oftentimes wonder if, after all, the old was not the best. As I look around today at the present condition of unrest it almost seems to me the old days were the best. However, I am glad and proud to think that I helped in some degree to bring the wonderful West to a state of peace and prosperity fit for millions to carve out their destinies and nations to be developed; here I will close, having talked long enough, as the campfire is dying low, knock the ashes out of my pipe, roll into my blankets, and sleep contented, so au revoir.

R.A. Bob Armstrong
Chief Scout NthWest Field Force 1885

APPENDICES

Appendix 1

RIEL'S APPREHENSION: MANY VERSIONS

T he first reports of Riel's capture were dispatches sent by General Middleton and by newspaper correspondents at the scene. Contemporary accounts also appeared in diaries and books, some published as early as 1885. Later, several principal participants in the conflict published their reminiscences. Subsequent accounts relied on these earlier publications and on interviews with those who were involved in, or were bystanders in, the Resistance. More recent histories have either restated a particular earlier version or limited their descriptions to a few lines. Before the accounts by the three captors of Riel are presented in Appendix 2, the portrayal of the event by General Middleton, by newspaper correspondents, by participants in the 1885 conflict, by early historians, and by later writers are presented here in turn.

GENERAL MIDDLETON'S ACCOUNTS

Middleton mentions Riel's capture on several occasions. His first announcement is a terse telegram to Minister of Militia and Defence A. P. Caron, dated May 15: "Riel is my prisoner. What is to be done with him? I await instructions here."[1] The next day Middleton wired a fuller description:

... I then sent off a party of mounted men to scour the woods. This was all seen by Riel who slipped behind the mounted party and gave himself up to two of my scouts whom they knew, one scout being a half-breed himself. They brought him quietly in and he walked into my tent before anybody knew. He had my note in his pocket and produced it saying, "General, I have come trusting to this." I assured him of protection. He was dreadfully frightened at first, fancying the soldiers would kill him. . . .[2]

The "half-breed" scout referred to here is Tom Hourie. Middleton's comment in this second telegram that Riel noticed the mounted search party and "slipped behind" them was not included in the first telegram or in any of his other communications.

Middleton's May 31, 1885, report to Parliament reads thus:

I sent out parties of mounted men, under Major Boulton, to scour the woods. In the afternoon two scouts, Armstrong and Hourie, who had been sent out with Boulton and had moved away by themselves, came upon Riel who gave himself up, producing my letter to him in which I summoned him to surrender and promised to protect him until his case was considered by the Canadian Government. The scouts brought him into my camp, and I made a prisoner of him, as you are aware.[3]

Middleton's report to Parliament alters his initial message in which he speaks of sending Boulton's scouts to search the countryside—but not his scouts (Hourie, Armstrong, and Diehl)—while in his report to Parliament, he states that his scouts "had been sent out with Boulton." This would be inconsequential except that Peter Hourie, Middleton's translator, states unambiguously that Middleton did not send "his scouts" on this search. Hourie points out that the three scouts set off on their own and that he advised his son not to go: "General Middleton knows that you are here, and if he wanted you to join the scouts he would have called on you."[4] Further, in a 1935 interview, Armstrong also indicates that they were not sent out by Middleton.[5] Middleton may have been uncomfortable with the fact that the captors of Riel did it on their own initiative, not unlike what happened in the taking of Batoche when the final charge occurred without his direct order. Much later, in 1894, however, Middleton adds a few more details, mentioning the names of all three scouts this time, and paying tribute to their work: "The next morning, May 15th, we commenced crossing the river, using one of the steamers for that purpose. I sent Boulton off with nearly all our mounted scouts to scour the woods as far back as Batoche. While he was beating the covers, the principal game was driven into the hands of three of my courier scouts, Hourie, son of the interpreter, Deal [sic], and Armstrong, all good men and true. . . ."[6]

NEWSPAPER REPORTS

Charles P. Mulvaney, in his history of the rebellion, wrote that seven correspondents wanted to interview Riel after he was brought to Middleton's camp.[7] Diehl, on the other hand, mentioned that only three reporters were there, and only Flinn met him when he arrived at camp—perhaps the others were elsewhere in the camp or out with Boulton's scouts, hoping to witness Riel's capture. Present at the camp were the reporters George A. Flinn (*Winnipeg Sun*), George H. Ham (*Toronto Daily News*), and an unknown *Toronto Globe* reporter.

Many newspapers reporting Riel's capture, and earlier stories, reprinted articles published in other papers without acknowledgments. On occasion they even intercepted their rivals' telegraphed messages, making it hard to trace the original source of the story. Mindful of that problem, Flinn attached his initials to his columns, as did Ham in his first report, and the *Globe* prefaced stories with "By our own reporter." Obtaining and using other reporters' dispatches became an issue for Flinn whose paper, the *Winnipeg Sun*, in its May 16 issue, compared the telegraph offices to dairies—"The despatch announcing the capture [of Riel] was brought to Clarke's Crossing, as he informs us by wire, by Mr. G. A. Flinn, the *Sun* correspondent, who made a ride over fifty miles for the purpose.

But through the 'milking' facilities which prevail at this telegraphic dairy, other newspapers were served as well."

Riel was taken into custody on May 15. Though dispatches were written that very afternoon, before they were delivered to the telegraph stations and then transmitted, it was too late for the news to be published on that day. Only on May 16, a Saturday, did the story make the headlines. Several newspapers carried a brief announcement on May 16, followed by a full account on Monday, May 18. On May 16 the *Winnipeg Sun* printed four items by Flinn. His first dispatches (and those of the reporter Ham and the *Toronto Globe*'s reporter), written in "real time" at Middleton's camp at Gardepuis' Crossing, are a primary source for learning what transpired that day and are reproduced here. These reports are the raw news, the descriptions by the captors before any biased revisions or contrived dialogue entered the story. Dispatches reporting Riel's apprehension were composed in two stages—first, when Diehl rode into camp before his companions and gave the news, and then, when Hourie, Armstrong, and Riel appeared. Diehl must have arrived sometime before 3:30 p.m. because at 3:30 Flinn writes, "Riel has not arrived yet, but the report of his capture is confirmed." It, of course, was confirmed by Diehl, whose statement is recorded in Flinn's first dispatch:

> Guardeput's [Gardepuis'] Crossing, May 15th. Wm. Diept [sic], Thomas Hurie [sic], and J. H. [sic] Armstrong, three daring scouts, captured Riel at noon to-day. He was on the road three miles north of Batoche's. He was in the company of three young men, two of whom were armed. He appeared unconcerned. Diept [sic] said to him "I am surprised to see you here." Riel answered, "I was coming to give myself up. My wife and family are across the river." While talking to him Boulton's scouts were seen coming up. Riel became afraid he was going to be shot, and begged his captors to take him into camp themselves. Accordingly Diept [sic] went off for a horse, but when a short distance away Boulton's scouts came closer and Hourie and Armstrong took Riel on one of their horses, and taking unfrequented

roads, will bring Reil [sic] into camp this afternoon. General Middleton gave an order that all men are to keep to their tents when Reil [sic] came in, as he was afraid of personal violence, many having sworn to shoot him on sight. No praise is too high for the three gallant men who effected the capture, who many times have risked their lives since the rebellion began, and this time ventured alone through the country this morning. G. A. F.[8]

That morning Armstrong had informed Flinn that "he was going out with Tom Hourie, the son of the official interpreter, to bring Riel in and that if I happened to be somewhere along the river trail in a few hours, I might see something of them."[9] After Diehl's announcement, Flinn, therefore, rode out of camp and met the other two scouts and Riel just as they were approaching Middleton's camp. After meeting the trio, Flinn returned to camp and wrote:

> May 15, 3:45 p.m. The letter Riel gave the courier was a letter Middleton sent to him. He beckoned the men to him. He knew nothing of Dumont. Riel said he stayed Tuesday and Wednesday nights in the bluffs one and a half miles north of Batoche. He wished for a fair trial. He asked Armstrong if he would get a civil or military trial. He wanted a civil trial. He was afraid of the scouts, but passing through them we brought him safely to camp. He said his wife and family were with a Half Breed woman nearby. Riel is now being interviewed by Middleton, while the men are standing idly around. No demonstration is being made. . . . G. A. F.[10]

The bulletin announcing Riel's apprehension dated May 16 in the May 19 *Regina Leader* is nearly a word-for-word copy of Flinn's dispatch, even incorporating the error in Armstrong's initials.[11] The *Montreal Witness* of the same date carried Flinn's story but also included the unlikely statement that Armstrong told Riel that he would be given a military trial. The May 16 *Saint Paul* (MN) *Globe* reveals how errors often occur in initial reports. In a news flash,

Diehl's and Hourie's names become altered such that they are wholly different ones: "Riel has been captured three miles north of Batoche's at noon yesterday by three scouts named Dript [sic], Thorne [sic] and Armstrong."

The *Toronto Globe*'s moment-by-moment description of Riel's apprehension as presented by Diehl when he arrived at Middleton's camp is more detailed than Flinn's similar account:

> Riel was captured to-day at noon by three scouts named Armstrong, Diehl and Howrie [sic] four miles north of Batoche. The scouts had gone out in the morning to scour the country, but there they separated from the main body, and just as they were coming out of the brush on an unfrequented trail leading to Batoche they espied Riel with three companions. He was unarmed, but the latter carried shot guns. All recognized Riel, and advancing towards him hailed him. They were then standing near a fence. No effort was made to escape, and after a brief conversation on expressing their surprise at finding him there, Riel declared that he intended to give himself up. His only fear was that he would be shot by the troops, but he was promised a safe escort to the General's quarters. His wife and children were not with him, and he said they were on the west side of the river to avoid the main body of scouts. Riel had [sic?] taken to a coulee near by and hidden while Diehl went off to corral a horse for him, the main body of scouts being seen in the distance. At the time when Diehl returned Riel and his companions disappeared, evidently to avoid the other scouts. Diehl says Riel was not in the least agitated when arrested and was willingly made captive. He was assured of a fair trial, which was all he seemed to want. During the interview he handed scout Armstrong a note, the contents of which have not yet been heard, as at the time of writing the party had not arrived in camp. Orders have been given to keep in tents so that no demonstrations can be made when Riel arrives. He is expected in an hour, but this is sent off by courier to Clark's Crossing before his arrival.

His capture is however assured. The boys in the camp are jubilant over the capture.[12]

On the same page on which the above report is printed, the *Globe* also includes a false article that appeared in a Cobourg, Ontario, paper: "There is great rejoicing here [Cobourg] over Riel's capture, especially as it was effected by commands of Majors Smith and Boulton, Cobourg citizens."

The May 16 *Toronto Daily Mail*'s first announcement of Riel's capture is brief: "Riel was brought in at half-past three this afternoon. There was no demonstration. He walked quietly to the General's tent. No one is allowed to see him. G. H. H." The evening issue of that day and the May 18 issue gave a full account, the information provided being similar to that in the *Globe* and the *Sun*. The nearly identical reports in the *Globe* and the *Daily Mail* may not be the result of one paper plagiarizing the other, but suggest that the two reporters may have decided to share a dispatch rather than send two separate riders to the telegraph office; or maybe, just as the *Sun* complained, one or the other obtained the telegram intended for their competitor. Slight variations in wording would then have been introduced by staff in the newspaper offices.

CONTEMPORARY ACCOUNTS, EARLY HISTORIES AND REMINISCENCES, AND MORE RECENT HISTORIES

Early histories depicting Riel's apprehension rarely include citations, but it is clear that in some cases the initial newspaper reports were copied. Other writers reformulated those descriptions by combining information from several sources. There are too many similar accounts to consider all of them here, but several are quoted to serve as representative samples, and others are mentioned if they provide information not noted elsewhere. It is a curiosity that the writers who describe Riel's arrest are silent about the contradictions or discrepancies occurring in the various accounts. The reasons may vary, but the two obvious ones are that they may not have consulted a sufficient number of sources to notice the contradictions, or they may just have had a preference for one particular version.

Charles Mulvaney's two accounts of Riel's surrender in his book published in 1885 repeat verbatim the first newspaper reports. G. Mercer Adam's description in *The Canadian North-West* (also published in 1885) relies on the same sources:

> The taking of Riel happened in this wise. While the country was being scoured to see that no number of armed insurgents were still lurking in the woods, a rumour reached the headquarters that the rebel chief was not far off. Three couriers, named Howrie [sic], Armstrong, and Deale [sic], who had diverged from the trail in an advance party of Boulton's Scouts, came upon four men at the edge of a wood. One of the four, Howrie [sic] recognized Riel, though he was coatless, hatless, and unarmed. His companions were young men, and they carried shotguns. The couriers rode up, and they called Riel by name, and he answered their salutation. They expressed surprise at his being there, and in reply Riel handed Armstrong a slip of paper—the note which General Middleton had sent him—informing him that if he would give himself up he would be protected, and given a fair trial. At the same time, he said: "I want to give myself up; but I fear the troops may hurt me." The couriers relieved Riel's mind on this point, and undertook to smuggle him into camp without molestation. This was ultimately done, and the rebel chieftain soon stood, a prisoner, in the tent of the General.[13]

Also appearing in the same year as the rebellion, Alexander Begg's *History of the North-West* relates that:

> General Middleton, hearing that Riel was somewhere in the neighborhood, sent out parties to scour the woods in search of the rebel leader, and two of these named Armstrong and Hourie, came upon him and took him prisoner. When he was captured he produced General Middleton's letter, promising him that if he surrendered he would be protected until handed over to the Canadian Government.

Armstrong and Hourie having promised that no harm would be done to Riel by the troops, until handed over to the proper authorities, managed to keep him out of sight until close to the camp, when they succeeded in bringing him to Middleton's tent. A man named Diehl, it is said, assisted in the capture, but his name is not given in the official report.[14]

While making their way to Middleton's camp, Riel and his captors encountered Boulton's scouts on at least one occasion. One of those scouts left a record of that encounter. He wrote that the scout beside him recognized Hourie and "called out jokingly, 'well, Tom, have you got Riel?' little thinking that the third man was the rebel chief. Hourie crossed the line of scouts unchallenged, slipped through the bluffs in front of the column until out of reach, and took his prisoner into camp whilst we went on scouring the country and our lariats hung unstretched at the saddle bows. His reason for avoiding us was that Riel was afraid the scouts would shoot him, and Hourie wanted the imaginary reward for himself."[15]

Roderick G. MacBeth, in three separate publications, has chosen to name two, one, or three captors of Riel respectively.[16] His first book, published in 1898, briefly mentions the capture and names Hourie and Armstrong as the captors; in *The Romance of Western Canada*, perhaps because he was personally acquainted with Hourie, MacBeth cites only Tom Hourie:

> Riel was found in a clump of bushes by Tom Hourie, one of Middleton's half-breed scouts. The giant lifted the rebel leader up behind him on his horse, and took him to Middleton's tent. . . . Tom Hourie, whom I knew well, was much lionized in Winnipeg and elsewhere for his capture of Riel.[17]

Much later, in 1931, MacBeth remarks: "And it is rather interesting to recall that it was big Tom Hourie, a Police interpreter, accompanied by two Police scouts, Armstrong and Diehl, who captured Riel and took him into Middleton's tent at Batoche."[18] (At that time Middleton's tent was no longer at Batoche, but at

Gardepuis' Crossing.) Another work, A. L. Haydon's *The Riders of the Plains*, shifts the focus to Armstrong:

> Constables Armstrong and Diehl were bearing dispatches from Colonel Irvine to General Middleton when, in company of a third scout, Howie [sic] by name, they came upon four men standing near a fence. One of the quartette, coatless and bareheaded, was easily recognized as Riel. His three companions carried rifles, he himself was unarmed. The scouts rode up. "You are Louis Riel?" asked Armstrong. "Yes, I am," was the answer; "I want to give myself up." Then he produced a slip of paper from his pocket. It was a note which General Middleton had sent him saying that if he would surrender he would be given a fair trial. A horse having been obtained for him, Riel was escorted to the camp at Battleford, whence on 23rd May he was conveyed to Regina.[19]

Haydon's account has several errors: Armstrong, Diehl, and Hourie were not carrying dispatches from Irvine on the day Riel was arrested—they were in Middleton's camp; Middleton's note did not offer him a fair trial—it promised him safety until he would be transferred to civilian authorities; and he was not escorted to Battleford, but to Middleton's camp at Gardepuis' Crossing, just north of Batoche, more than sixty-two miles from Battleford.

Major Boulton published his reminiscences in 1886. He linked himself to Riel's capture by writing, "Hourie, Deal[sic], and Armstrong, three scouts who knew the country and the people, accompanied me about a half a mile in advance of the column, and on the main trail Riel had surrendered to them. . . ."[20] It is possible that Boulton rode alongside the scouts for awhile; however, though Boulton's scouts are mentioned, Armstrong, Hourie, and Diehl do not make any reference to Boulton. Boulton's version of his scouts' encounter with Riel and his captors omits the oft-repeated remark about Riel being a cook but adds that Hourie claimed to have lost his horse, a detail absent in other accounts: ". . . when about five miles from the trail they passed through some of my scouts, who did not know Riel, and Hourie in his anxiety to take him into camp himself, gave no intimation of his capture, sending word that he had lost his horse and was going back to camp for another."[21]

Reporter Flinn, in his reminiscences, reconstructed the event and dramatized the episode with questionable dialogue, adding the fascinating detail about receiving a souvenir bullet from Armstrong:

> "Will I get a civil trial?" he asked Armstrong.
>
> "No, you will be court-marshalled," replied the Scout, who apparently was not favourably impressed with his prisoner. Riel thereupon prayed a little and then put his hand in a vest pocket and produced a small 22-caliber revolver which he held out to Armstrong with the remark: "See what I might have done to you. I am acting in good faith though." Armstrong took the little weapon, held it on his open hand and extracted five small cartridges from it, one of which he handed to me for a souvenir. He looked at Riel with something as near being a smile as it was possible for his Missouri features to assume, and shoved the weapon in his own vest pocket. . . .[22]

It is something of a puzzle why Flinn wrote that Armstrong was not suitably disposed to Riel or that Riel would be court-martialled when other reports show that Riel was informed that he would get a fair trial. Further, Armstrong told Charlotte Gordon that Riel was notified that he would get a "fair British trial" and William McCartney Davidson that he found Riel a likable man.[23] Riel did not surrender his revolver when he met his captors, only later, and before his encounter with Flinn so it is equally odd that Flinn's account of the receipt of a souvenir bullet and other details practically suggest that he was present at Riel's apprehension.

The portrayal by R. C. Laurie, a lieutenant in Middleton's force, is strange and not corroborated by any eyewitnesses:

> Orders were given that all men were to be confined to their tents and no demonstration was to be made on Riel's arrival. In a short time, a democrat wagon drew up at the entrance

to the tent and I saw a man get down and walk into the tent. This was the only glimpse I had of Riel. . . . He [Boulton] was very anxious to be the one to capture Riel and was out with his troop in extended order sweeping up the country in search for the leader of the Rebellion. Three scouts, Wm. Diehl, Wm. [sic] Anderson [sic] and Tom Hourie, with a fourth man behind one of them on his horse came riding through their ranks. To an enquiry, "who have you there" the reply was "some old man, probably Riel's cook.[24]

Laurie's glimpse of Riel disembarking from a "democrat" is refuted by all accounts—he may have witnessed a different prisoner being transported in that manner and confused him with Riel.[25] Quoting Laurie, Don McLean, in *1885: Metis Rebellion or Government Conspiracy?*, says ". . . but Louis Riel quietly, and of his own accord, rode up and turned over his only weapon, a small .22 revolver, to police scouts William Diehl and Robert Armstrong with the remark, 'Perhaps it is better if you had this.'"[26] That Riel rode up to his captors on a horse is as unfounded as Riel disembarking from a democrat. Further, Riel handed his revolver either to Armstrong or Hourie, not Diehl and Armstrong.

Hugh Nelson, a participant in the military operations, writes in his *Four Months Under Arms* that "Riel . . . was making his way to the Catholic mission house at St. Laurent, when he was captured by three volunteer scouts from Prince Albert—Thos. Horrie [sic], Robert Armstrong, and Wm. Deihl [sic]."[27] John G. Donkin, a former corporal in the NWMP, in *Trooper and Redskin in the Far North-West*, simply states, "Riel was found wandering in the woods and captured by two scouts, Armstrong and Howrie [sic] on the afternoon of the 15th."[28] Colonel Steele, a NWMP officer and commander of scouts with the Alberta Field Force, notes that three scouts captured Riel but names only Diehl and Armstrong, possibly because these two began their activities with Colonel Irvine of the NWMP while Hourie did not.[29] Norman Black, in *History of Saskatchewan and the North West Territories* says, "Two of these scouts, Armstrong and Hourie, fell in with him on the 15th and brought him to Middleton's tent."[30] John Hawkes, who interviewed

Peter Hourie, includes Peter Hourie's description of Tom's activities during the rebellion in *The Story of Saskatchewan and Its People*.[31] John Peter Turner's *The North-West Mounted Police 1873–1893* offers this account:

> William Diehl a rancher from near Fort Carlton, Bob Armstrong[,] an old Indian fighter and scout from the United States, both of whom were special scouts for the Mounted Police, and Tom Hourie[,] half-breed guide who had accompanied Middleton's column from Qu'Appelle, also took up the hunt. . . . After consultation with some of his councillors, Riel decided he would not attempt escape, that he would give himself up and stand trial, believing that in that way, public attention would be directed to the injustice to which he considered the halfbreeds had been subjected by the Government of Canada. He was not far away, and was soon located. With little hesitation the hapless instigator of revolt surrendered to Tom Hourie.[32]

In *The Birth of Western Canada* and in *Louis Riel*, George Stanley, who met Armstrong, relates in the first instance that Riel gave himself up to two scouts and in the second book to three NWMP scouts.[33] According to Joseph Howard, in *The Strange Empire of Louis Riel*, Hourie is the principal actor, but Joseph Howard concedes that it was Armstrong who presented Riel to Middleton:

> Unarmed, but accompanied by three Métis carrying shotguns, Louis left his hiding place and set off on foot for Batoche. As they neared the river they were discovered by three scouts, Tom Hourie, Bob Armstrong and William Deale [sic]. Hourie, a local man, instantly recognized Riel even though his face was haggard, his beard dirty and untrimmed, and his usually neat clothing stained and torn. The Métis party offered no resistance when Hourie called upon him to surrender, and Riel handed the scout the note he had received from Middleton. "I want to give myself up," he said, "but fear the troops may hurt me." Hourie assured him that he would

not be molested. While they talked they heard a large party of Boulton's scouts approaching and the three men who had "captured" Louis—his companions were not held—hid him in a coulee until the others had passed. An effort was made to bring him into camp secretly, but within a few moments everyone knew that the shabby, dejected 'half-breed' who had been escorted into Middleton's tent was the fabulous Louis Riel. Curious militiamen swarmed around the headquarters area and were ordered to disperse. When the group entered the tent Armstrong said, "General, this is Riel."[34]

On the other hand, in *The Man Who Had to Hang: Louis Riel*, E. B. Osler repeats some of the information provided by Armstrong in the 1920s interviews.[35] Also emphasizing Armstrong's role, Frank Anderson, in his unpublished manuscript, *Louis Riel: Patriot and Rebel*, writes:

That same afternoon, the fifteenth, still hesitant, he [Riel] met three armed Métis near a farm fence some four miles north of Batoche and entered into conversation with them on the matter of the army scouts who were known to be searching the woods for him. While they were still talking, they observed three horsemen riding towards them from the north. Though the Métis gripped their shotguns more tightly, Riel waited with folded arms until the three riders stopped before him. The spokesman, Constable Armstrong of the North West Mounted Police, asked him if he was Louis Riel. Louis replied that he was, adding that he wished to give himself up. He then took the above note from his pocket and handed it to Armstrong. . . . The little cavalcade was unmolested and Louis Riel, dressed in a dark, threadbare woollen suit, was unrecognized as they passed several groups of Major Boulton's scouts, who were searching the woods around, and entered the army camp.[36]

In a later publication, *Riel's Saskatchewan Rebellion*, Anderson presents a similar story with additional details:

Riel was standing beside a trail with three Métis when Constable Robert Armstrong rode up, accompanied by Special Constable William Diehl and an interpreter, Tom Hourie. Armstrong asked him if he was the Métis leader and Riel confirmed his identity, adding that he wished to surrender and that he had a safe conduct pass from General Middleton. Armstrong advised that he was on his way to Batoche and invited Riel to ride along with them. There was no animosity shown to Riel—he was not even a prisoner at that point—and it was only later that stories began to appear giving a dramatic account of "his capture." Though they passed several search parties along the road, none of these recognized Riel and they reached Batoche without incident.[37]

Anderson's sources are unknown, but he alone turns the surrender into an invitation by Armstrong to Riel to join him for a ride to Batoche. (Actually, as has already been mentioned, they went in the opposite direction, to Gardepuis' Crossing.) The encounter may not have been as casual as Anderson portrays it, although, in one of his interviews, Armstrong does describe the ride to Middleton's tent as an interesting and cordial trip.

Most recent histories and biographies of Riel give little or no attention to Riel's surrender/capture. Maggie Siggins, in *Riel: A Life of Revolution*, writes: "Later that afternoon, two Canadian scouts and an army translator of Cree found a weary, disheveled Métis dressed in a Hudson Bay coat, with a white handkerchief tied around one sleeve, an out-of-shape Stetson, and his pants rolled up over sockless feet, walking on the trail near Guardepuis [Gardepuis'] crossing. They asked him who he was and he answered, 'Louis Riel.' Armed only with Middleton's letter, he had come to surrender."[38] Douglas W. Light informs that "Louis Riel surrendered to N.W.M.P. scouts Robert Armstrong and William Diehl who were accompanied by Middleton's scout, Thomas Hourie. He was immediately escorted by these scouts to Middleton's tent."[39] Ruth Wright Millar provides a brief, fair account, favouring Hourie, but acknowledges that other versions exist.[40]

Appendix 2

RIEL'S APPREHENSION:
ACCOUNTS BY THE THREE CAPTORS

ROBERT ARMSTRONG'S ACCOUNT

Robert Armstrong put forward his recollection of Riel's apprehension in his memoir and in several interviews. He told his story
to Charlotte Gordon in 1923; to Howard Angus Kennedy in 1926;
to William McCartney Davidson, possibly in 1927;[1] and to an
unknown reporter in 1935.[2] The version in Armstrong's memoir
appears in Part Two of this book, "Robert Armstrong's Memoir,"
while the accounts by the other writers are presented here in turn.
A commentary on these five versions follows.

Charlotte Gordon Interview
Charlotte Gordon would have seen Armstrong's memoir when
she met with him in 1923. In her article she quotes directly from
it, paraphrases some parts, and at times includes information that
was not in the memoir but which she acquired in her meeting
with Armstrong. Only the portions of her article that differ from
the account in the memoir are included here. She begins by saying
that Armstrong met Riel in Montana, and "His second meeting
with the notorious rebel was in Prince Albert in the Fall of 1884,

and in attendance at some of the public meetings held by the agitators." Armstrong's version according to Gordon:

> As we went up, he [Riel] started to move away and I called to him. He immediately turned and ran to me, with his hands up, thinking I was going to kill him. Then he fell on his knees and began to pray in French. I told him to get up, that it was too late to pray. He should have done that some time ago. He stood up and I gave him General Middleton's order of surrender. Riel [sic] took charge of the other men while Hourie attended to the horses. I knew that Major Boulton and some of his men were on the hunt, also "Gatling Gun Howard," so I decided to take Riel to Batoche, four miles away, through the bushes, for Major Boulton had sworn to "shoot Riel on sight," while General Middleton had said, "Try to bring Riel in alive.". . . I sent Riel [sic] ahead to tell General Middleton of our capture, while Hourie and I looked after our notorious prisoner. I instructed Riel to keep his mouth shut if we met anyone. Finally we came on several advance scouts who inquired as to who our man was. Riel was a very short man, not of prepossessing appearance, and I answered that it was Riel's cook. They cried out, "Why don't you shoot him, I would not take a little thing like that to camp."
>
> As Hourie talked with the scouts, I moved on with Riel who was behind me on my horse. We got about a half a mile from the rest when Riel drew a small .32 derringer pistol from his inside pocket and handed it to me, saying I had missed it when I examined him. "I will be honest with you Mr. Armstrong, take this pistol too." I said, "Why did you not use that on me from your point of vantage—escape on my horse and save your neck?" He answered, "I could not kill a man in cold blood, especially as I knew you in Montana. Will they hang me in camp?" Mr. Armstrong told him that he would have a fair British trial.[3]

Kennedy, a war correspondent in 1885, also must have glanced at Armstrong's manuscript because his brief summary of Armstrong's life parallels the story in the memoir. Kennedy, like Gordon, introduces expressions into the story that are his own:

> After the Battle of Batoche, most of the Métis surrendered, but their chief, Riel, and his generalissimo, Gabriel Dumont, fled. Armstrong, Hourie, and Diehl, hunting them almost at random, south-east [sic] of Batoche, came upon a little halfbreed camp. One of the Métis women, angry with Riel because her sons had been killed fighting for him, told the scouts that he had come to her tepee the night before and had started westward. Away rode the scouts by the trail pointed out.
>
> "Presently," Bob told me, "we caught sight of five halfbreeds on foot. Four miles from Batoche they stopped near a shanty and seemed to be having a conference. We crept up, hidden by timber, got within forty yards of them and charged in. We disarmed four of them, without a word said on either side. The fifth started walking quietly away, but incautiously looked back over his shoulder and I recognized him at once as Louis Riel. I had seen him three years before in Montana where he was teaching school."
>
> When he heard me call out "that's Riel," he turned and gave up. His men had a saddle and bridle and had been trying to find a horse for him. Gabriel Dumont had got away already for Montana. Some of the other scouts came up while I had sent Diehl back for the pony and said they would shoot Riel on sight if they found him. They asked me who I had got and I said, "Riel's cook." "Shoot him and let him die," the man said. Riel did look a pretty hard customer in the Hudson's Bay coat with capote, and what had been a fine Stetson hat, a pair of shoe packs, pants rolled up and bare legs.
>
> I left Hourie to keep the other scouts talking, while I got Riel up behind me on the pony and started for the General's camp. Half a mile away, he passed a pistol over my shoulder,

saying, "Mr. Armstrong, I'll act square with you." "You're a fool," said I, "you could have stuck me up and got away. If you ain't soft!" He said, "Often last winter I saved your life. I told my men to get you but not to kill you, though they may have to cripple you." We didn't keep to the road, but made a shortcut through the woods to the camp. Diehl had gone ahead and reported the capture to the general. We came up to the general's tent, and I said, "This is Riel." The general said to him, "I am glad to meet you. Sit down on my cot." The general brought his chair and while they talked I went out to eat.[4]

William McCartney Davidson Interview
William McCartney Davidson's conversation with Armstrong is included in his book *Louis Riel, 1844–1885: A Biography*. About the same time as the book was published, it was serialized in abridged form in *The Albertan*. Davidson writes:

Riel gave himself up on the morning of Friday, May 14th [sic], to Robert Armstrong, one of Middleton's scouts, who with two others, Houri [sic] and Diehl, were searching three or four miles north-east of Batoche. Armstrong, who is still living (1927), in Calgary, declares that his party came upon Riel and some other Metis as the latter were making their way toward the protection of the river bottom. Riel and the Metis have given emphatic evidence that Riel surrendered voluntarily.

Riel was unusually fortunate in his capture. Armstrong was an adventurous buffalo hunter, a pioneer of the plains, who knew all the ways of the wilds and had full knowledge of the natives. He had come into the Canadian forces after the battle of Fish Creek, to act as courier and scout for Middleton himself, taking orders directly from the General and no one else. He had done good service. He stood beside Middleton when the General wrote the message offering protection to the Metis leader if he would surrender and beside the General he saw the final charge that captured Batoche, scattered the Metis, and ended the resistance.

Riel had known Armstrong in Montana, and was greatly relieved when he recognized him. "God has sent you here to arrest me. Had some of those Canadians arrested me, they might have shot me, but you are an American and without any prejudices against me," said Riel, and he showed Armstrong the letter from Middleton offering him protection. Armstrong ventured no opinion about the ways of Providence or whether he had been despatched especially by supernatural authority. "I have seen that bit of paper before," he told Riel as the latter produced the Middleton note. "I saw the General write it." He took Riel under formal arrest.

Not being very certain of the temper of the soldiery, he decided to conceal his prisoner from others for a time. Houri [sic] gave his attention to the Metis who accompanied Riel, and Diehl went in advance of the party to announce the arrest, but apparently lost touch with the others. "There was some talk about martial law couple of days ago, when some of the boys seemed to be getting out of hand, but it is all right now," said Armstrong reassuringly. Riel was cautious but not excited or alarmed.

Then began an unusual journey, possible only upon the Canadian plains, and there only in pioneer days. Riel handed to Armstrong a revolver that had been concealed in his shirt and had been overlooked by his captor in his casual search. Armstrong mounted his horse and the prisoner started on foot. But the buffalo hunter, with his prairie-bred habits of feeling, could not be happy with conditions so unequal. "I knew Riel and liked him," said Armstrong telling the story later. "He was a decent fellow and I didn't feel right riding while he was walking." He looked about. No person was in sight. "I gave him a hand, pulled him up behind me, and then we rode on and were both more comfortable," explained Armstrong.

In such manner they rode during the forenoon, the prairie scout acting as captor, and Riel, the man over whose resistance the whole of Canada was in turmoil, and for whose arrest the Dominion had raised a total force of about eight thousand men at a cost of about five million dollars, a volunteer prisoner—the two chatting in friendly fashion. "In the afternoon we came upon a pony loose on the range," Armstrong has related. "We dismounted and rounded up the animal. Then I rigged up a makeshift saddle using some blankets I had; and Riel rode the pony and I kept on my own horse." When they neared the camp of Middleton the informality of easy prairie ways gave place to military discipline. They dismounted, recovered Armstrong's blankets, turned the pony loose again, and Riel marched behind his captor in proper order.

"Of course, as you say, it was a mistake that I ever left Montana," Armstrong has reported Riel as saying on the way. "I was getting along well enough there. We were all happy. I liked my work. They seemed to like me."

"Why did you ever quit Montana?" asked Armstrong.

"Some of my friends up here wanted me to help them, and I thought I could do something for them," Riel replied. "I didn't expect any trouble like this when I came."

"How did you get into all of this trouble with the shooting and the fighting?"

"We just drifted into it. One thing led to another. I can't explain how it did happen," Riel said to Armstrong. They talked continually from the time of the arrest until they arrived in camp. Armstrong does not recall that Riel said anything to him about religion, but adds that he was not greatly interested because their religion was different and he was not much interested in that phase of Riel. . . . News of the capture preceded their arrival at camp, and as they passed along the tents the soldiers rushed out, calling, "Is that Riel you've got there?" "No, it is only his cook," Armstrong shouted back. He took no chances on the formation of a mob even that near headquarters. "General, this is Mr. Riel," was Armstrong's direct and simple introduction to Middleton, as they entered the General's tent. Middleton shook hands with the Metis leader, and invited him to sit on the bed, which was the only available seat. It was 4:30 in the afternoon. The journey had begun at 10:30 in the morning. Armstrong then left the tent.[5]

1935 Interview
An interview with Robert Armstrong and J. A. Fraser published in a July 17, 1935, newspaper yields some additional details but also introduces some errors.[6] The reporter seemed unprepared for the interview—he did not know the names of the three men who had taken Riel into custody and allowed Mr. Fraser to be one of the three. No mention of Hourie is made by Armstrong or by Fraser. Understandably, the remarks of two old men, sipping scotch and recalling their youthful experiences, are not expected to be rigorously accurate. The 1935 article in part:

> Robert Armstrong of Gleichen, and J. A. Fraser of 11219 99th avenue, visitors to the Exhibition, got together Tuesday noon for a talk. Visualize the redoubtable Col. William (Buffalo Bill) Cody. That's Bob Armstrong at 86 years, little white goatee and all. Visualize a tall, buckskin-clad wiry trail scout of the old school—and that's Mr. Fraser at 76. . . . They sat and siped [sic] their Scotch with relish as they reminisced. The dynamic glint of the old daring lighted their eyes as they recalled the redoubtable escapades which made the campaign a history-weaving classic—for these two were prime central figures in the capture of Riel, the rebel and they were living it over again.
>
> In 1885 Robert Armstrong who had been a buffalo-killer in Montana and Texas found himself attached to the forces of General Middleton as special guide and scout, and two days after the battle of Batoche, the 15th of May, 1885, to be exact, he found himself with the Middleton forces at Gurtipee's [sic] Ferry. Some of Bolton's [sic] agents, hot upon the trail of the rebellious Riel, drifted into the Middleton camp—and from them Bob Armstrong conceived the idea that he would undertake the capture of the rebel chief.

At the Carlton trading post near-by was Billy Deal [sic], a New Yorker. Deel [sic] was good and sore for Riel forces had raided his stock. . . . Bob Armstrong, following this adventure pressed on with Deal [sic] and Ashley [sic] to affect the capture of the rebel chief. At Manitchinatch [sic] Hills the scouts saw an Indian encampment and a pair of white man's pants upon a line aroused their suspicions. This was but a few miles from Batoche, and from the old Indian women in the camp the Three Musketeers learned that the famous Riel had been there at midnight preceding. Picking up his trail they ultimately surprised Riel and a small following seated upon the ground in a small garden. Deal [sic], says Bob Armstrong, was all for killing the rebel and his crowd without further ado but instead Bob Armstrong ran the ragged rebel down, searched him and made him prisoner.

Searching Riel, the old scout overlooked a vest pocket, apparently, for after he had mounted his prisoner behind him, Riel, he says, handed over to him a .38 caliber revolver which he had in his inside vest pocket. This was Riel's way of expressing appreciation for the fact that Armstrong had circled with his prisoner around a patrol of Bulton's [sic] scouts whose sole mission was to shoot the rebel chief on sight. "You being a Yankee, I have nothing against you, but if you were a Canadian I'd have let you have it through the back of the head" was Riel's way of being appreciative said the old scout.

Riel was subsequently ridden in to General Middleton's camp by Bob Armstrong who was surprised to find the camp apparently deserted—not a man in sight. He later learned that advance word of the capture had resulted in a general order for all men to remain in their tents, for fear of summary vengeance by individuals.[7]

Variations in these descriptions do not necessarily imply inconsistencies, and, in many cases, they are supplementary. Decades separated the event from these interviews. Oral accounts, typically, vary somewhat with each telling—incidental details can get mixed up or even forgotten. Some differences are superficial embellishments meant to dramatize the event and do not alter the more significant aspects of the story. Yet, there are some clear contradictions.

In the 1935 interview, Armstrong claims that the decision to go after Riel was his own, not because of an order from Middleton. Yet in Gordon's version, Armstrong's remark that General Middleton said, "Try to bring Riel in alive," suggests the opposite. Though seemingly contradictory, it is possible to imagine how both scenarios can be reconciled. After Middleton had sent off Boulton's scouts, Armstrong and Hourie decided on their own that they were going after Riel. Tom remarked, "Let us go for our horses," at which time Armstrong may have decided to inform Middleton and was told, "Try to bring Riel in alive." But, more likely, "bring him in alive" is meant to make the story sound more thrilling.

An inconsequential discrepancy occurs when, in his memoir, Armstrong writes that when Riel was spotted, he crept closer to the group and then returned to Hourie and Diehl. Elsewhere, he says that "we" crept closer before charging the group. In all likelihood, no one was creeping. Armstrong also reports in his memoir that Hourie went to find a pony for Riel while Diehl looked after the Métis who were with Riel; but elsewhere he states that Diehl went after a horse and Hourie looked after the other captives. The first instance is an inadvertent slip because further in the memoir Armstrong indicates that Hourie joined him after settling matters with the other Métis (rather than having gone off to find a horse).

In the 1935 interview, Armstrong says that upon arrival at Middleton's camp the place was deserted because of an order for everyone to be in their tents, but in another account he recalls talking to bystanders. There is evidence that men were peering out of their tents to see the arrival of the trio; so, though the camp may have at first appeared deserted, Armstrong could have spoken with the onlookers who were at the thresholds of their tents.

Armstrong, in one interview but not in the others, says that he found a pony and Riel rode on it for a while. A horse for Riel could have been obtained at some point. Haydon, in *The Riders of the Plains*, mentions, "A horse having been obtained for him, Riel was escorted to the camp. . . ."[8] The search for horses for Riel and his companions was a reasonable undertaking. There were many Métis horses on the loose—the combatants who were hiding in the woods thought they would be safer if they abandoned their horses. Comprehensive accounts are not possible in interviews, so a "pony for Riel" may not have come up in the other interviews.

Other than the blurring of memory, it is hard to explain how Armstrong, in his memoir, says he started off alone with Riel, ran into Boulton's scouts alone, and only later was joined by Hourie, while elsewhere he informs that Hourie was with him when they encountered Boulton's search party.

There are instances where the inaccuracies are the fault of the journalists. For example, when Gordon writes, "I sent *Riel* ahead to tell General Middleton of our capture . . ." or that "Peter *Diel* [sic]" was Middleton's interpreter (rather than Peter Hourie).[9] In the 1935 article, initially, Fraser is named as a central figure in the capture of Riel (he had no role in the capture), but further on, the columnist writes that "Ashley" was the third scout—the reporter, apparently, did not know of Tom Hourie.

Gordon's interview, Flinn's writings, and some other reports create the impression that Armstrong was hostile to Riel. This is at odds with what Armstrong told William McCartney Davidson: he liked Riel, considered him a decent fellow, and they chatted in a friendly manner. Gordon's use of "notorious rebel" in her writing and then her insertion of the very same words in Armstrong's dialogue demonstrates how journalists of the time coloured their stories and distorted what they may have been told. Similar epithets applied by others lead one to believe that in the presence of individuals with a hostile attitude to Riel, Armstrong might have gone along with the mood; or more likely, those inflamed words were devised by the writers, either for sensation or to match the mean-spirited sentiments many of their readers had regarding the Métis.

TOM HOURIE'S ACCOUNT

Tom Hourie did not provide his side of the story directly, but his exploits were described by his father (and others noted in Appendix 1). Just when Peter Hourie recorded his son's role in Riel's capture is not certain, but it would have been after his son's death in December 1908 and before his own in 1910, thus some twenty years after the event:

There was Tom and an American named Armstrong and a man named Deal [sic]. These two were friends of Tom's. They had been living in Prince Albert. General Middleton did not send Tom after Riel at all. Tom and Deal [sic] and this Armstrong heard them talking about Riel. Of course, it was heard that there was $1500 reward for whoever would capture Riel or Gabriel. Tom said: "Let us go for our horses," and I called out to Tom from the tent where I was lying and said: "General Middleton knows that you are here, and if he wanted you to join the scouts he would have called on you. If you come across Gabriel or any of them they might put bullets through you. You had better stay where you are." Tom said, "To hell with them."

Of course, they got on their horses and away they went. They had not gone two miles before they caught up with the crowd, who had started out to look for Riel. Major Boulton was head of the party of scouts to capture Riel and Gabriel. Tom and the other two men had set off after them, and now they caught them up.

We have been trading from Red River to Carlton and Tom knew what road to take as there were two roads. There was a road went down the river and a road across country and that was the road Tom made use of when he was carrying General Middleton's messages. He knew the direction the deserters going to Batoche would probably take. In fact, he was sure he knew the road they had gone. Major Boulton only made a guess and the scouts were to scour the country abreast. They never saw Tom at all. Tom took the other direction. Tom went to the Mountain behind Batoche on the north side of the river to head Riel off. They went full tilt, as fast as their horses would carry them.

All at once, Tom said: "This trail is fresh.["] They followed up this fresh trail. Major Boulton's men could not have done this, no one but Tom could have done it. Armstrong and Deal [sic] were green horns at the trail, but Tom could follow a trail. They caught up with a party of women and children. Tom asked, "Where was Gabriel?" They said they did not know, and that the last time they saw him he was in Batoche. Then Tom said: "Where is Riel?" They said they did not know at all, but they did know for they were hiding him; Riel and six other men were with them. Tom still followed up tracking them, losing the trail sometimes and picking it up again where it would show at all. They came out on the prairie from the mountainside, and lo and behold Tom says: "By Jove, we will now take them by surprise," for he saw a party of men walking ahead of them, walking to Batoche as fast as they could. It was rolling country. They came on within three or four hundred yards of the men, and then just called to them and before they had time to do anything with their guns. Tom spoke to them and said, "Hold on don't fire." They knew Tom the same as their own brother. There were Riel and five other men and Deal [sic] and Armstrong. They did not know Riel, only Tom. Tom had seen Riel all the winter. Riel was properly disguised. He had an old slouch grey hat and an old Hudson Bay duffel overcoat. These fellows all quit when they heard Tom's voice. Here was Riel in the crowd. He was walking backwards facing Tom. Tom says: "Mr. Riel we want you." Then he begged Tom that if he would take him in safety to General Middleton he would go with him. Tom promised he would. Riel had a revolver but no rifle. The other men had guns. Tom says: "Give up your arms boys," so Tom took their guns from them and all their bullets and powder and they went away back on the same trail they came. Tom was afraid all the time that Boulton's scouts would be upon them so they went riding back as fast as they could with all their speed. Some of Major Boulton's scouts came upon them who called out, "Tom, what is it you have there? Who is it you have got there?" What does Tom do? When Tom captured Riel he made Riel get on his horse. He told Riel to get on behind, so they were on the same horse. Deal [sic] and Armstrong had the ammunition. When they were riding along they threw away their guns and all the powder and bullets. They let the other five men go on to Batoche. They only took Riel. When they were riding along Riel said: "Oh, by the way Tom, here is my revolver." Tom turned around on the horse and said: "Hand it here," and Riel handed it to him.

Deal [sic] and Armstrong were riding along side. They said, "Let me see it." They wanted to see Riel's revolver, and Tom handed it to him. Armstrong said, "By Jove Tom, let me have the revolver.["] Tom said, "Keep it," but see there is another loaded.[10] Riel could have shot Tom and the others but he was too much afraid. It was never known how Riel was captured. Boulton's scouts would not have known Riel if they had caught him but Boulton would have known him. Tom said they would take Riel to General Middleton, and they might get some good news out of him (this probably refers to major Boulton's scouts)[11] and that was the reason why they let the scouts go on free and never bothered them anymore. They were away off the trail, but they went back on the same trail that they went out in.

When they were approaching General Middleton's camp Tom sent Deal [sic] ahead to tell General Middleton that he (Tom) had Riel. I (Peter Hourie) was in camp at the time. Orders were given by General Middleton that all soldiers were to keep [to] their tents. I was in camp and saw Deal [sic] riding in. I was very anxious to get word from Deal [sic] because I did not know what had become of Tom. I thought he had got shot perhaps. Deal [sic] came over to my tent. I said, "Hello Deal [sic] what is the news?" Deal [sic] said, "Tom and Armstrong are bringing in Riel." I said: "And all is well?" "Yes," he said. In the matter of an hour or a little while longer perhaps here we see Tom and Armstrong walking leading horses with Riel between them. This was at Guarde Pie's [sic] Crossing. They went right into General Middleton's tent and put Riel in the tent and that was the last of him. I said, "By George, everything is all right." I had been very anxious about Tom and now I was very pleased. Of course, the scouts were all out at the time looking for Riel. At night they all came in and they had no word of anything. They came in heavily armed and here the head leader of the rebellion was in General Middleton's tent.[12]

Hourie contributes some details of Riel's apprehension not reported by the other two scouts: Middleton did not send the trio in search of Riel; the three scouts may have been motivated by the possibility of reward money; Peter Hourie witnessed Diehl's arrival at camp; and Tom Hourie, Armstrong, and Riel showed up about one hour after Diehl.

There are some boastful assumptions and false claims: "no one but Tom could have done it. Armstrong and Deal [sic] were green horns at the trail, but Tom could follow a trail," or "There were Riel and five other men and Deal [sic] and Armstrong. They did not know Riel, only Tom." Peter Hourie probably did not know if the other two scouts knew Riel or not. Armstrong says he had met Riel when they were in Montana and saw him again in Prince Albert. Diehl also might have seen Riel in Prince Albert or elsewhere. Some of the early writings mention that "they" or "all" recognized Riel. W. J. Carter, living in Prince Albert at the time, writes, "These three men [Armstrong, Diehl, Hourie] were employed by Colonel Irvine in carrying messages to and from General Middleton and all three happened to be at Batoche the day of the big show, and but for the fact that these three men all knew Riel it is probable that he would have made his escape back to Montana with several other leaders."[13]

Hourie writes, "Tom sent Deal [sic] ahead to tell General Middleton that he (Tom) had Riel." This could not be so. When Riel was located, Diehl went off to find a horse for him. When he returned to where he had left Riel and the other two scouts, they were nowhere to be seen so he returned alone to Middleton's camp. He, therefore, could not have been "sent ahead" by anyone.

Peter Hourie, like Armstrong, told his stories of the Resistance with occasional embellishment and with some suspect descriptions. For example, Hourie's account of Captain French's death goes beyond exaggeration. Peter Hourie says French addressed his dying words to Tom after the captain was shot through an upstairs window—"Well, Tom, I'm shot, but never mind; we were the first that came here."[14] Captain French was not alone, nor just with Tom and Armstrong, but with some of his own scouts, and the testimony of one of them suggests that the remark, "Well, Tom, I'm shot," is most unlikely. E. C. Maloney and H. F. Boyce were two of French's scouts who escorted French's body after he was killed. In a letter dated May 1, 1945, Boyce writes, "I was nearby when Capt. French was shot, he fell into Maloney's arms, I was right behind, I think the Captain uttered words indistinctly to Maloney but did not hear them."[15] So, French fell back against Maloney, Boyce was beside Maloney, and French uttered something indistinctly.

A multitude of different "last words" have been attributed to Captain French by different individuals. Anyone shot through the heart would not be capable of making any statement, and the indistinguishable sounds Boyce described were probably the death groans of Captain French and not an address to Tom Hourie or anyone else. Of course, his last words may have been spoken when he entered the house and before he rushed upstairs and was shot, as is recalled by Armstrong. One of French's scouts and a participant in the fight, Harold Rusden, in his recollection, is more convincing: "He fell dead and never spoke a word."[16]

WILLIAM DIEHL'S ACCOUNT

A number of Diehl's activities during the Resistance were described in an article written circa 1932:

> Acting for a forgotten Winnipeg newspaperman [Flinn], representing the Winnipeg *Star* [*Sun*], he scooped the world on that capture of Riel which put an end to the

Riel Rebellion. Being the first to reach General Middleton's camp at Batoche [sic] with the news of the surrender of the rebel leader, he gasped out the great story that Riel was taken. Three newspapermen were attached to the headquarters staff as war correspondents, but two of them were absent from the camp with scouting parties. Only the Winnipeg *Star* [*Sun*] man had remained behind. To him fell the great scoop and he hired William Diehl to gallop his bulletin to the telegraph line at Clarke's [sic] Crossing. Mr. Diehl was paid $80 for the ride. . . . Mr. Diehl had many thrilling days and nights during the two months that he was a scout for General Middleton. He scouted and carried dispatches between Prince Albert, Battleford and the army camps; he rode through rebel lines and camps on venturesome night errands; he recaptured a favorite horse from a rebel camp a few days after it had been stolen from his own ranch; he outran, in a night ride of 16 miles, two enemy half-breeds; but, greatest of all, he was in on the capture of Riel and flashed the news to the outside world.[17]

Diehl, in his own words, describes the capture of Riel in an affidavit sworn on September 30, 1919, in the town of Marcelin, Saskatchewan:

With reference to Louis Riel's capture and a certain extract from Colonel S. B. Steele's book "Forty Years in Canada" chapter XI, page 210, that starting from Gariepy's [Gardepuis'] Crossing, with Bolton's [sic] scouts, Tom Hourey [sic], R. Armstrong and I, we branched off and were riding alongside the river. When we reached within about 3 miles from Batoche, we sighted through the bush five armed men, standing as if they were holding a conference.

One of the party called them in cree [sic] to surrender, and they immediately dropped their arms and marched towards us. When they came within speaking distance, we noticed to our surprise that it was Riel with four guards.

We then turned back towards Middleton's camp, 16 odd miles away, and as we did not have enough horses to carry the party, William Diehl was sent forward on horseback with a half-breed to try and get hold of a few stray horses to carry the party back to camp. In the meantime, and fearing that our errand had not met with success, the rest of the party started for the camp afoot, and when I got back to where I have left them, they were gone. Riding back towards camp, I arrived there just a moment before Riel was brought in to General Middleton's tent. That event took place on May 16th as far as I can remember and two days after the Battle of Batoche.[18]

What prompted Diehl to make this declaration nearly thirty-four years after the event is a mystery. His reference to a certain extract in Steele's book does not provide a motive as Steele's comment was simply: "After the battle at that place [Batoche] Diehl and Armstrong, scouts sent out by Colonel Irvine with dispatches to General Middleton, were two of the three who captured the rebel leader."[19] The declaration may have been intended to support a request for a pension or some other petition.

Diehl's direct style, lacking in self-aggrandizement, contrasts with the presentations of the other two scouts. Some of his revelations do not appear in the Armstrong and Hourie stories. In particular, he reports that one of his companions called out to Riel in Cree. (This would have been Hourie.) Diehl's statement that he was accompanied by one of Riel's companions in his search for stray horses suggests that initially the intention may have been to bring in the entire group, not just Riel. It is interesting to note that he says, "we noticed to our surprise that it was Riel . . . ," implying that all three recognized Riel, not just Tom Hourie. Diehl places Riel's apprehension on May 16 (it occurred on May 15) and also states that Riel was brought in just a moment after he arrived—Riel probably was brought in about fifteen minutes later.

Having made his sworn statement thirty-four years after the event, it is to his credit that he says, "as far as I can remember." However, far more important is his description of Riel's capture recorded by reporters the moment he arrived with the news at Middleton's camp. Recapitulating only the most significant points made by Diehl as reported by the correspondents Flinn, Ham, and the unknown *Toronto Globe* reporter on May 15, 1885 (see Appendix 1): Riel was spotted with three companions; Riel was unarmed (so he was unaware of Riel's concealed pistol) but his companions had shotguns; no effort was made to escape; after a brief conversation, Riel expressed his wish to surrender but was afraid of being shot; he was assured of a fair trial; during the conversation, Riel handed Armstrong a note; Riel was hidden from Boulton's scouts in a coulee while Diehl went searching for a horse; when Diehl returned to where he had left his companions, they were gone so he went on alone to Middleton's camp.

NOTES

INTRODUCTION

1   Howard Angus Kennedy, "Riel's Captors Would Accept No Cash Award," *Saskatoon Phoenix*, May 17, 1926. This article appeared in other newspapers, and under the title "Robert Armstrong: Buffalo Hunter" in *Old & New Furrows: The Story of Rosthern* (Rosthern, SK: Rosthern Historical Society, 1977), 313–17. The story in *Old & New Furrows* was reprinted from the *Saskatchewan Valley News*, December 8, 1943.

2   All quotes attributed to Robert Armstrong that are not cited are from his memoir, printed in Part Two of this book.

CHAPTER ONE: BEFORE ROBERT ARMSTRONG

1   See the introductory paragraph of Armstrong's memoir, page 111 of this book.

2   Ella Melendrez, e-mail message to author, August 17, 2011.

3   Robert Armstrong / Irvin Mudeater should not be confused with another Robert Armstrong, a noted leader of the Wyandots.

4   Ella Melendrez, e-mail message to author, August 17, 2011. A possible candidate for the person whose name was adopted is considered further in the story; see page 36.

5   Census of the United States: 1910 Population, Oklahoma, Ottawa District, Wyandotte Township, Enumeration District 167, sheet 1b, accessed November 15, 2013, www.ancestry.com.

6   Census of Canada, 1901. NWT, District of Saskatchewan, Rosthern, polling sub-division 17, page 19, accessed November 17, 2013, http://www.bac-lac.gc.ca/eng/census/Pages/census.aspx.

7   Census of the United States: 1910 Population, sheet 1b.

8   The Quapaw Agency was located in northeast Oklahoma where the Wyandot reserve was. The agency's agent was the contact between the federal government and tribal members.

9   Census of Manitoba, Saskatchewan and Alberta, 1916. Alberta, District of Calgary East, Enumeration District 12, page 43, accessed February 2, 2011, http://www.bac-lac.gc.ca/eng/census/Pages/census.aspx.

10   Census of the United States: 1940, California, Los Angeles, Ward 55, Enumeration District 60-953, page 6a, accessed November 2013, www.ancestry.com.

11   Various spellings have been used—from Wendat came the English version of Wyandot (sometimes, Wyandott) and the French spelling, Wyandotte. Wyandotte is the spelling used in Oklahoma and Kansas, though Wyandot is commonly used when referring to individuals. Further, when the Wyandots first established a settlement in Kansas, the village (town) was called Wyandotte and so was the county where it was situated. The town later lost that identity as it merged with Kansas City, Kansas; but there still is a Wyandotte County in Kansas. The Wyandots who settled in Oklahoma established a town called Wyandotte in Ottawa County, so presently there is a Wyandotte County in Kansas and a town of Wyandotte in Oklahoma.

12   This cemetery, in a prime location in Kansas City, Kansas, was the source of contention for many decades between developers and the Wyandots of Oklahoma and the Wyandots of Kansas City. It is now listed in the National Register of Historic Sites. Huron Indian Cemetery appears on the sign to the cemetery, but in many written sources the name is just Huron Cemetery. Matthew Mudeater's mother and one of his children, deceased at birth, are buried in the cemetery.

13   William E. Connelley, ed., *The Provisional Government of Nebraska Territory and the Journals of William Walker, Provisional Governor of Nebraska Territory* (Lincoln, NE: The Nebraska State Historical Society, 1899),

234–35, n. 1, accessed November 7, 2013, http://www.archive.org/details/ provisionalgoveroooconn/. William Walker was born in Michigan. He was a well-educated man who was active on behalf of the Wyandots. Walker was chief of the Wyandots while still in Ohio and moved with his people to Kansas during their migration in 1843. In 1853 he was appointed provisional governor of Kansas Territory.

14 Rusha Chaplog, a Wyandot, had enlisted in the Fifth Cavalry during the Civil War. Perhaps a mispronunciation of Rusha by early writers resulted in the name "Russia."

15 Connelley, *Provisional Government*, 237–38.

16 "Huron Cemetery: Wyandotte National Burial Ground," accessed November 7, 2013, http://www.wyandotte-nation.org/culture/history/ cemetery-lists/huron-cemetery/.

17 The year 1812 is inscribed on his cemetery marker and is mentioned in other sources. He belonged to the Big Turtle Clan—but his children belonged to the Porcupine Clan because clan was determined through the matrilineal line.

18 Connelley, *Provisional Government*, 234–35, n. 1. Crawford was captured while attacking a combined force of several tribes and British soldiers during the American Revolutionary War in 1782.

19 1860 Federal Census of Kansas Territory, Wyandott [sic] Township, Wyandott [sic] County, page 3(3) [33?], accessed November 17, 2013, www.ancestry.com. See also 1865 Kansas State Census, Wyandott [sic] Township, Wyandott [sic] County, page number illegible, 474th house enumerated, accessed November 17, 2013, www.ancestry.com.

20 The map can be viewed by choosing culture/history/maps/ at http://www. wyandotte-nation.org/.

21 William G. Cutler, *History of the State of Kansas* (Chicago, IL: A. T. Andreas, 1883), Indian History, Wyandotte County, Part 20, Biographical Sketches Quindaro Township, Frank H. Betton, accessed December 15, 2011, http://www.kancoll.org/books/cutler/.

22 Connelley, *Provisional Government*, 234-235, n.1. Also 1865 Kansas State Census.

23 Cutler, *History*, Indian History, Wyandotte County, The Wyandot Nation, Part 2.

24 Ibid.

25 Connelley, *Provisional Government*, 234–35, n.1.

26 "Passing of a Landmark," *Kansas City Star*, November 17, 1904.

27 William E. Connelley, ed., *Collections of the Kansas State Historical Society*, Vol. 15 (Topeka, KS: Kansas State Historical Society, 1923), 141. A map in volume 15 displays the allotments that were assigned and shows Mudeater's location.

28 U.S. Congress, *Report of the Secretary of the Interior, Being Part of the Message and Documents Communicated to the Two Houses of Congress at the Beginning of the Second Session of the Forty-Second Congress*, W. R. Irwin and O. S. Witherell, "Investigation of Action of Wyandotte Guardians. Wyandotte, Kansas, July 14, 1871. No. 8.—Case of Mathew Mudeater, guardian" (Washington, DC: Government Printing Office, 1871), 621.

29 Ibid.

30 John P. Bowes, *Exiles and Pioneers: Eastern Indians in the Trans-Mississippi West* (Cambridge, UK: Cambridge University Press, 2007), 212.

31 U.S. Congress, House, *Reports of Committees of the House of Representatives. Thirty-Sixth Congress, Second Session, 1860–61* (Washington, DC: Government Printing Office, 1861), 1666–67.

32 Grant W. Harrington, *Historic Spots or Mile-Stones in the Progress of Wyandotte County, Kansas* (Merriam, KS: Mission Press, 1935), 115–16.

33 "1870 Roll," transcribed by Charles Garrad, accessed November 7, 2013, http://www.wyandotte-nation.org/.

34 Powell's report was titled *Wyandot Government: A Short Study of Tribal Society*. This short book is available online at http://www.gutenberg.org/. The photograph of Matthew Mudeater is at the Department of Rare Books and Special Collections at Princeton University Library and can be viewed at http://pudl.princeton.edu/objects/z316q203q/.

35 Bland Cemetery is located on two acres (0.8 ha) of farm land in Ottawa County, Oklahoma, about 2.5 miles (4 km) southeast of Wyandotte.

36 Oklahoma did not become a state until 1907. In the last decade of the nineteenth century, and until 1907, the region of the present-day state was divided into Oklahoma Territory and Indian Territory. The Wyandots were settled in the northeast part of Indian Territory. Annual censuses of the Wyandots provide a record of the Mudeaters for the late nineteenth and early twentieth centuries. (In researching for the writing of this book, the author examined records for 1885–1937.) Just how the names of those not resident there were entered is unclear. The list of names at times was incorrect and incomplete. In 1891, when Florence was only two years old,

for example, she was given an age of eight. In 1892 Irvin is registered as Irvin P. In addition to Florence, an Irvin P. Jr. is inexplicably listed. Since this individual is two years younger than Florence, Cora, not Irvin P. Jr., should have been recorded. For some time, Julia was listed before Cora. Much later, the confusion was corrected and all of Armstrong's children were properly registered—Florence, Cora, Julia, Dawson, and Jane (Myrtle).

37   1934 and 1937 Indian Census Rolls of the Wyandotte reservation.

38   Connelley, *Provisional Government*, 234–35, n.1.

39   Perhaps the earliest official list of the Mudeater family was recorded in 1855 when the Wyandotte reservation was partitioned and allotments made: Mathew [sic], 38; Nancy, 37; Susannah, 14; Dawson, 12; Zalinda [sic], 10; Mary, 8; Irvin, 6; Benjamin, 4; Alfred, 2; and Mathew Jr. [sic], 1. In the 1860 U.S. Federal Census of Kansas Territory, Matthew Mudeater listed his children and their ages: Dawson, 17; (Sindi), 15; Mary, 13; Irvin, 11; Benjamin, 9; Alfred, 7; and Mathew [sic], 5. Susannah, not listed here, was married and enumerated separately with her husband, Frank Betton. The name Sindi most likely refers to Zelinda. In the 1865 Kansas State Census, the same names are repeated, except Peter appears in place of Benjamin. This is not repeated elsewhere and must be an error. Peter may have been Armstrong's second name—in several Indian census entries he is listed as Irvin P. The 1885 Register of Wyandots in Oklahoma gives the following Mudeater children's names and their ages: Dawson, 43; Zalinda [sic], 40; Irvin, 38; Benjamin, 34; Alfred, 31; and Ida, 26.

40   Jeremiah Hubbard, *Forty Years Among the Indians: A Descriptive History of the Long and Busy Life of Jeremiah Hubbard* (Miami, OK: Phelps Printers, 1913), 154.

41   U.S. Congress, House, *The Executive Documents of the House of Representatives for the First Session of the Fiftieth Congress, 1887–88, Report of the Secretary of the Interior,* "Table Giving Names, Positions, Periods of Service, Salaries Per Annum, etc. Cheyenne and Arapaho Agency" (Washington, DC: Government Printing Office, 1889), 410.

42   William C. Barry, "New Fruits in 1879," in *Brief Essays on New Fruits, Ornamental Trees and Plants* (Rochester, NY: Evening Express Paper Co., 1880), 3.

43   Nadine Grant and Della Vineyard, comps., *History of Wyandotte, Oklahoma* (Miami, OK: Timbercreek Ltd., 1987), 10.

44 Connelley, *Provisional Government*, v, vi.

45 *Miami (ok) Daily News-Record*, July 19, 1929. Miami, Oklahoma, is a town near Wyandotte.

46 Census of the United States: 1910 Population, sheet 14a.

47 From Phoenix and California telephone directories.

48 Thomas I. Tullock, "Capt. Robert Neal, Senior and his Wife, Margaret Lear Neal. Their Descendants and Family Connections," *The Granite Monthly* 4, no. 7 (1881): 270. The Wyandot Tribal Roll of 1867 confirms her marriage to an Armstrong: "Armstrong, Mary, wife of Winfield S. [Scott] and daughter of Mathew [sic] Mudeater."

49 1880 U.S. Federal Census of Kansas, Quindaro Township, Wyandotte County, Enumeration District 191, page 34, accessed November 18, 2013, www.ancestry.com.

50 Cutler, *History*, Indian History, Wyandotte County, Part 20, Biographical Sketches, Quindaro Township, Frank H. Betton.

51 "Passing of a Landmark," *Kansas City Star*, November 17, 1904.

52 "Deaths in Kansas City," *Kansas City (mo) Times*, August 23, 1912.

CHAPTER TWO: YOUTH TO 1885

1 Billy Dixon, *Life and Adventures of "Billy" Dixon of Adobe Walls, Texas Panhandle: A Narrative in which is Described Many Things Relating to the Early Southwest, with an Account of the Fight Between Indians and Buffalo Hunters at Adobe Walls, and the Desperate Engagement at Buffalo Wallow, for which Congress Voted the Medal of Honor to the Survivors*, comp. Frederick S. Barde (Guthrie, ok: Co-Operative Publishing Co., 1914), 22. See also Zona A. Withers, *Handbook of Texas Online*, "Withers, Marcus Allen [Mark]," accessed September 20, 2016, http://www.tshaonline.org/handbook/online/articles/fwibc.

2 Kennedy, "Robert Armstrong: Buffalo Hunter," 315.

3 In his memoir, Armstrong reports, in order, joining Union forces during the Civil War, going to Denver, going to school in Ohio, and then his adventure with the Blanchard wagon train. This could not be the correct sequence. The Blanchard episode occurred in August 1864. He relates going to school just after his trip to Denver. However, he registered for the 1865–66 school term and, therefore, if he went to school shortly after his Denver trip as he says, then the Denver trip probably occurred in the spring of 1865. (He

speaks of wintery weather.) In all likelihood, the sequence of events was either Civil War, Blanchard wagon train, Denver trip, school in Ohio; or Blanchard wagon train, Civil War, Denver trip, school in Ohio.

4 Benjamin Capps, *The Great Chiefs*, The Old West Series, rev. (Alexandria, VA: Time-Life Books, 1982), 26.

5 Gregory F. Michno and Susan J. Michno, *Forgotten Fights: Little-Known Raids and Skirmishes on the Frontier, 1823 to 1890* (Missoula, MT: Mountain Press Publishing Co., 2008), 206.

6 W. H. Ryus, *The Second William Penn: A True Account of Incidents that Happened along the Old Santa Fe Trail in the Sixties* (Kansas City, MO: Frank T. Riley Publishing Co., 1913), 165–73. W. H. Ryus was a stage-coach driver on the Santa Fe route who was sometimes called the second William Penn. Chapter 24, "Colonel Moore's Graphic Description of a Fight with Cheyennes," describing the Blanchard disaster, was written by Colonel Milton Moore.

7 Ibid., 171.

8 Information provided by Louise Kiefer, university historian at Baldwin-Wallace University, e-mail to author, March 26, 2010.

9 Cutler, *History*, Indian History, Wyandotte County, Part 20, Biographical Sketches, Quindaro Township, Frank H. Betton.

10 William F. Cody (Buffalo Bill), *True Tales of the Plains* (New York, NY: Cupples & Leon Company, 1908), 68. See also Nellie Snyder Yost, *Buffalo Bill: His Family, Friends, Fame, Failures, and Fortunes* (Chicago, IL: The Swallow Press, 1979), 15.

11 Cody, *True Tales of the Plains*, 68.

12 Daniel Fitzgerald, *Ghost Towns of Kansas: A Traveler's Guide* (Lawrence, KS: University Press of Kansas, 1988), 241, 242.

13 "Ghost Town of Sheridan," accessed June 1, 2014, http://travelwallace-county.com/2014/01/ghost-town-sheridan/.

14 George Armstrong Custer, *My Life on the Plains: Or, Personal Experiences with Indians* (New York, NY: Sheldon & Co., 1874), 47.

15 Ibid., 99–100.

16 Susan K. Salzer, "Medicine Bill Comstock: Saga of the Leatherstocking Scout," accessed November 7, 2013, Historynet.com. According to Salzer, "Comstock was born in Michigan in 1842, the son of a prosperous Michigan lawyer and state legislator."

17 Ibid. Salzer gives the wood merchant's name as H. P. Wyatt. Armstrong's son-in-law, while putting down to paper Armstrong's stories may have erred. "Wyatt" sounds similar to "White."

18 Paul I. Wellman, "Some Famous Kansas Frontier Scouts," *The Kansas Historical Quarterly* 1, no. 4 (1932): 352.

19 "About People," *Pacific Marine Review* 18 (1921): 536.

20 Amos Jay Cummings, "Over the Kansas Plains, A Second Pleasing Incident," *New York Sun*, June 6, 1873, accessed July 28, 2016, http://nyshistoricnewspapers.org/lccn/sn83030272/1873-06-06/ed-1/seq-3/.

21 Paul Howard Carlson, *The Buffalo Soldier Tragedy of 1877* (College Station, TX: Texas A & M University Press, 2003), 23.

22 John Hanner, "Government Response to the Buffalo Hide Trade, 1871–1883," *Journal of Law and Economics* 24, no. 2 (1981): 239–71.

23 Dixon, *Life and Adventures of "Billy" Dixon*, 200, 207.

24 Ibid., 234.

25 Mike Duke Venturino, "The Battle of Adobe Walls, Myth vs. Reality," *Guns Magazine*, June 2005.

26 T. Lindsay Baker and Billy R. Harrison, *Adobe Walls: The History and Archeology of the 1874 Trading Post* (College Station, TX: Texas A & M University Press, 1986), 75. The first part of this book is the result of a comprehensive study of the written documents and literature pertaining to the trading post and the conflict on June 27, 1874. The second part presents the findings of an excavation of the site in the 1970s.

27 Ibid., 79. "Who Was Really There?" (Chapter 4 of Baker and Harrison's study) examines the claims of some who purport to have been at the Adobe Walls fight.

28 Dixon, *Life and Adventures of "Billy" Dixon*, 198.

29 Ryus, *The Second William Penn*, 68.

30 Baker and Harrison, *Adobe Walls*, 75.

31 Baker and Harrison, *Adobe Walls*, 57–58. One participant in the fight later suggested that the owner of the saloon was aware of the impending attack, fired a rifle during the night, and claimed the sound was that of a cracking ridgepole. This apparent ruse was meant to have the men awake rather than asleep when the Indians attacked. If informed sooner, the hunters and others might have fled and left the place more vulnerable to attack.

32 S. C. Gwynne, *Empire of the Summer Moon: Quanah Parker and the Rise and Fall of the Comanches, the Most Powerful Indian Tribe in American History* (New York, NY: Scribner, 2010), 272.

33 In September 1874 Cheyenne warriors attacked the Germain/Germaine (sometimes spelled German) family, killing all except four sisters, whom they took with them. Two were recaptured in November. When Stone Calf surrendered, he arranged for the release of the remaining two girls on February 25, 1875, who were then returned to Darlington Agency (beside Fort Reno) on March 1. Stan Edward Hoig, *Fort Reno and the Indian Territory Frontier* (Fayetteville, AR: University of Arkansas Press, 2005), 32–33.

34 William B. Shillingberg, *Dodge City: The Early Years, 1872–1886* (Norman, OK: The Arthur H. Clark Co., 2009), 149.

35 "The Armstrong Surveying Party," *Leavenworth Daily Commercial,* August 18, 1874.

36 "Restoration of the Monument at the Initial Point of the Public Land Surveys of Oklahoma," *Chronicles of Oklahoma* 3, no. 1 (1925): 82.

37 Gwynne, *Empire of the Summer Moon,* 83.

38 Ibid., 263.

39 "Fort Reno Historical Information: Cheyenne & Arapaho, the Indian Scouts and the Indian Wars," accessed November 4, 2013, http://www.fortreno.org.

40 "Tom Green County Courthouse, San Angelo, Texas," accessed July 22, 2016, http://www.254texascourthouses.net.

41 He may have been involved in these matters in some way, but there is no corroboration that he ever was formally a deputy. Golda Foster, who compiled a list of all area city marshals, special deputies, and, finally, chiefs of police, states that Mudeater (Armstrong) was not among those listed. Golda Foster is the chairman of the Tom Green County Historical Commission. (San Angelo is located in Tom Green County.) Golda Foster, e-mail to author, April 10, 2012.

42 Among the fourteen saloons in San Angelo in 1883 was one called the First and Last Chance Saloon. Jacqueline M. Moore, *Cowboys and Cattle Men: Class and Masculinities on the Texas Frontier, 1865–1900* (New York, NY: New York University Press, 2010), 172.

43 Carlson, *Buffalo Soldier Tragedy,* 126.

44 John R. Cook, *The Border and the Buffalo* (1907; repr., New York, NY: Citadel Press, 1967), 267.

45 The 10th U.S. Cavalry, established at Fort Leavenworth, Kansas, in 1866, was composed of white officers and black recruits. In April 1875 it relocated to Fort Concho, Texas.

46 Charles L. Cooper, "A Thrilling Texas Story," *New-York Daily Tribune*, September 8, 1877, http://chroniclingamerica.loc.gov/lccn/sn83030214/1877-09-08/ed-1/seq-5/.

47 Ibid.

48 Ibid.

49 Carlson, *Buffalo Soldier Tragedy*, 108. Carlson provides the names of all the soldiers and hunters who were on the Staked Plains expedition.

50 Cooper, "A Thrilling Texas Story."

51 Ibid.

52 Cook, *The Border and the Buffalo*, 366–67.

53 From an information plaque at White's gravesite.

54 In the period 1865–68, the U.S. Army established Fort Reno, Fort Phil Kearny, and Fort C. F. Smith to offer protection to travellers along the Bozeman Trail. Numerous attacks by Red Cloud—leader of the Oglala Sioux (Lakota)—and his warriors resulted in the 1868 Treaty of Fort Laramie, whereby the army abandoned these forts, which were destroyed by the Indians soon after their abandonment. Armstrong would have come to this area about a decade after their destruction.

55 R. Michael Wilson, *Outlaw Tales of Wyoming: True Stories of the Cowboy State's Most Infamous Crooks, Culprits, and Cutthroats* (Guilford, CT; Helena, MT: TwoDot Publishers, 2008), 27.

56 "Big Nose George," Wikipedia, accessed October 27, 2013.

57 Burton S. Hill, "Bozeman Trail Trek: The Trabing Trading Post," *Annals of Wyoming: The Wyoming Historical Journal* 36, no. 1 (1964): 55–57.

58 Mark H. Brown, *The Plainsmen of the Yellowstone: A History of the Yellowstone Basin* (Lincoln, NE: University of Nebraska Press, 1961), 406–407.

59 James T. Annin, *They Gazed on the Beartooths*, Vol. 2 (Billings, MT: J. Annin, 1964), 3. The Gilmer and Salisbury Stage Company was a large company that hired many employees to work on its network of routes in the Northwest. Coulson was located about two miles (3.2 km) from where Billings, Montana, is today. Coulson existed only for the period 1877–82 and, apparently, had no schools or churches but plenty of saloons. Billings was

founded in 1882, the year Armstrong left for Canada. Stillwater, Montana, to avoid confusion with Stillwater, Minnesota, was renamed Columbus.

60 Robert H. Lowie, "The Culture-Type of the Plains Indians," in *The North American Indians: A Source Book*, ed., Roger C. Owen et al. (Toronto, ON: The MacMillan Co., 1967), 489.

61 James Willard Schultz, *Blackfeet and Buffalo: Memories of Life among the Indians* (Norman, OK: University of Oklahoma Press, 1981), 37.

62 Joseph Kinsey Howard, *The Strange Empire of Louis Riel* (Toronto, ON: Swan Publishing Co. Ltd., 1970), 300.

63 Ibid., 290.

64 Ella Melendrez, e-mail message to author, August 17, 2011.

65 Frank W. Anderson, *Louis Riel: Patriot and Rebel* [1949?], 326. Typescript, Special Collections, University of Saskatchewan Library, Shortt Collection, FC3217.1 R36A73 1949. Anderson is mistaken about the crime being committed in California. There is a double irony here. Anderson also was convicted of murder and spent fifteen years in a penitentiary. He educated himself in prison and took post-graduate studies when released. He was eventually pardoned by Prime Minister Trudeau and was appointed to the National Parole Board in 1974. Frank Anderson died on April 10, 2008.

66 Ella Melendrez, e-mail message to author, February 6, 2010.

67 Michelle Massine, deputy clerk of District Court, Yellowstone County, e-mail message to author, March 12, 2012. A search of the index of the court's records did not have an entry for Mudeater. Huntley is now a suburb of Billings, Montana.

68 Stanley D. Hanson, "Policing the International Boundary Area in Saskatchewan, 1890–1910," *Saskatchewan History* 19, no. 2 (1966): 62.

69 Walter P. Stewart, *A Photo-Journalist Looks at the Town of Maple Creek, Saskatchewan* (Winnipeg, MB: W. P. Stewart Consultant, 1977), 9.

70 *Qu'Appelle, Footprints to Progress: A History of Qu'Appelle and District* (Qu'Appelle, SK: Qu'Appelle Historical Society, 1980), 9. The man described in this book is identified as L. W. Mulholland. Armstrong calls his companion Lou "Mullholand." There is no absolute proof that these two are the same person, but it would be surprising if it was not so.

71 John Hawkes, *The Story of Saskatchewan and Its People*, Vol. 2 (Chicago, IL, and Regina, SK: S. J. Clarke Publishing Company, 1924), 1012.

72 W. J. Carter, *Forty Years in the North-West*, 1920, Typescript, accessed December 18, 2013, http://folklore.library.ualberta.ca.

1   For a full discussion of First Nations involvement in the events of 1885, see Blair Stonechild and Bill Waiser, *Loyal Till Death: Indians and the North-West Rebellion* (Calgary, AB: Fifth House Publishers, 1997).

2   Carter, *Forty Years in the North-West*.

3   Manon Lamontagne et al., eds., comps., *Voice of the People: Reminiscences of the Prince Albert Settlement's Early Citizens, 1866–1895* (Prince Albert, SK: Prince Albert Historical Society, 1985), 162.

4   Acheson Gosford Irvine, Copy of Official Diary of Lieut.-Col. Irvine (Ottawa: s.n., 1885), accessed October 27, 2013, http://peel.library.ualberta.ca/bibliography.

5   Barry J. Degenstein, "Colonel Irvine's Report," in *The Pursuit of Louis Riel: A Journey Back in Time* (Battleford, SK: B. J. Degenstein, 2008), 714.

6   Samuel Benfield Steele, *Forty Years in Canada: Reminiscences of the Great North-West with Some Account of His Service in South Africa*, ed. Mollie Glenn Niblett (Winnipeg, MB: Russel Lang and Co.; London: Herbert Jenkins Ltd., 1915), 210.

7   Ernest J. Chambers, *The Royal North-West Mounted Police: A Corps History* (Montreal-Ottawa: The Mortimer Press, 1906), 90.

8   A. N. Mowat (Mouat), Diary, MG3 C9, Archives of Manitoba.

9   Desmond Morton, *The Last War Drum: The North West Campaign of 1885* (Toronto, ON: Hakkert, 1972), 94. Writers have used many spellings for the name of this ferry crossing; among those noted are Gariépy, Gariepy, Gardepuis, Guardepuis, Guardapais, Guardeput, Gaurdapuy, GuardePie, and Gurtipee. According to Bill Barry, "Although the family name was Gariépy [the family operating the ferry], they were usually known to their neighbours and customers as Gardepuis or Gardipee." Accordingly, the spelling Gardepuis is used in this book. Bill Barry, *Geographic Names of Saskatchewan* (Regina, SK: People Places Publishing, 2005), 156.

10   George A. Flinn, Memoirs, George A. Flinn fonds, MG3 C13, Archives of Manitoba. A slightly abridged version of this manuscript was published in the *Winnipeg Free Press* on June 1, 1935, as part of the fiftieth anniversary of the 1885 conflict.

11   Douglas W. Light, *Footprints in the Dust* (North Battleford, SK: Turner-Warwick Publications, 1987), 216. Other writers also have combined or confused the roles of the two Houries—Peter, the translator, and his son Tom, the courier and scout. Armstrong is referred to as Middleton's

chief scout in articles written by individuals who interviewed him; this, however, is simply what they were told by Armstrong rather than information obtained from some other objective source.

12 General Sir Frederick Dobson Middleton, *Suppression of the Rebellion in the North West Territories of Canada 1885*, G. H. Needler, ed., University of Toronto Studies: History and Economic Series, 11 (1886; repr., Toronto, ON: University of Toronto Press, 1948), 56.

13 List of Members of the Militia Force lately on Active Service in the North-West, in 1885 claiming to be entitled to "Grants of Land" under the provisions of 48-49 Victoria, Chapter 73, Dominion of Canada, Library and Archives Canada. Copy of document shown to author by Eleanor Peppard.

14 Isabelle Vandal, "Heroines of the 1885 Resistance: Isabelle Branconnier Vandal," accessed May 6, 2012, http://www.metismuseum.ca/.

15 *Winnipeg Daily Times*, May 26, 1885. The newspaper published extracts from his letters to his wife.

16 Desmond Morton and Reginald H. Roy, *Telegrams of the North-West Campaign 1885* (Toronto, ON: The Champlain Society, 1972), 285.

17 As reported in the *Prince Albert Times*, February 12, 1886.

18 Ibid.

19 Ibid.

20 Lewis Redman Ord, Richard Scougall Cassels, and Harold Penryn Rusden, *Reminiscences of a Bungle, by One of the Bunglers, and Two Other Northwest Rebellion Diaries*, ed. R. C. Macleod (1887; repr., Edmonton, AB: University of Alberta Press, 1983), 299.

21 Alexander Laidlaw, *From the St. Lawrence to the North Saskatchewan: Being Some Incidents Connected with the Detachment of "A" Battery, Regt. Canadian Artillery, Who Composed Part of the North West Field Force in the Rebellion of 1885* (Halifax, NS: J. Bowes, 1885), 35. Laidlaw was part of "A" Battery of the Canadian Artillery Regiment.

22 Flinn, Memoirs.

23 Morton and Roy, *Telegrams*, 297.

24 William E. Young, Diary, Edinburgh Square Heritage and Cultural Centre, Caledonia, Ontario.

25 Ibid.

26 Peter Hourie, Reminiscences, NW Rebellion, 1885 veterans, R-E3023, Provincial Archives of Saskatchewan.

27　As reported in Hawkes, *The Story of Saskatchewan*, Vol. 1, 253.

28　A short biography of his life is available in Ruth Wright Millar, "Big Tom Hourie: Saskatchewan's Paul Revere," *Saskatchewan Heroes and Rogues* (Regina, SK: Coteau Books, 2004), 39–55. Commissioner Irvine, in his Diary, mentions Tom Hourie and his courier activities.

29　A lengthier description of Diehl's life can be found in Rose Bonin and Marguerite Grenier, eds., *History of Marcelin and District* (Marcelin, SK: Marcelin Historical Society, 1980), 87–89. Diehl is mentioned several times in Commissioner Irvine's Diary.

30　The *Globe* and *Sun* suggest different times for Diehl's and Riel's arrivals at Middleton's camp. The times prefacing the newspaper articles are the times the notes were written, not the time of the events; nevertheless, they can be used to make a fair estimate of when the events occurred. The *Globe*'s first item suggests Diehl arrived at 1:30 p.m. At 2:30 the reporter writes that Riel and the other scouts had not yet arrived, while his 2:40 dispatch indicates that they were now at camp. Since Diehl, in his affidavit (see Appendix 2: William Diehl's Account), says he arrived ". . . just a moment before Riel . . ." there is something amiss when the *Globe* puts Riel arriving more than an hour later than Diehl. It could be that the reporter had mistaken the times. If he was off by one hour, then his latter two times would align with those Flinn reports: 3:30 and 3:45. Ham, on the other hand, does not indicate the time of his dispatch but makes a clear statement that Riel was brought in at 3:30, thus giving credence to Flinn's times.

31　"Full Details of the Capture of Riel," *Toronto Globe*, May 18, 1885. The newspaper informs that the report is "by our own reporter." Joseph Howard, who casts Hourie as the principal scout, appears to be alone in saying that Riel received the note from Hourie. His statement, made sixty-five years after the event, cannot negate the first-hand account presented at the time of the event by an independent participant (Diehl). Howard, *The Strange Empire*, 411.

32　"Captured," *Winnipeg Sun*, May 16, 1885.

33　Millar argues that Riel probably surrendered to Hourie rather than to Armstrong because Tom knew Riel: Millar, "Big Tom Hourie," 49. Hourie most likely had seen Riel at some prior time, but that is not a proof that the other two scouts had not. Further, Armstrong claims he met Riel in Montana.

34 Roderick George MacBeth, *The Romance of Western Canada* (Toronto, ON: William Briggs, 1918), 216.

35 Kennedy, "Riel's Captors Would Accept No Cash Award."

36 Flinn, Memoirs.

37 Howard, *The Strange Empire*, 411.

38 Irvine, Diary. Irvine recorded the weather in Prince Albert, but it would have been similar where Riel was found.

39 "Rebellion Veterans Reunited Recount Days of Adventure," July 17, 1935, newspaper clipping, Alberta Folklore and Local History Collection, University of Alberta Libraries, accessed December 18, 2013. http://folklore. library.ualberta.ca. The newspaper from which the clipping was taken is not identified, but it most likely was a Calgary paper.

    Presumably the phaeton was brought to camp by Tom Hourie. Peter Hourie relates how, after the end of the fighting at Batoche, "my son Tom had gone over to the stable there, and found a horse and buggy. He hitched the horse to the phaeton and took them to camp." Hourie, Reminiscences.

40 Davin, founder of the *Regina Leader*, was a Member of Parliament for Assiniboia West, 1887–1900.

41 Kennedy, "Riel's Captors Would Accept No Cash Award."

42 Morton and Roy, *Telegrams*, 298.

43 Kennedy, "Robert Armstrong: Buffalo Hunter," 313–14.

44 Canada, Parliament, Office of the Auditor General, "Expenditure Under Appropriation of $2,300,000 to Defray Expenses and Losses Arising Out of Troubles in the North-West Territories, from 1st July 1885 to 15th March, 1886," 1886 *Sessional Paper*, no. 50:12.

45 Medallions were handed out to the militia and civilians who participated in the 1885 campaign: Hugh A. Halliday, "Medals for the Volunteers: Queen Victoria Honours the Victors of the North-West Rebellion," *The Beaver* (June–July 1997): 4–7.

46 Charlotte Gordon, "Mr. Robert Armstrong—the Captor of Louis Riel," *Western Home Monthly* (May 1923): 16.

47 The village of Batoche was named after François Xavier Letendre who was commonly called "Batoche." (François Xavier Letendre dit Batoche.) In his memoir, Armstrong may have confused Batoche, the man, with Bremner when he mentions the compensation that was paid for stolen furs.

48 Ord et al., *Reminiscences of a Bungle,* 71. Later, Middleton "appropriated" the furs belonging to a Métis named Charles Bremner. When hostilities in the Northwest were over, Middleton was honoured as a hero. However, Bremner, determined to recover his losses for that theft, took his case to Parliament, where a public enquiry disgraced Middleton, and he left Canada to spend the rest of his years in Great Britain. "Middleton, Sir Frederick Dobson" in *Dictionary of Canadian Biography,* accessed September 29, 2016, http://www.biographi.ca/en/bio/middleton_frederick_dobson_12E.html.

49 Irvine, Diary, May 19, 20, 21.

50 *Prince Albert Times,* June 5, 1885.

51 Charles A. Boulton, *Reminiscences of the North-West Rebellions: With a Record of the Raising of Her Majesty's 100th Regiment in Canada, and a Chapter on Canadian Social and Political Life* (Toronto, ON: Grip Printing and Publishing Co., 1886), 372; Ord et al., *Reminiscences of a Bungle,* 52; Steele, *Forty Years in Canada,* 227–28.

52 Boulton, *Reminiscences,* 370.

53 Steele, *Forty Years in Canada,* 227–28.

54 Quoted in Sarah Carter, *Capturing Women: The Manipulation of Cultural Imagery in Canada's Prairie West* (Montreal, QC; Kingston, ON: McGill-Queen's University Press, 1997), 72.

55 Morton and Roy, *Telegrams,* 342, 346.

56 When Riel was apprehended, he and his companions were without horses. It is doubtful that Armstrong would have known whose horse he had seized.

57 Hourie, Reminiscences.

58 Ord et al., *Reminiscences of a Bungle,* 48.

59 Light, *Footprints in the Dust,* 442–43.

60 Light, *Footprints in the Dust,* 505.

61 Armstrong, in his memoir, reversed the sequence of events—he mentions finding the hostages first and then going to Beaver River.

62 Morton and Roy, *Telegrams,* 354.

63 W. J. McLean, "Tragic Events at Frog Lake and Fort Pitt During the North West Rebellion," *Manitoba Pageant* 18, no. 3 (Spring 1973), accessed November 8, 2013, http://mhs.mb.ca/docs/pageant/18/tragicevents5.shtml.

64 Gordon, "Mr. Robert Armstrong," 32.

65 McLean, "Tragic Events."

66 Thomas Bland Strange, *Gunner Jingo's Jubilee* (London, UK: Remington and Company, 1893), accessed November 8, 2013, https://archive.org/stream/gunnerjingosjubioostra#page/n7/mode/2up.

67 Gordon, "Mr. Robert Armstrong," 32.

68 Ibid., 32.

CHAPTER FOUR: 1885 TO 1940

1 In McPhillips' directory of 1888, Armstrong is listed as a painter. *McPhillips' Alphabetical and Business Directory of the District of Saskatchewan, N.W.T., Together with Brief Historical Sketches of Prince Albert, Battleford and the Other Settlements in the District* (Qu'Appelle, N.W.T.: n.a., 1888), 71.

2 Letter to Armstrong's daughter, Myrtle Jane Kroeker, then living in Rosthern, Saskatchewan. She had made an enquiry regarding the naturalization of her father in August 1941. Letter provided by Ella Melendrez in 2013.

3 "Man Who Captured Riel Seeks Old Age Pension, But He May Not Get It," *Edmonton Journal*, October 25, 1929.

4 Westmount in *Old & New Furrows: The Story of Rosthern* (Rosthern, SK: Rosthern Historical Society, 1977), 313. Westmeath in family notes.

5 Ibid., 313. As reported by Mrs. Julia Wheeler, daughter of Robert Armstrong and Adeline Burke.

6 Single handwritten sheet of paper dated 1973; writer's identity illegible, but with this introduction: "from memory as told—by Mrs. Armstrong and to my own personal knowledge." Copy shown to author by Eleanor (Wheeler) Peppard.

7 Census of Canada, 1891, NWT, District No. 200 Saskatchewan, S. District Prince Albert, page 15, accessed October 22, 2008, http://www.bac-lac.gc.ca/eng/census/Pages/census.aspx. The enumeration occurred on April 24, 1891. The ages given for Robert and Adeline, 30 and 24 respectively, are more than ten years below what they should be. Ages provided in later censuses are more accurate but still vary from one to another.

8 *Old & New Furrows*, 594.

9 Information provided by Ella Melendrez. The 1901 census includes the same birthdays as recorded in 1891 for the family members but has Florence born on April 2, 1890, a mistake made at the time of enumeration.

10   Information provided by Trevor Wheeler, great-grandson of Robert Armstrong. His grandfather was Percy Wheeler, who married Armstrong's daughter, Julia.

11   Single handwritten sheet of paper dated 1973; writer's identity illegible, but with this introduction: "from memory as told—by Mrs. Armstrong and to my own personal knowledge." Copy shown to the author by Eleanor (Wheeler) Peppard.

12   "About Land Records," Oklahoma Historical Society, accessed October 27, 2013, http://www.okhistory.org/research/land.

13   The map can be seen at http://www.wyandotte-nation.org/; choose culture/history/maps/1888-reservation/.

14   Census of Manitoba, Saskatchewan and Alberta, 1906, Saskatchewan, District 16, Sub-district 15, page 20, accessed November 19, 2013, http://www.bac-lac.gc.ca/eng/census/Pages/census.aspx. The census confirms that Cora and Florence had gone with Armstrong. Listed as living in the house of Percy Wheeler are Adeline Armstrong, boarder, and only three of her children, Julia, Myrtle, and Dawson.

15   Conversation with Ella Melendrez, June 19, 2013.

16   Census of the United States: 1910 Population, sheet 1a, 1b.

17   From the Calgary Henderson's Directories.

18   Ibid. In 1912–1913, Cora and her husband and son lived on 1216 5 St. E. In 1914, when Armstrong joined them, they were at 2015-7 Ave. E. Subsequently, their addresses were: 1916, 2215-15a St. E.; 1917, 2207-15a St. E.; 1918–1919, no data; 1920–1921, 1328-10 Ave. E; 1922–1925, 1440-11 Ave. E.; 1926, no data; 1927–1929, 1013-8 Ave E.; 1930–1933, 1328-10 Ave. E.; and 1934, 1208-10 Ave. E. Though Armstrong, Cora, and Irven had departed for California in 1939, Richard Humphrey continued living at 1208-10 Ave. E. into the 1950s.

19   Census of Canada, 1921, Province of Alberta, District 3, Calgary E., Enumeration Sub-district 28, page 23, accessed November 20, 2013, www.ancestry.com

20   Gordon, "Mr. Robert Armstrong," 16.

21   Ibid., 16.

22   Ibid., 36.

23   "Jubilee, Historical Pageant and Stampede Parade," *Calgary Daily Herald*, July 4, 1925. Writing about the 1925 exhibition in the November 26, 1959, issue of the *Western Producer*, Frank W. Anderson quotes Bert Mosley, an

old-timer from the Buffalo Hills: "Bobby Armstrong, one of the fellows who captured Riel, was guest of honor."

24 William McCartney Davidson, *Louis Riel, 1844–1885: A Biography* (Calgary, AB: Albertan Publishing Co., 1955), 185–86.

25 Kennedy, "Riel's Captors Would Accept No Cash Award."

26 *Miami (*OK*) Daily News-Record*, July 19, 21, 1929.

27 "Man Who Captured Riel Seeks Old Age Pension."

28 "Rebellion Veterans Reunited."

29 Manifest, Port of Eastport, Idaho, June 27, 1937.

30 Census of the United States: 1930, Missouri, Jasper County, Joplin, Enumeration District 49-6, sheet 3A; Index to Register of Voters, 1934. California, Los Angeles City, Precinct no. 524. The 1930 census has the couple living on East Ninth Street in Joplin and the 1934 voters list locates them at 931 Bixel Street, Los Angeles.

31 The 1940 voters' list has Richard Humphrey living alone in his Calgary home.

32 Census of the United States: 1940, page 6a.

33 Remarks entered at the back of her border entry card.

34 Conversation with Ella Melendrez, June 19, 2013.

35 Besides being an activity centre, the Memorial Building houses an archive and library. One of the former directors of the centre was Judy Lalonde—a granddaughter of Florence Armstrong, that is, Armstrong's great-granddaughter. Armstrong's grandson, Irven, reportedly died in a motorcycle accident on July 9, 1966. Though Cora moved to California in 1939 without her husband, there are photos of her taken in Calgary in 1943 and 1948. It is not clear whether she had moved back for a few years after Armstrong's death, or those photos were taken during visits to Calgary. Cora died in Los Angeles on July 1, 1984, but she was buried in Calgary. Richard Humphrey spent his last years in Vancouver.

36 Middleton, *Suppression of the Rebellion*, 56.

37 Degenstein, "Colonel Irvine's Report," 714.

38 Flinn, Memoirs.

39 Kennedy, "Riel's Captors Would Accept No Cash Award."

40 *Old & New Furrows*, 315.

41 Gordon, "Mr. Robert Armstrong," 16.

PREFACE TO ARMSTRONG'S MEMOIR

1 Kennedy, "Riel's Captors Would Accept No Cash Award"; Gordon, "Mr. Robert Armstrong."

APPENDIX 1

1 Morton and Roy, *Telegrams*, 288.

2 Ibid., 297.

3 Canada, Parliament, "Report Upon the Suppression of the Rebellion in the North-West Territories, and Matters in Connection therewith, in 1885," 1886 *Sessional Report*, no. 6. Appendix 1C: 33.

4 Hourie, Reminiscences.

5 "Rebellion Veterans Reunited."

6 Middleton, *Suppression of the Rebellion*, 56.

7 Charles Pelham Mulvaney, *The History of the North-West Rebellion of 1885* (Toronto: A. H. Hovey & Co., 1885), 317.

8 *Winnipeg Sun*, May 16, 1885.

9 Flinn, Memoirs.

10 *Winnipeg Sun*, May 16, 1885.

11 At that time, the *Regina Leader* was a weekly paper. The May 19 issue was the first to appear after Riel's capture.

12 "Full Details of the Capture of Riel," *Toronto Globe*, May 18, 1885.

13 Mulvaney, *The History of the North-West Rebellion*), 310, 316–17; Graeme Mercer Adam, *The Canadian North-West: Its History and Its Troubles, from the Early Days of the Fur-Trade to the Era of the Railway and the Settler; with Incidents of Travel in the Region, and the Narrative of Three Insurrections* (Toronto, ON: Rose Publishing Company, 1885), 365–66.

14 Alexander Begg, *History of The North-West*, Vol. 3 (Toronto, ON: Rose Publishing Company, 1885), 231. The report referred to at the end of the quote is General Middleton's—in a later account, Middleton does mention Diehl's name.

15 Ord et al., *Reminiscences of a Bungle*, 49–50.

16 See Roderick George MacBeth's, *The Making of the Canadian West: Being the Reminiscences of an Eye-Witness* (Toronto, ON: William Briggs, 1898), 187; *The Romance of Western Canada*, 216; and *Policing the Plains: Being the Real-Life Record of the Famous Royal North-West Mounted Police* (Toronto,

ON: Musson, 1931), 118. In this latter book, MacBeth responds to claims of inactivity by the NWMP during the 1885 conflict.

17 MacBeth, *The Romance of Western Canada*, 216.

18 MacBeth, *Policing the Plains*, 118.

19 A. L. Haydon, *The Riders of the Plains: A Record of the Royal North-West Mounted Police of Canada, 1873–1910* (London, UK: Andrew Melrose; Toronto, ON: Copp Clark, 1910), 153.

20 Boulton, *Reminiscences*, 298–99.

21 Ibid.

22 Flinn, Memoirs.

23 Gordon, "Mr. Robert Armstrong," 30; Davidson, *Louis Riel*, 184.

24 Richard Carney Laurie, *Reminiscences of Early Days in Battleford and with Middleton's Column* (Battleford, SK: *Saskatchewan Herald*, 1935), 63–64. Laurie was a surveyor who in 1903 took over the *Saskatchewan Herald*, a paper published in Battleford by his father.

25 Peter Hourie, Middleton's interpreter, states that he witnessed the arrival of Riel and his captors: ". . . we see Tom and Armstrong walking, leading the horses, with Riel between them." Recorded in Hawkes, *The Story of Saskatchewan*, Vol. 1, 256.

26 Donald George McLean, *1885: Metis Rebellion or Government Conspiracy?* (Winnipeg, MB: Pemmican Publications Inc., 1985), 117.

27 Hugh S. Nelson, *Four Months Under Arms: A Reminiscence of Events Prior to and During the Second Riel Rebellion* (Nelson, BC: *Nelson Daily News*, 1940), 16.

28 John G. Donkin, *Trooper and Redskin in the Far North-West: Recollections of Life in the North-West Mounted Police, Canada, 1884–1888* (London: Sampson Low, Marston, Searle, and Rivington, 1889), 144.

29 Steele, *Forty Years in Canada*, 210.

30 Norman Fergus Black, *History of Saskatchewan and the North West Territories*, Vol. 2 (Regina, SK: Saskatchewan Historical Company, 1913), 549.

31 Hawkes, *The Story of Saskatchewan*, Vol. 1, 254–56.

32 John Peter Turner, *The North-West Mounted Police, 1873–1893*, vol. 2 (Ottawa, ON: King's Printer, 1950), 188–89.

33 George Francis Gillman Stanley, *The Birth of Western Canada: A History of the Riel Rebellions* (1936; repr., Toronto, ON: University of Toronto Press, 1978), 372; *Louis Riel* (Toronto, ON: The Ryerson Press, 1963), 339.

34 Howard, *The Strange Empire*, 411. Unfortunately, Howard died before including citations in his book, thus making his sources unknown. He, alone, suggests that Riel handed his note to Hourie. Even Peter Hourie does not make that claim.

35 Edmund Boyd Osler, *The Man Who Had to Hang: Louis Riel* (Toronto, ON: Longmans, Green, and Co., 1961), 289–91.

36 Anderson, *Louis Riel*, 325–26.

37 Frank W. Anderson, *Riel's Saskatchewan Rebellion* (Humboldt, SK: Gopher Books, 1999), 80.

38 Maggie Siggins, *Riel: A Life of Revolution* (Toronto, ON: HarperCollins Publishers Ltd., 1994), 409.

39 Light, *Footprints in the Dust*, 458. More accurately, Riel was not escorted by those three scouts to Middleton's tent, only by Armstrong and Hourie.

40 Millar, "Big Tom Hourie," 48–49.

APPENDIX 2

1 The author says that research for his book was done mainly in 1926–1928, but the information from interviews was mostly collected earlier. He also mentions that Armstrong was still alive in 1927, so that may be a possible date of the interview. Davidson, *Louis Riel*, Foreword, 184–86.

2 "Rebellion Veterans Reunited."

3 Gordon, "Mr. Robert Armstrong," 16, 30, 32, 36. Unfortunately, the magazine blundered and overlaid her description of the initial stage of Riel's arrest with some advertisements. Future issues did not carry a correction.

4 Kennedy, "Robert Armstrong: Buffalo Hunter," 315–16.

5 Davidson, *Louis Riel*, 184–86. Davidson interviewed a host of participants from both sides of the 1885 conflict.

6 "Rebellion Veterans Reunited."

7 Ibid.

8 Haydon, *The Riders of the Plains*, 153. Haydon's book was published in 1910, quite some time before Armstrong wrote his memoir or gave his interviews. It is not known how Haydon learned that Riel was provided with a horse.

9 Gordon, "Mr. Robert Armstrong," 30, 16.

10   The meaning of "but see there is another loaded" is unclear and is omitted in Hawkes's reprinting of Peter Hourie's account. Tom might have been requesting confirmation that Riel had no other concealed pistol. However, this phrase is not included in Tom's quoted response to Armstrong: "Keep it."

11   The addition of "this probably refers to Major Boulton's scouts" in parenthesis suggests that the individual who typed Peter Hourie's narrative, or someone else, made this comment. Hawkes replaces this phrase with the more probable: "this probably refers to the reward." The incomplete sentence about the scouts letting them go free seems to refer to the episode when the captors of Riel encountered Boulton's scouts. The enclosure of "Tom" and "Peter Hourie" in parentheses in the following sentences also appears to be the work of someone other than Peter Hourie.

12   Hourie, Reminiscences.

13   Carter, *Forty Years in the North-West*.

14   Hawkes, *The Story of Saskatchewan*, 258.

15   H. F. Boyce, Correspondence, NW Rebellion, 1885 veterans. SHS 160, Provincial Archives of Saskatchewan. In an August 7, 1945, letter, Boyce repeated his testimony.

16   Ord et al., *Reminiscences of a Bungle*, 288.

17   William Diehl, Affidavit, Box 32, Bill Smiley Archive, Prince Albert Historical Society. This is a two-page typescript (c. 1932). See also William Diehl, "Aided in Riel's Capture, William Diehl, 85, Dies," Biog., Clippings, Provincial Archives of Saskatchewan. The latter item, a two-page transcription from a newspaper announcement of Diehl's death (1936), reproduces much of the c. 1932 article. Both include Diehl's 1919 affidavit. (See next note.)

18   William Diehl, William Diehl Affidavit, MG3 C16, Archives of Manitoba. A nearly identical document is located in Box 32, Bill Smiley Archives, Prince Albert Historical Society (per previous note). The Prince Albert document might be a draft for the Manitoba one. They are nearly identical except, strangely, in one case the date of the Riel's capture is May 14 (Prince Albert), in the other May 16 (Winnipeg)—May 15 is the correct date.

19   Steele, *Forty Years in Canada*, 210.

BIBLIOGRAPHY

The following bibliography includes not only the sources cited in this book but also some titles that were important to the author while conducting research.

1860 Federal Census of Kansas Territory. Wyandott [sic] Township. Wyandott [sic] County.

1865 Kansas State Census. Wyandott [sic] Township. Wyandott [sic] County.

1880 U.S. Federal Census of Kansas. Quindaro Township. Wyandotte County. Enumeration District 191.

"About Land Records." Oklahoma Historical Society. Accessed October 27, 2013. http://www.okhistory.org/research/land.

"About People." *Pacific Marine Review* 18 (1921): 536. Accessed November 4, 2013. https://archive.org/details/pacificmarinerev1821paci.

Abrams, Gary William David. *Prince Albert: The First Century, 1866–1966.* Saskatoon, SK: The Modern Press, 1966.

Adam, Graeme Mercer. *The Canadian North-West: Its History and Its Troubles, from the Early Days of the Fur-Trade to the Era of the Railway and the Settler; with Incidents of Travel in the Region, and the Narrative of Three Insurrections.* Toronto, ON: Rose Publishing Company, 1885.

Anderson, Frank W. *Louis Riel: Patriot and Rebel* [1949?]. Typescript. Special Collections. University of Saskatchewan Library. Shortt Collection. FC3217.1 R36A73 1949.

——. *Riel's Saskatchewan Rebellion.* Humboldt, SK: Gopher Books, 1999.

Annin, James T. *They Gazed on the Beartooths*, Vol. 2. Billings, MT: J. Annin, 1964.

Arora, Ved Parkash, comp. *Louis Riel: A Bibliography*. Regina, SK: Provincial Library, Bibliographic Services, 1972.

Asfar, Dan, and Tim Chodan. *Louis Riel*. Edmonton, AB: Folklore Publishing Ltd., 2003.

Atkin, Ronald. *Maintain the Right: The Early History of the North West Mounted Police, 1873–1900*. London, UK: Macmillan, 1973.

Baker, T. Lindsay, and Billy R. Harrison. *Adobe Walls: The History and Archeology of the 1874 Trading Post*. College Station, TX: Texas A & M University Press, 1986.

Barnholden, Michael, trans. *Gabriel Dumont Speaks*. Vancouver, BC: Talonbooks, 1993.

Barry, Bill. *Geographic Names of Saskatchewan*. Regina, SK: People Places Publishing, 2005.

Barry, William C. "New Fruits in 1879." In *Brief Essays on New Fruits, Ornamental Trees and Plants*. Rochester, NY: Evening Express Paper Co., 1880. Accessed November 27, 2013, https://babel.hathitrust.org/cgi/pt?id=hvd.32044103113726;view=1up;seq=1.

Beal, Bob, and Rod Macleod. *Prairie Fire: The 1885 North-West Rebellion*. Edmonton, AB: Hurtig, 1984.

Begg, Alexander. *History of the North-West*. Vol. 3. Toronto, ON: Rose Publishing Company, 1895.

Black, Norman Fergus. *History of Saskatchewan and the North West Territories*, 2 Vols. Regina, SK: Saskatchewan Historical Company, 1913.

Bonin, Rose, and Marguerite Grenier, eds. *History of Marcelin and District*. Marcelin, SK: Marcelin Historical Society, 1980.

Boulton, Charles A. *I Fought Riel: A Military Memoir*. Edited by Heather Robertson. Toronto, ON: James Lorimer and Co., 1985.

——. *Reminiscences of the North-West Rebellions: With a Record of the Raising of Her Majesty's 100th Regiment in Canada, and a Chapter on Canadian Social and Political Life*. Toronto, ON: Grip Printing and Publishing Co., 1886.

Bowes, John P. *Exiles and Pioneers: Eastern Indians in the Trans-Mississippi West*. Cambridge, UK: Cambridge University Press, 2007.

Boyce, H. F. Correspondence. NW Rebellion, 1885 veterans. SHS 160. Provincial Archives of Saskatchewan.

Brown, Mark H. *The Plainsmen of the Yellowstone: A History of the Yellowstone Basin*. Lincoln, NE: University of Nebraska Press, 1961.

Canada. Parliament. "Report Upon the Suppression of the Rebellion in the North-West Territories, and Matters in Connection therewith, in 1885." 1886 *Sessional Report*, no. 6. Appendix 1C: 27–37.

——. 1886 *Sessional Paper*, no. 43:120.

——.1886 *Sessional Paper*, no. 45c:5-6.

Canada. Parliament. Office of the Auditor General. "Expenditure Under Appropriation of $2,300,000 to Defray Expenses and Losses Arising Out of Troubles in the North-West Territories, from 1st July 1885 to 15th March, 1886." 1886 *Sessional Paper*, no. 50:12.

Capps, Benjamin. *The Great Chiefs*. The Old West Series, rev. Alexandria, VA: Time-Life Books, 1982.

Carlson, Paul Howard. *The Buffalo Soldier Tragedy of 1877*. College Station, TX: Texas A & M University Press, 2003.

Carter, Sarah. *Capturing Women: The Manipulation of Cultural Imagery in Canada's Prairie West*. Montreal, QC; Kingston, ON: McGill-Queen's University Press, 1997.

Carter, W. J. *Forty Years in the North-West*. 1920. Typescript. Accessed December 18, 2013. http://folklore.library.ualberta.ca.

Census of Canada, 1891. NWT. District No. 200 Saskatchewan. S. District Prince Albert.

Census of Canada, 1901. NWT. District of Saskatchewan. Rosthern. Polling sub-division 17.

Census of Canada, 1921. Province of Alberta. District 3. Calgary E. Enumeration Sub-district 28.

Census of Manitoba, Saskatchewan and Alberta, 1906. Saskatchewan. District 16. Sub-district 15.

Census of Manitoba, Saskatchewan and Alberta, 1916. Alberta. District of Calgary East. Enumeration District 12.

Census of Manitoba, Saskatchewan and Alberta, 1916. Saskatchewan. Prince Albert. District 25. Enumeration District 9.

Census of the United States: 1910 Population. Oklahoma. Ottawa District. Wyandotte Township. Enumeration District 167.

Census of the United States: 1930. Missouri. Jasper County. Joplin. Enumeration District 49-6.

Census of the United States: 1940. California. Los Angeles. Ward 55. Enumeration District 60-953.

Chambers, Ernest J. *The Royal North-West Mounted Police: A Corps History.* Montreal-Ottawa: The Mortimer Press, 1906.

Charlebois, Peter. *The Life of Louis Riel in Pictures.* Rev. ed. Toronto, ON: NC Press, 1978.

Clark, W. Leland. "Assignment: 'The 1885 Rebellion.'" Manitoba Pageant 23, no. 2 (1978). Accessed January 22, 2013. http://mhs.mb.ca/docs/pageant.

Cody, William F. (Buffalo Bill). *True Tales of the Plains.* New York, NY: Cupples & Leon Company, 1908.

——. "Hunting Buffalo to Feed the Railroad Builders." *America: Great Crises in Our History Told by Its Makers.* Vol. 9. Kansas City, MO: Veterans of Foreign Wars of the United States, 1925. Accessed May 19, 2013. http://www.unz.org/Pub/VFW-1925v09-00043.

Connelley, William E., ed. *The Provisional Government of Nebraska Territory and the Journals of William Walker, Provisional Governor of Nebraska Territory.* Lincoln, NE: The Nebraska State Historical Society, 1899. Accessed November 7, 2013. http://www.archive.org/details/provisionalgoveroooconn/.

——. *Collections of the Kansas State Historical Society.* Vol. 15. Topeka, KS: Kansas State Historical Society, 1923.

Cook, John R. *The Border and the Buffalo.* 1907. Reprint. New York, NY: Citadel Press, 1967.

Crissey, Forrest. *The Young Newspaper Scout: An Interesting Narrative of a Boy's Adventures in the Northwest During the Riel Rebellion.* Chicago, IL: W. B. Conkey, 1895.

Crutchfield, James Andrew. *The Santa Fe Trail.* Plano, TX: Republic of Texas Press, 1996.

Custer, George Armstrong. *My Life on the Plains: Or, Personal Experiences with Indians.* New York, NY: Sheldon & Co., 1874. Accessed March 27, 2014. https://archive.org/details/my_life_on_plains_1106_librivox.

Cutler, William G. *History of the State of Kansas.* Chicago, IL: A. T. Andreas, 1883. Accessed October 27, 2013. http://www.kancoll.org/books/cutler/.

Davidson, William McCartney. *Louis Riel, 1844–1885: A Biography.* Calgary, AB: Albertan Publishing Co., 1955.

Degenstein, Barry J. "Colonel Irvine's Report." In *The Pursuit of Louis Riel: A Journey Back in Time*. Battleford, SK: B. J. Degenstein, 2008.

Diehl, William. William Diehl Affidavit. MG3 C16. Archives of Manitoba.

——. Affidavit. Box 32. Bill Smiley Archives. Prince Albert Historical Society.

——. "Aided in Riel's Capture, William Diehl, 85, Dies." Biog. Clippings. Provincial Archives of Saskatchewan.

Dixon, Billy. *Life and Adventures of "Billy" Dixon, of Adobe Walls, Texas Panhandle: A Narrative in which is Described Many Things Relating to the Early Southwest, with an Account of the Fights Between Indians and Buffalo Hunters at Adobe Walls, and the Desperate Engagement at Buffalo Wallow, for which Congress Voted the Medal of Honor to the Survivors*. Compiled by Frederick S. Barde. Guthrie, OK: Co-Operative Publishing Co., 1914.

Donkin, John G. *Trooper and Redskin in the Far North-West: Recollections of Life in the North-West Mounted Police, Canada, 1884–1888*. London, UK: Sampson Low, Marston, Searle, and Rivington, 1889.

Dumont, Gabriel. *Gabriel Dumont: Memoirs. The Memoirs as Dictated by Gabriel Dumont and Gabriel Dumont's Story*. Edited by Denis Combet. Translated by Lise Gaboury-Diallo. Saint-Boniface, MB: Les Éditions du Blé, 2006.

Dunn, Jack F. *The Alberta Field Force of 1885*. Calgary, AB: Jack Dunn, 1994.

Fitzgerald, Daniel. *Ghost Towns of Kansas: A Traveler's Guide*. Lawrence, KS: University Press of Kansas, 1988.

Flinn, George A. Memoirs. George A. Flinn fonds. MG3 C13. Archives of Manitoba.

"Fort Reno Historical Information: Cheyenne & Arapaho, the Indian Scouts, and the Indian Wars." Accessed November 4, 2013. http://www.fortreno.org.

Gordon, Charlotte. "Mr. Robert Armstrong—the Captor of Louis Riel." *Western Home Monthly*, May (1923).

Grant, Nadine, and Della Vineyard, comps. *History of Wyandotte, Oklahoma*. Miami, OK: Timbercreek Ltd., 1987.

Grinnell, George Bird. *The Fighting Cheyennes*. Norman, OK: University of Oklahoma Press, 1956.

Gwynne, S. C. *Empire of the Summer Moon: Quanah Parker and the Rise and Fall of the Comanches, the Most Powerful Indian Tribe in American History*. New York, NY: Scribner, 2010.

Halliday, Hugh A. "Medals for the Volunteers: Queen Victoria Honours the Victors of the North-West Rebellion." *The Beaver* (June–July 1997): 4–7.

Ham, George Henry. *Reminiscences of a Raconteur, Between the '40s and the '20s*. Toronto, ON: Musson Book Co. Ltd., 1921.

Hamilton, Z. M. Correspondence. NW Rebellion, 1885 veterans. SHS 160. Provincial Archives of Saskatchewan.

Hanson, Stanley D. "Policing the International Boundary Area in Saskatchewan, 1890–1910." *Saskatchewan History* 19, no. 2 (1966): 61–63.

Hanner, John. "Government Response to the Buffalo Hide Trade, 1871–1883." *Journal of Law and Economics* 24, no. 2 (1981): 239–71. Accessed November 5, 2013. http://econpapers.repec.org.

Harrington, Grant W. *Historic Spots or Mile-Stones in the Progress of Wyandotte County, Kansas*. Merriam, KS: Mission Press, 1935.

Haultain, Theodore Arnold. *A History of Riel's Second Rebellion and How It Was Quelled*. Toronto, ON: Grip Printing and Publishing Co., 1885.

Hawkes, John. *The Story of Saskatchewan and Its People*. 3 Vols. Chicago, IL, and Regina, SK: S. J. Clarke Publishing Company, 1924.

Haydon, A. L. *The Riders of the Plains: A Record of the Royal North-West Mounted Police of Canada, 1873–1910*. London, UK: Andrew Melrose; Toronto, ON: Copp Clark, 1910.

Hill, Burton S. "Bozeman Trail Trek: The Trabing Trading Post." *Annals of Wyoming: The Wyoming Historical Journal* 36, no. 1 (1964): 55–56. Accessed October 27, 2013. https://archive.org/stream/annalsofwyom36121964wyom#page/n63/mode/2up.

Hoig, Stan Edward. *Fort Reno and the Indian Territory Frontier*. Fayetteville, AR: University of Arkansas Press, 2005.

Hougham, Robert H. Correspondence. M-539-13. Robert H. Hougham fonds. Glenbow Archives, Calgary.

Hourie, Peter. Reminiscences. NW Rebellion, 1885 veterans. R-E3023. Provincial Archives of Saskatchewan.

Howard, Joseph Kinsey. *The Strange Empire of Louis Riel*. Toronto, ON: Swan Publishing Co. Ltd., 1970.

Hubbard, Jeremiah. *Forty Years Among the Indians: A Descriptive History of the Long and Busy Life of Jeremiah Hubbard*. Miami, OK: Phelps Printers, 1913.

"Huron Cemetery: Wyandotte National Burial Ground." Accessed November 7, 2013. http://www.wyandotte-nation.org/culture/history/cemetery-lists/huron-cemetery/.

Index to Register of Voters: 1934. California, Los Angeles City, Precinct no. 524.

Irvine, Acheson Gosford. Copy of Official Diary of Lieut.-Col. Irvine. [Ottawa: s.n., 1885]. Accessed October 27, 2013. http://peel.library.ualberta.ca/bibliography.

"Kansas Pacific Railway, Union Pacific Eastern Division." UtahRail.Net. Accessed November 4, 2013. http://utahrails.net/up/kansas-pacific.php.

Kappler, Charles J., comp., ed. "Absentee Wyandotte Indians." In *Indian Affairs: Laws and Treaties*, Vol. 3 *Laws*. Chapter 1767. Accessed November 7, 2013. http://digital.library.okstate.edu/kappler/Vol4/html_files/v4p1032b.html.

Kennedy, Howard Angus. *The North-West Rebellion*. Toronto, ON: Ryerson Press, 1928.

———. "Robert Armstrong: Buffalo Hunter." In *Old & New Furrows: The Story of Rosthern*. Rosthern, SK: Rosthern Historical Society, 1977. 313–17. Reprinted from the *Saskatchewan Valley News*, December 8, 1943.

Kitchener, Frederick Marshall. Diary. M 635. Frederick Marshall Kitchener fonds. Glenbow Archives, Calgary.

Laidlaw, Alexander. *From the St. Lawrence to the North Saskatchewan: Being Some Incidents Connected with the Detachment of "A" Battery, Regt. Canadian Artillery, Who Composed Part of the North West Field Force in the Rebellion of 1885*. Halifax, NS: J. Bowes, 1885. Accessed November 5, 2013. http://peel.library.ualberta.ca/bibliography/1477/3.html.

Lamontagne, Manon, et al., eds., comps. *Voice of the People: Reminiscences of the Prince Albert Settlement's Early Citizens, 1866–1895*. Prince Albert, SK: Prince Albert Historical Society, 1985.

Laurie, Richard Carney. *Reminiscences of Early Days in Battleford and with Middleton's Column*. Battleford, SK: *Saskatchewan Herald*, 1935.

Leeson, Michael A., ed. *History of Montana. 1739–1885: A History of Its Discovery and Settlement, Social and Commercial Progress, Mines and Miners,*

Agriculture and Stock-growing, Churches, Schools and Societies, Indians and Indian Wars, Vigilantes, Courts of Justice, Newspaper Press, Navigation, Railroads and Statistics, with Histories of Counties, Cities, Villages and Mining Camps . . . Chicago, IL: Warner, Beers & Co., 1885.

Lewin, Charlotte. "The Powell Family of Early Pleasants County." Accessed November 7, 2013. http://www.wvgenweb.org/pleasants/powell-history.htm.

Light, Douglas W. *Footprints in the Dust*. North Battleford, SK: Turner-Warwick Publications, 1987.

Lowie, Robert H. "The Culture-Type of the Plains Indians." In *The North American Indians: A Sourcebook*, edited by Roger C. Owen et al. Toronto, ON: The MacMillan Co., 1967.

MacBeth, Roderick George. *The Making of the Canadian West: Being the Reminiscences of an Eye-Witness*. Toronto, ON: William Briggs, 1898.

——. *The Romance of Western Canada*. Toronto, ON: William Briggs, 1918.

——. *Policing the Plains: Being the Real-Life Record of the Famous Royal North-West Mounted Police*. Toronto, ON: Musson, 1931.

MacDonald, J. S. *The Dominion Telegraph*. Battleford, SK: Canadian North-West Historical Society, 1930.

McLean, Donald George. *1885: Metis Rebellion or Government Conspiracy?* Winnipeg, MB: Pemmican Publications Inc., 1985.

McLean, W. J. "Tragic Events at Frog Lake and Fort Pitt During the North West Rebellion." *Manitoba Pageant* 18, no. 3 (Spring 1973). Accessed November 8, 2013. http://www.mhs.mb.ca/docs/pageant.

Macleod, R.C. *The North West Mounted Police, 1873–1919*. Ottawa, ON: Canadian Historical Association, 1978.

McPhillips' Alphabetical and Business Directory of the District of Saskatchewan, N.W.T., Together with Brief Historical Sketches of Prince Albert, Battleford and the Other Settlements in the District. Qu'Appelle, N.W.T.: n.a., 1888.

Michno, Gregory F., and Susan J. Michno. *Forgotten Fights: Little-Known Raids and Skirmishes on the Frontier, 1823 to 1890*. Missoula, MT: Mountain Press Publishing Co., 2008.

Middleton, General Sir Frederick Dobson. *Suppression of the Rebellion in the North West Territories of Canada 1885*. ed. G. H. Needler, University of Toronto Studies: History and Economic Series, 11. 1886. Reprint. Toronto, ON: University of Toronto Press, 1948.

Mika, Nick, and Helma Mika. *The Riel Rebellion, 1885.* Belleville, ON: Mika Silk Screening, 1972.

Millar, Ruth Wright. "Big Tom Hourie: Saskatchewan's Paul Revere." *Saskatchewan Heroes and Rogues.* Regina, SK: Coteau Books, 2004.

Molony (Moloney), E. C. R-1454. File VI. 5. Provincial Archives of Saskatchewan.

Moore, Jacqueline M. *Cow Boys and Cattle Men: Class and Masculinities on the Texas Frontier, 1865–1900.* New York, NY: New York University Press, 2010.

Morgan, Perl W., ed. and comp. *History of Wyandotte County Kansas and Its People.* Chicago, IL: The Lewis Publishing Company, 1911.

Morton, Desmond. *The Last War Drum: The North West Campaign of 1885.* Toronto, ON: Hakkert, 1972.

Morton, Desmond, and Reginald H. Roy. *Telegrams of the North-West Campaign 1885.* Toronto, ON: The Champlain Society, 1972.

Mowat (Mouat), A. N. Diary. MG3 C9. Archives of Manitoba.

Mulvaney, Charles Pelham. *The History of the North-West Rebellion of 1885.* Toronto, ON: A. H. Hovey & Co., 1885.

Needler, G. H. *Louis Riel: The Rebellion of 1885.* Toronto, ON: Burns & MacEachern, 1957.

Nelson, Hugh S. *Four Months Under Arms: A Reminiscence of Events Prior to and During the Second Riel Rebellion.* Nelson, BC: *Nelson Daily News,* 1940.

Old & New Furrows: The Story of Rosthern. Rosthern, SK: Rosthern Historical Society, 1977.

Oppen, William A., ed. *The Riel Rebellions: A Cartographic History. Le récit cartographique des affaires Riel.* Toronto, ON: University of Toronto Press in association with the Public Archives of Canada and the Canadian Government Publishing Centre, 1979.

Ord, Lewis Redman, Richard Scougall Cassels, and Harold Penryn Rusden. *Reminiscences of a Bungle, by One of the Bunglers, and Two Other Northwest Rebellion Diaries.* Edited by R. C. Macleod. 1887. Reprint. Edmonton, AB: University of Alberta Press, 1983.

Osler, Edmund Boyd. *The Man Who Had to Hang: Louis Riel.* Toronto, ON: Longmans, Green, and Co., 1961.

Otter, William Dillon. Brigade Orders: Otter. O/B/Ot8. William Dillon Otter fonds. Archives of British Columbia.

Pilon, Barthélémi. "Testimony of the Last Days of Freedom of Louis Riel as Reported by Madame Barthélémi Pilon." Accessed May 27, 2013. http://piloninternational.ca/international/archives/christine/echristine.html.

Powell, John Wesley. *Wyandot Government: A Short Study of Tribal Society.* N.p.: Bureau of American Ethnology, c. 1880. Accessed January 15, 2014. www.gutenberg.org.

Qu'Appelle, Footprints to Progress: A History of Qu'Appelle and District. Qu'Appelle, SK: Qu'Appelle Historical Society, 1980.

"Rebellion Veterans Reunited Recount Days of Adventure," July 17, 1935, newspaper clipping, Alberta Folklore and Local History Collection, University of Alberta Libraries. Accessed December 18, 2013. http://folklore.library.ualberta.ca.

"Restoration of the Monument at the Initial Point of the Public Land Surveys of Oklahoma." *Chronicles of Oklahoma* 3, no. 1 (1925): 81–85. Accessed November 5, 2013. http://digital.library.okstate.edu/Chronicles/v003/v003p081.html.

Russell, Ralph Clifford. *The Carlton Trail: The Broad Highway into the Saskatchewan Country from the Red River Settlement, 1840–1880.* Saskatoon, SK: Prairie Books, 1971.

Ryus, W. H. *The Second William Penn: A True Account of Incidents that Happened along the Old Santa Fe Trail in the Sixties.* Kansas City, MO: Frank T. Riley Publishing Co., 1913.

Salzer, Susan K. "Medicine Bill Comstock: Saga of the Leatherstocking Scout." Accessed November 7, 2013. Historynet.com.

Schultz, James Willard. *Blackfeet and Buffalo: Memories of Life among the Indians.* Norman, OK: University of Oklahoma Press, 1981.

Shillingberg, William B. *Dodge City: The Early Years, 1872–1886.* Norman, OK: The Arthur H. Clark Co., 2009.

Siggins, Maggie. *Riel: A Life of Revolution.* Toronto, ON: HarperCollins Publishers Ltd., 1994.

Silliman, Eugene Lee. *We Seized Our Rifles: Recollections of the Montana Frontier.* Missoula, MT: Mountain Press Publishing Co., 1982.

Silver, A. I., and Marie-France Valleur. *The North-West Rebellion.* Vancouver, BC: Copp Clark Publishing Co., 1967.

Stanley, George Francis Gillman. *Louis Riel.* Toronto, ON: The Ryerson Press, 1963.

———. *The Birth of Western Canada: A History of the Riel Rebellions*. 1936. Reprint. Toronto, ON: University of Toronto Press, 1978.

Steele, Samuel Benfield. *Forty Years in Canada: Reminiscences of the Great North-West with Some Account of His Service in South Africa*. Ed. Mollie Glenn Niblett. Winnipeg, MB: Russel Lang & Company; London: Herbert Jenkins Ltd., 1915.

Stewart, Sharon. *Louis Riel: Firebrand*. Montreal, QC: XYZ Publishing, 2007.

Stewart, Walter F. Diary. Stewart family fonds. Microfilm 1885. Archives of Manitoba.

Stewart, Walter P. *A Photo-Journalist Looks at the Town of Maple Creek, Saskatchewan*. Winnipeg, MB: W. P. Stewart Consultant, 1977.

Stobie, Margaret R. *The Other Side of Rebellion: The Remarkable Story of Charles Bremner and His Furs*. Edmonton, AB: NeWest Press, 1986.

Stonechild, Blair, and Bill Waiser. *Loyal Till Death: Indians and the North-West Rebellion*. Calgary, AB: Fifth House Publishers, 1997.

Strange, Thomas Bland. *Gunner Jingo's Jubilee*. London, UK: Remington and Co., 1893. Accessed November 8, 2013. https://archive.org/stream/gunnerjingosjubi00stra#page/n7/mode/2up.

Stuart, Granville. *Forty Years on the Frontier as Seen in the Journals and Reminiscences of Granville Stuart, Gold-Miner, Trader, Merchant, Rancher and Politician*. Lincoln, NE: University of Nebraska Press, 1925.

Telfer, W. P. *Humboldt on the Carlton Trail*. Saskatoon, SK: Modern Press, 1975.

"Tom Green County Courthouse, San Angelo, Texas." Accessed July 22, 2016. http://www.254texascourthouses.net.

Tremblay, Emil. *The Shadow of Riel*. Ituna, SK: Icon Press, 1984.

Tullock, Thomas L. "Capt. Robert Neal, Senior, and his Wife, Margaret Lear Neal. Their Descendants and Family Connections." *The Granite Monthly* 4, no. 7 (1881): 270. Accessed November 5, 2013, from Google Books.

Turner, John Peter. *The North-West Mounted Police, 1873–1893*, 2 Vols. Ottawa, ON: King's Printer, 1950.

U.S. Congress. *Report of the Secretary of the Interior Being Part of the Message and Documents Communicated to the Two Houses of Congress at the Beginning of the Second Session of the Forty-Second Congress*. Irwin, W. R., and O. S. Witherell. "Investigation of Action of Wyandotte Guardians.

Wyandotte, Kansas, July 14, 1871. No. 8.—Case of Mathew Mudeater, guardian." Washington: Government Printing Office, 1871. Accessed November 7, 2013, from Google Books.

U.S. Congress. House. *Reports of Committees of the House of Representatives. Thirty-Sixth Congress, Second Session, 1860–61.* Washington, DC: Government Printing Office, 1861. Accessed November 4, 2013, from Google Books.

——. *The Executive Documents of the House of Representatives for the First Session of the Fiftieth Congress. 1887–88.* "Report of the Secretary of the Interior. Table Giving Names, Positions, Periods of Service, Salaries Per Annum, etc. Cheyenne and Arapaho Agency." Washington: Government Printing Office, 1889. Accessed November 4, 2013, from Google Books.

Vandal, Isabelle. "Heroines of the 1885 Resistance: Isabelle Branconnier Vandal." Accessed October 27, 2013. http://www.metismuseum.ca.

Venturino, Mike Duke. "The Battle of Adobe Walls, Myth vs. Reality." *Guns Magazine*, June 2005.

Wadmore, Lieutenant R. Lyndhurst. Diary. Pamphlet/VF LXII-42. Special Collections. University of Saskatchewan Library.

Wellman, Paul I. "Some Famous Kansas Frontier Scouts." *The Kansas Historical Quarterly* 1, no. 4 (1932): 345–59. Accessed November 5, 2013. http://www.kshs.org/p/some-famous-kansas-frontier-scouts/12557.

Wiebe, Rudy, and Bob Beal, comps. and eds. *War in the West: Voices of the 1885 Rebellion.* Toronto, ON: McClelland and Stewart, 1985.

Wilson, R. Michael. *Outlaw Tales of Wyoming: True Stories of the Cowboy State's Most Infamous Crooks, Culprits, and Cutthroats.* Guilford, CT; Helena, MT: TwoDot Publishers, 2008.

"Yellowstone County—Its Beginnings." Accessed October 27, 2013. http://www.rootsweb.ancestry.com/~mtygf/county/yellowstone.htm.

Yost, Nellie Snyder. *Buffalo Bill: His Family, Friends, Fame, Failures, and Fortunes.* Chicago, IL: The Swallow Press, 1979.

Young, William E. Diary. Edinburgh Square Heritage and Cultural Centre, Caledonia, Ontario.

INDEX

ABOUT THE AUTHOR

John D. Pihach received a B.Sc. degree
in physics from the University of British Columbia, studied studio fine arts
at Vancouver Community College,
and spent many years wandering about
Europe and Asia. He is the author of
Ukrainian Genealogy and currently lives
in Yorkton, Saskatchewan.